Portrait Jewels

Diana Scarisbrick

Portrait Jewels

Opulence and Intimacy from the Medici to the Romanovs

With 356 illustrations, 341 in color

1 *page 1* Pendant with an onyx cameo traditionally identified as Mary Stuart, Queen of Scots, in an enamelled frame embellished with gems and pearls, *c.* 1560–70. (See Ills 21, 22.)

2 *frontispiece* Detail of a self-portrait of Martin van Meytens, court painter to the Empress Maria Theresa, 1740s. He holds a miniature portrait of the Empress and wears a portrait medal of her husband, the Emperor Franz I. (See Ill. 189.)

3 *opposite* Column table portrait with a miniature of Nicholas II, Emperor of Russia, 1910. The column is by Henrik Wigström, workmaster for Carl Fabergé. (See Ill. 313.)

© 2011 Thames & Hudson Ltd, London
Text © 2011 Diana Scarisbrick

Designed by Karolina Prymaka

All Rights Reserved. No part of this publication may be reproduced or transmitted in any form or by any means, electronic or mechanical, including photocopy, recording or any other information storage and retrieval system, without prior permission in writing from the publisher.

First published in 2011 in hardcover in the United States of America by Thames & Hudson Inc., 500 Fifth Avenue, New York, New York 10110

thamesandhudsonusa.com

Library of Congress Catalog Card Number 2010936780
ISBN 978-0-500-51557-0

Printed and bound in China by C & C Offset Printing Co. Ltd

The author acknowledges with gratitude the information, advice and assistance she has received from the following: Benjamin Zucker, whose collection provides the nucleus of the book; Earl Fortescue, the Earl of Portarlington and Lord Stafford, descendants of Mrs Fitzherbert's heirs; the Marquis of Lansdowne; the Earl of Sandwich; Baroness Willoughby d'Eresby; Count Andrew Ciechanowiecki; Count Charles-André Walewski; Derek Adlam; Mrs Noel Annesley; Florence Evans of the Weiss Gallery; Kate Fielden; Etienne Grafe, Christopher Hartop, Judith Kilby Hunt; Dr John and Mrs Zoe Kurtz; David Lavender; Mr and Mrs Alain Moatti; Nicholas, Jonathan and Francis Norton and Max Michelson of S. J. Phillips; Peter and Paul Schaffer; Lindsay Stainton; and Mrs Sarah Troughton. Special thanks are due to colleagues in the salerooms, especially Camilla Lombardi of Bonhams; Raymond Sancroft Baker, Jo Langston and Francis Russell of Christie's; and Victor de Baux, Julia Clarke, Leonora Gummer, Daniela Mascetti, Sabrina O'Cock, Ludovic Shaw Stewart, the Hon. James Stourton, and Gemma Williams of Sotheby's. Colleagues abroad include in Boston Susan Ward and Yvonne Markowitz; in Brussels Christophe Vachaudez; in Copenhagen Charlotte Christianson, J. Greve of the Royal Silver Collection, and Jørgen Hein of Rosenborg Castle; in The Hague René Brus; in Paris Mathilde Avisseau of the Cabinet des Médailles, Roselyne Hurel of the Musée Carnavalet, Beatrice de Plinval and Melanie Sallois of Chaumet, and Emmanuel Ducamp and Isabelle Lucas; and in Stockholm Magnus Olausson of the Nationalmuseum. Valuable support for my research has come from Amanda Corp of the London Library, and from Adrian James of the Society of Antiquaries. I owe much to the generosity of Richard Falkiner for sharing his knowledge of medals, and to Stefano Papi who made elusive Russian images available to me. I must also thank Jo Walton, my picture researcher, Karolina Prymaka, who has married my text and images with art and logic, Susanna Friedman, who oversaw the production, and Emily Lane, my editor, who has taken such a close interest in every detail that this really is 'our book'.

Contents

Introduction 6

1 *Renaissance Europe*, 1500–1625 8

2 *The Baroque Interpretation*, 1625–1715 78

3 *Eighteenth-Century Absolutism, Elegance and Sentiment*, 1715–1800 154

4 *Dynastic Pride and Private Affection from Napoleon to World War I*, 1800–1916 224

5 *The Portrait Diamond*, 1613–1906 320

The Engraved Diamond Portrait 344

Notes 345
Bibliography 348
Acknowledgments for Illustrations 349
Index 351

4 *opposite* Interior of a locket that contained a miniature of James I of England and Ireland and VI of Scotland, finely enamelled in various colours. (See Ills. 67–69.)

Introduction

From the Renaissance onwards 'portraits in little' of famous personalities – political, military, literary, artistic – as well as of private individuals have inspired goldsmiths and jewellers to design settings in precious materials to enhance their beauty and emphasize their significance for both donor and recipient. Surviving rings, pendants, lockets, bracelets and *objets de luxe* show that the desire for these jewelled portraits was international, ranging from Lisbon to Moscow, from Stockholm to Naples, from London to Paris to New York. Yet while cameo and intaglio portraits, medals and miniatures have been extensively surveyed, their settings do not seem to have attracted the same attention. This is surprising.

The story begins with the 16th-century portraits by Jacopo da Trezzo, Giancristoforo Romano, François Clouet and Nicholas Hilliard of the powerful Habsburg, Medici, Valois, Bourbon and Tudor monarchs. In their turn, these diminutive masterpieces provided the most celebrated jewellers – François Dujardin and Etienne Delaune in Paris, George Heriot in Edinburgh and London, Gabriel Gipfel in Dresden – with a new and attractive means of artistic expression, echoing the elaborate frames surrounding the paintings hanging on the walls of palaces and mansions. These creations set the standard for the following periods and successive artistic styles.

The superb series of 17th-century portrait medals and miniatures are surrounded by enamelled swags of fruit, flowers and leaves deriving from the contemporary passion for botany, and the *boîtes à portraits* enriched with diamond-studded borders associated with Louis XIV strike a new note of luxury. Similarly, the Rococo and Neoclassical elegance of 18th-century settings shows the influence of that great arbiter of taste, the Marquise de Pompadour, an enthusiastic patroness of cameo-cutters, medallists and miniaturists. The variety of 19th-century frames illustrates the eclecticism reigning in the arts of that time. The photograph struck a death blow to the miniature, but its popularity resulted in an increased demand for frames to be worn as jewels and for display on desk or bedside table, epitomized by the splendid creations of Fabergé.

Finally, in a chapter of its own, which will be a revelation to many, there is a discussion of those few precious jewels in which diamonds not only surround but cover the miniature, followed by a short history of the even rarer portraits engraved on diamonds.

Like a portrait gallery in miniature, these images bring to life five centuries of extraordinary events and personalities, and at the same time illustrate an aspect of the history of jewelry never explored to this degree.

I *Renaissance Europe*
1500–1625

During the Renaissance the reawakening of interest in human individuality and character which reached its highest expression in the portraits of Raphael, Antonello da Messina and Titian is also reflected in images on a much smaller scale. These carved hardstone cameos and intaglios, portrait medals and miniatures painted on vellum served various purposes: to glorify heads of state, as diplomatic gifts, and as private tokens of love and friendship. Whether hidden or openly displayed, most were worn as jewels, and were therefore mounted in enamelled gold and gem-encrusted frames which affirmed their value and made an additional statement about the person portrayed.

5 *opposite* A portrait medal of Cosimo I de' Medici, Grand Duke of Tuscany (1519–74), set in a pendant, is displayed by his young daughter, Bia: detail of her portrait by Agnolo Bronzino (see Ill. 35).

Cameos and Intaglios

The revival of the ancient art of gem engraving – in relief as cameos or incised as intaglios – began in 15th-century Italy, where so many gems were being unearthed from Roman sites. These discoveries, which coincided with contemporary humanist admiration for classical culture, stimulated the emergence of a new school of gem engravers, not only in Rome but also in the regional centres of Florence, Milan, Verona and Padua. The fame of these masters soon attracted patrons beyond the Alps: Matteo del Nazzaro was summoned to France by François I, Jacopo Caraglio to Poland by Sigismund II, and Jacopo da Trezzo to Spain by Philip II. Just as the Roman emperors had required that the gem engravers produce official images in which they appeared as aloof, ideal, calm embodiments of power, so too did the rulers of the Renaissance. As guardians of the law and order on which public peace and prosperity depended, an Italian, Valois, Habsburg or Tudor monarch wished to be seen, in the words of Baldassare Castiglione (in *The Courtier*), as

> most wise, most continent, most temperate, most just, full of liberalitie, majestie, holinesse and mercy . . . most glorious and most dearely beloved to God and man: through whose grace he shall attaine unto that heroicall and noble virtue that shall make him pass the boundes of the nature of man and shall rather be called a demy God than a man mortal . . . Thus, just as in heaven the sun and moon and other stars show the world as in a mirror some likeness of God, so on earth a much liker image of God is found in those good princes who love and revere Him, and show their people the shining light of His justice and a reflection of His divine reason and mind.

6, 7 Front and back of a pendant with an onyx cameo portrait of the Emperor Charles V (1500–1558), in an enamelled gold frame embellished with table-cut rubies between scrolls, hooks and flowers. The back is enamelled with the crowned Habsburg coat of arms between columns (the Pillars of Hercules) entwined with Charles V's motto, and the insignia of the Order of the Golden Fleece. Cameo North Italian; setting Netherlandish, 1556/58. H 54 mm.

8, 9 *left and opposite* Front and back of a pendant with an onyx cameo bust of Philip II, King of Spain (1527–98), in armour, with the inscription PHILIPPUS REX HISPANIAE. The cameo is set in a gold frame embellished with eight table-cut diamonds alternating with raised quatrefoils, and a pearl drop. The back is enamelled with a trophy of arms echoing the military character of the portrait. Cameo Italian, from the circle of Jacopo da Trezzo (*c.* 1515–89); setting Spanish, *c.* 1560. 47 × 31 mm.

This concept was understood by Shakespeare, whose King of Denmark tells his wife 'There's such divinity doth hedge a king' (*Hamlet*, IV. v), and whose Richard II is described by the Bishop of Carlisle as sacred, 'The figure of God's majesty / His captain, steward, deputy elect / Anointed, crowned' (*Richard II*, IV. i).

As the most powerful sovereign in Europe, the Emperor Charles V was portrayed by the best artists of the period. A realistic cameo bust in which the Emperor wears contemporary dress is set as a pendant edged with scrolls enamelled in various colours interspersed with table-cut rubies [6, 7]: his prestige and power are further conveyed on the back by his device of the Pillars of Hercules and motto PLUS ULTRA, declaring that whereas the empire of the Romans was bounded by these columns (representing the Straits of Gibraltar), his extended to the new world beyond. The collar of the Order of the Golden Fleece and the arms of Austria and Castille surmounted by three crowns complete this statement of imperial authority.

Philip II, son of Charles V, is shown in each of his surviving cameo portraits in the role recommended by Niccolò Machiavelli in *The Prince*, as a military leader and man of action, in armour as if directing his troops in the wars against the English, the French, the Portuguese and his rebellious subjects in the Netherlands. This theme is emphasized in one of these portraits, bordered by table-cut diamonds, which is enamelled with a trophy of arms – pikestaff, arquebus, sword, helmet, powder flask and drum – at the back [8, 9]. Another pendant is enamelled with a pattern of white moresques on a ground of red, green and black [10, 11], similar to designs published in 1554 by Balthasar Sylvius in *Variarum Protractionum quas vulgo Maurusias vocant* [12]. A third is more dynastic.

10, 11 Front and back of a pendant with a sardonyx cameo bust of Philip II in armour, within a border outlined in black, the top and base marked by green leaves. The back is patterned with varicoloured interlaced moresques outlined in white. Cameo and setting c. 1550–75. 33 × 28 mm.

12 Moresque ornament on the titlepage of a collection of moresque designs published by Balthasar Sylvius (Balthasar van den Bos, 1518–80) of Antwerp, *Variarum Protractionum quas vulgo Maurusias vocant . . .*, 1554.

13, 14 *above, left and right* Double-sided gold pendant, the front with an onyx cameo bust of Philip II wearing armour, the back with an onyx cameo bust of his son, Don Carlos (1545–68), in armour ornamented with a Medusa mask. The cameos are set within a white border interspersed with coloured ovals, surrounded by a partly translucent red and dark blue frame. Cameos Italian, from the circle of Jacopo da Trezzo, *c.* 1559; setting Spanish, contemporary. 42 × 34.5 mm.

15 *opposite* Isabel Clara Eugenia, Infanta of Spain (1566–1633), with Magdalena Ruiz, her dwarf attendant: detail of a portrait from the school of Alonso Sanchez Coello, *c.* 1586. Magnificently dressed and bejewelled, she displays the cameo portrait of her father, Philip II. Magdalena Ruiz herself holds a miniature.

It is double-sided, with a portrait bust of the heir, Don Carlos, at the back [13, 14]. The enamelled inner frame, which is white interspersed with coloured ovals, is enclosed within a convex border decorated with translucent red and opaque blue ornamental motifs.

A similar onyx cameo bust of Philip II is held as if it were her most precious possession by his daughter, the splendidly bejewelled Infanta Isabel Clara Eugenia, in a portrait [15], and another, in a cartouche frame, hangs from a chain round the neck of the funeral effigy of his beloved sister, Doña Juana of Portugal, in the chapel of the convent of the Descalzas Reales in Madrid,[1] demonstrating the prestige attached to these hardstone images. Doña Juana was given by her nephew, Don Carlos, who also patronized Jacopo da Trezzo, his portrait engraved on a diamond, set in a nielloed ring and inscribed with his name and title.[2] Whereas black niello harmonized well with the diamond, coloured enamels seem to have been chosen to brighten the frames of onyx cameos. This style of decoration enhanced the portrait of the Habsburg princess Anna of Austria, who married her widower uncle Philip II in 1570 and died in 1580, which is listed complete with setting in his posthumous inventory: 'An oval grey and white cameo portrait of Queen Anna, our sovereign, within a rope twist border and mounted in a gold frame enamelled red, blue and green'.[3]

In Florence the art of gem engraving encouraged by Lorenzo the Magnificent was also patronized by his Medici successors, and most notably by Grand Duke Cosimo I, founder of the Grand Duchy of Tuscany. His onyx portrait cameo bust, dressed as a warrior, which has survived intact [16] with the beaded inner border surrounded by a frame of enamelled strips, is edged with four attachment loops, a clear indication that the cameo was to be worn on the hat or dress.

16 *opposite* Hat or dress jewel with an onyx cameo bust of Cosimo I de' Medici, Grand Duke of Tuscany (1519–74), wearing armour and the insignia of the Golden Fleece. The cameo is set within a beaded border surrounded by a frame of strips radiating outwards enamelled with touches of blue alternating with white. Cameo attributed to Giovanni Antonio de' Rossi (1517–c. 1574), after 1546; setting contemporary. 43 × 32 mm.

17 *opposite* Alternative designs (to the right and left) by Giorgio Vasari for a figurative frame for the *grandissimo* cameo by Giovanni Antonio de' Rossi depicting Cosimo I de' Medici, his first wife, Eleonora da Toledo, and their five children, *c.* 1559.

Depicted at the height of his powers, strong, handsome and courageous, he was regarded as the incarnation of Machiavelli's Prince, 'joining daring to talent and prudence, capable of great cruelty yet practising mercy when required'.

The extraordinary dynastic cameo by Giovanni Antonio de' Rossi of Cosimo I, his wife Eleonora of Toledo and their five children is now fragmentary and without a frame, but alternative designs survive that display the imaginative powers of the 16th-century Florentine goldsmiths. Flanking the cameo, Giorgio Vasari's drawing, *c.* 1559 [17], shows two alternative proposals that are essentially figurative and architectural, and includes a representation of Cosimo's collar of the Order of the Golden Fleece, the Medici-Toledo coat of arms and ducal crown below, and a plaque at the top inscribed COSMUS / MED / DUX / FLO II. On a smaller scale, a similar figurative design for the frame of a bust of an old man by Domenico Ghirlandaio recalls the heights which the Renaissance artist could attain.[4] Less ambitious is the narrow enamelled border framing a cornelian cameo double portrait of Cosimo II and Maria Maddalena of Austria, although the crowned Medici arms between elegant scrolls on the back of the pendant make an uncompromising statement of sovereignty.[5]

Although François I of France was portrayed in cameo, as was his heir Henri II, no images of these two monarchs have survived in their original settings. Still intact, however, in a gold border of table-cut rubies, is the onyx portrait bust of Catherine de Médicis, wearing the badge of the Order of St Michel, dating from soon after her marriage with the future Henri II [20]. Their daughter-in-law, Mary Stuart, Queen of Scots and widow of François II – described by Michel de Montaigne as 'the fairest Queen in Christendom' – is traditionally identified as the subject of a distinctive group of cameos of

18, 19 *left and below* Front and back of a pendant with an onyx cameo bust traditionally identified as Mary Stuart, Queen of Scots (1542–87), who married the future François II of France in 1558. The cameo is set in an enamelled red border. The back is patterned with red, green and white flowers. Cameo Italian, 1566; setting French, contemporary. 38 × 28 mm.

20 Pendant with an onyx cameo of the young Catherine de Médicis (1519–81), future Queen of France, wearing the Order of St Michel with court dress. The frame is embellished with twenty-nine table-cut rubies, close set in gold. Cameo French, c. 1540; setting French, later. 31 × 26 mm.

a well dressed and beautiful young woman, in their original settings. The earliest, of *c.* 1560, is mounted in a pendant within a frame enamelled in a black and white egg-and-dart pattern interspersed with rubies and diamonds and hung with a baroque pearl, the back covered with a pattern of red quatrefoils and white daisies: it is attributed to the Parisian goldsmith and court jeweller Etienne Delaune.[6] Dated 1566 is another of the same shape and quality, the back also patterned with flowers [18, 19]. Quite different in character is a third, said to have been sent by Mary to her suitor, Thomas, 9th Duke of Norfolk, whose desire to marry her led to his execution on Tower Hill at the age of thirty-four in 1572. It is mounted in a wide scrollwork frame set with a turquoise, amethysts and a peridot and hung with three pearls [21, 22]. More symbolic is a fourth, set in an enamelled gold 'bleeding' heart.[7]

Because of the death and destruction wrought by the War of the League, it was not until Henri IV brought peace and prosperity to France that the art of gem engraving was again put at the service of the monarchy. A symbolic portrait presents him as the Gallic Hercules [23] crowned with the skin of the Nemean Lion, thereby associating the first of the labours of the mythological hero with King Henri's restoration of law and order so that civilization might once again flourish.[8] This image is further emphasized by the frame of enamelled gold trophies of arms linked by lover's knots with a lion crouching at the base and a royal crown at the top: it is a more elaborate version of a similar frame on a military theme probably designed in Paris *c.* 1550–73 by Etienne Delaune [24]. After King Henri's assassination in 1610 his heir, the young Louis XIII, and his widow, Marie de Médicis, who acted as regent for their son, are represented in bloodstone intaglios set in rings enamelled mauve.[9]

21, 22 Front and back of a pendant with an onyx cameo traditionally identified as Mary Stuart, Queen of Scots, bejewelled and wearing court dress, in a wide enamelled gold frame covered with scrolls and set with a turquoise, two amethysts and a peridot, hung with three pearls. The back is enamelled with a symmetrical pattern of scrolls and leaves. Cameo and setting *c.* 1560–70.

Renaissance Europe, 1500–1625   25

23 *opposite* Pendant with a sardonyx cameo of Henri IV, King of France (1553–1610), like Hercules wearing a lion skin, alluding to his qualities of strength and courage. These are also represented in the enamelled gold frame surmounted by the crown of France, by the motifs of four military trophies, linked by lover's knots, and by the lion crouching at the base. Cameo and setting French, *c.* 1600. 88 × 66 mm.

24 Drawing attributed to Etienne Delaune (1518–80) of a frame with military trophies consisting of two helmets, two shields superimposed on palmettes, two leather corselets hanging on swords, a helmeted head at the top and a lion's mask at the base, both superimposed on palmettes, with scrolls and strapwork between, *c.* 1550–73.

25 *opposite* Pendant set with an opal cameo of the infant Louis XIII of France (1601–43) wearing the ribbon of the Order of the St Esprit, within an octagon. The openwork frame is enamelled white, black and dark green in the *cosses de pois* or 'peapod' style. Cameo French, *c.* 1610; setting French, *c.* 1620–30. 63 × 43 mm.

26 Titlepage of a collection of *cosses de pois* designs for goldsmiths by Balthazar Lemersier (fl. 1625–34). The *cosses de pois* garland, similar to that framing the cameo opposite, is tied with a ribbon hung with goldsmith's tools. The putto in the centre with a chain in one hand and three burins in the other holds over his arms a cloth identifying the artist and the engraver – Balthazar Moncornet – and giving the place and date of publication – Paris, 1626.

27 Watercolour of the sardonyx cameo of Elizabeth I, Queen of England and Ireland (1533–1603), worn in his hat by the Earl of Essex.

A new style of decoration, *cosses de pois*, derived from peapods, like an openwork garland enamelled in green, black and white, frames an opal cameo of the young Louis XIII [25]. It is close to a design by Balthazar Lemersier [26].[10]

In England, throughout her long reign Queen Elizabeth I required artists to represent her as Spenser's 'most royall queene or empresse' and 'most vertuous and beautifull lady'. Perhaps influenced by Jacopo da Trezzo's images of her brother-in-law, Philip II of Spain, she commissioned hardstone portraits of herself, usually shown in the left profile, idealized, her dress and jewels meticulously rendered, which were set in rings, brooches and pendants. Worn as badges of loyalty by those closest to her, these can be seen in the portraits of Sir Francis Walsingham and Sir Christopher Hatton [29] and of Lord Burghley, who wore his pinned to the front of his hat, as did the Earl of Essex [27]. Some settings are documented: one of the earliest instances is in 1586, when the Earl of Rutland paid Peter Van Lore £80 for 'a brooch of Her Majestie's picture in an agatt set with 53 diamondes',[11] while the 1607 will of Thomas Sackville, Earl of Dorset, bequeaths as an heirloom 'one picture of our late famous Queen Elizabeth, being cut out of an agate with excellent similitude, oval fashion and set in gold, with 26 rubyes about the circle of it, and one oriental pearle pendant to the same'.[12] The Queen's own collection included 'A tablet of gold with an agatt graven with the Queenes Ma[jestie']s picture garnished with three meane diamonds and four meane table rubies and a cluster of four little pearles pendant and a piece of unicorn's horn in it',[13] an 'Armlet of gold . . . with a ruby in the middest thereof cut with her Maiesties picture, received as a New Year's gift in 1588,[14] and in 1603, the year of her death, 'One jewell of gold like a dasye and small flowers about it garnished with sparks of diamonds and rubies with Her

28 The Wild Jewel, a pendant set with a turquoise cameo of Queen Elizabeth, in an enamelled gold scrolled frame with forget-me-nots embellished with rubies and point-cut diamonds, hung with three pearls, c. 1590. It was given by the Queen to her god-daughter, Elizabeth Wild. H 55 mm.

Majestie's picture graven within a garnet and a sprig of three branches garnished with sparkes of rubies and pearle in the topp and a small pendaunt of sparkes of diamonds'.[15]

All the surviving portrait cameo jewels of the Queen date from the last thirty years of the 16th century. They include the Wild Jewel [28], a turquoise cameo surrounded by an open scrolled border set with rubies and point-cut diamonds, given with a lace christening gown to a god-daughter, Elizabeth Wild: the ewer used for the ceremony is engraved on the back of the cameo. Others are bordered by flat enamelled gold frames interspersed with rubies or garnets. A very large example is set within a border reserved in the stone, framed in gold enamelled with red and white twists interspersed with table-cut diamonds with a pearl hanging below [30]; a portrait of Sir Francis Walsingham shows a similar pendant hanging round his neck.[16] Alluding to the Queen's virginity are the pansies and eglantines decorating a portrait cameo ring, enamelled in black, white and various other colours.[17] Several others, including a locket with sapphire cameo portrait on the cover,[18] are mounted in settings enamelled in a *cosses de pois* pattern. The most significant of these is the Barbour Jewel [31, 32]. The frame, which is set with rubies and diamonds, is surmounted by a diamond crown and hung with a cluster of pearls like a bunch of grapes. Traditionally, the oak tree on the back alludes to the circumstances that won the Protestant William Barbour his reprieve from execution as ordered by Mary I, for it was while reading under an oak tree at Hatfield that the young Elizabeth had received the momentous news of her accession.

Crowns come in different kinds, depending on the status of the ruler: the enamelled gold frame of a fine rock crystal intaglio portrait of Albrecht V of Bavaria of 1580–81 is surmounted by a closed royal crown [33].

29 *opposite* Portrait of Sir Christopher Hatton (1540–91), Lord Chancellor of England and Knight of the Garter, attributed to Cornelius Ketel, *c.* 1589. He wears a cameo pendant of Queen Elizabeth within a frame of table-cut diamonds with pearl drop, hanging from long gold chains.

30 Pendant set with a sardonyx cameo of Queen Elizabeth within a border reserved in the stone; the frame is enamelled with red and white twists interspersed with table-cut diamonds in box collets with a pearl drop below. Cameo English or French, *c.* 1575–79; setting English, contemporary. 92 × 60 mm.

Renaissance Europe, 1500–1625 33

31, 32 Front and back of the Barbour Jewel, a pendant with a sardonyx cameo of Queen Elizabeth, within a reserved border, in a frame hung with a pearl cluster. The front of the frame is enamelled white dotted with black and dark green, embellished with alternate table-cut rubies and diamonds, and surmounted by three rectangular diamonds forming a crown. The back is enamelled with an oak tree. The jewel was traditionally owned by William Barbour, a Protestant, condemned to death by Mary I and saved by the accession in 1558 of Elizabeth, who received the news while sitting under an oak tree at Hatfield. Cameo English or French, c. 1575; setting English, c. 1615–25. H 60 mm.

Renaissance Europe, 1500–1625

33 Pendant with a rock crystal intaglio portrait of Albrecht V, Count Palatine of the Rhine and Duke of Bavaria (1528–79), in armour, wearing the collar of the Order of the Golden Fleece, inscribed with his titles, in a gold frame of addorsed C scrolls with foliage enamelled in bright colours and surmounted by a closed royal crown. Intaglio by Valentin Drausch (1546–1610); setting by Heinrich Wagner (d. 1607), 1580–81. 66 × 50 mm. The jewel was commissioned after Albrecht's death by his heir, Duke Wilhelm.

Portrait Medals

Since every aspect of the ancient Roman way of life – texts, coins, the sculptural portrait – was of interest to the humanist scholars, this led to a revival of the medallic portrait bust. Whereas cameos and intaglios, each of which is unique, were rare, rulers could distribute medals marking events and anniversaries, not only individually but in groups as rewards for good service and loyalty. Since the proud recipients – military leaders, artists and writers – wanted to show off these tokens of royal favour, like the engraved gem portraits they were often converted into jewels, as brooches to pin in the hat and as pendants hanging from gold chains.

Originating in 15th-century Italy, the most famous early survival of a medallic portrait jewel is that of Isabella d'Este by Giancristoforo Romano, *c*. 1500 [34]. The gold profile medal of the celebrated patroness of the arts is surrounded by a wide frame embellished with diamonds cut to spell out her name in black-letter rather than Roman lettering, amidst enamelled gold flowers in relief within a border of entwined branches. The suspension loop indicates that the portrait was to be worn as a pendant.

On the evidence of portraits and surviving medals, most were framed in plain gold borders or cartouches. Bia, the young natural daughter of Cosimo I de' Medici, was painted by Bronzino as a princess in a white silk dress, bejewelled in diamond and pearl earrings, a pearl necklace, gold chains round her waist and at the neck, the latter chain hung with a gold medallic portrait of her father [5, 35]. The chased oval frame is bordered with scrolls at the top and bottom, with swags of flowers and leaves between. All three medallic portraits of Grand Duke Ferdinand I by Michele Mazzafirri, which were found in his tomb and that of his wife, Christine of Lorraine, have three chains attached to loops on the top border

34 *opposite* Pendant with a gold medal of Isabella d'Este (1474–1539) inscribed with her name and title, Marchesa of Mantua. The gold frame has her Christian name in diamond Gothic letters (starting at one o'clock) between flowers within rope twist borders, outlined with intertwined branches. Medal by Giancristoforo Romano (1465–1512), *c.* 1500; setting contemporary. D 69 mm.

35 *right* Bia de' Medici (1536–42), painted by Agnolo Bronzino in 1542. She wears a portrait medal of her father, Grand Duke Cosimo I (1519–74), shown in profile like an ancient Roman, within a fluted border outlined by swags of laurel and scrolls. (For a closer view, see Ill. 5.)

Renaissance Europe, 1500–1625

36 *Gnadenpfennig* of Archduke Maximilian III of Austria (1558–1618). The inscribed medal is set in an enamelled gold frame with scrolls and flowers between four coats of arms alluding to his titles and functions, and hangs from three chains supported by the coat of arms of Austria. Medal Italian, by Alessandro Abondio (*c*. 1570–1648), 1612; setting German, contemporary. H 96 mm.

and joined together at a single loop, to be worn as pendants, probably from a ribbon or a chain at the neck.[19] In Titian's portrait the art dealer Jacopo Strada wears such a medal, hanging from three short gold chains which are attached not to a ribbon but to a long gold chain wound four times round his neck, setting off his splendid red and black dress and fur cloak.[20]

In the German-speaking lands the unmounted gold or silver-gilt medal attached to gold chains developed by the end of the 16th century into the *Gnadenpfennig*, a pendant enriched with a wrought gold and enamelled frame.[21] The number of suspension chains can vary from three to one only, and the loop to which they are attached might hang from decorative scrollwork or an armorial cartouche. The armorial theme is also applied to the frames, and the shields of arms, declaring pride of rank and birth, vary in numbers. The *Gnadenpfennig* of Archduke Maximilian III of Austria, of 1612 [36], has four between scrolls, fleurs-de-lis and flowers in various colours, hanging from three chains at the top of which is a cartouche enclosing an oval shield under a crown: on one side are the arms of Austria, on the other the black cross of the Teutonic Order on white. Exceptionally, the oval portrait medal of 1611 depicting Johann Georg I, Elector of Saxony, on one side and his wife, Magdalena Sibylla, on the other [37] is bordered by no less than ten shields, hung with three pearls, and the three suspension chains are united by an armorial cartouche crowned by the electoral bonnet. It was made by the Dresden goldsmith Abraham Schwedler. Another Dresden goldsmith, Gabriel Gipfel, framed the Tobias Wolff medal of the Electress Sophia in an openwork border of coloured scrolls (1589) [38]. The three suspension chains unite at a scrollwork cartouche, and the surface of the portrait is enamelled like a painting. This use of enamel varies: in some cases there is none, in others it covers

37 Gold *Gnadenpfennig* of Magdalena Sibylla of Saxony (1587–1659), bordered by ten shields of arms, suspended from three chains meeting at an armorial cartouche crowned by an electoral bonnet, and hung with three pearl drops. Medal by Daniel Kellerthaler (1600–?1656) and setting by Abraham Schwedler (active 1612–47), Dresden, 1611 – the year of the accession of Magdalena Sibylla's husband, Johann Georg I, as Elector. 111 × 53 mm.

Renaissance Europe, 1500–1625 39

the background only, or is applied to highlight details of dress. Following contemporary designs for jewelry, a group of medals are framed in laurel crowns [39], in borders of military trophies [40], in convex borders decorated with five-petalled flowers and putti heads [41] or with strapwork and winged grotesque half figures [42], and it is clear that the more important the setting the greater the honour conferred by the presentation medal. A portrait of a young woman of the Hamburg family of Remstede (1621) shows her wearing a *Gnadenpfennig* of Duke Friedrich III of Holstein-Gottorp along with three gold medals hanging from gold chains wrought in different patterns.[22]

Whereas the *Gnadenpfennige* or medallic badges of loyalty and honour can be regarded as the German lands' contribution to the history of Renaissance jewelry, the custom of wearing them was adopted in England, and Shakespeare alludes to it in *The Winter's Tale*: 'He that weares her like her Medall hanging about his neck' (I. ii. 307). Two outstanding English versions are both associated with Queen Elizabeth I. In the Phoenix Jewel [43, 44], the medallic bust of the Queen, cut out in an open silhouette which bears her emblem – a phoenix in flames – under the royal monogram at the back, is enclosed within a crown of green leaves and white and red Tudor roses asserting her descent from the Houses of York and Lancaster, united by her grandfather, Henry VII. Her commanding presence is evoked by the regal pose, magnificent dress and jewelry, and the mythical phoenix, with its power of rising anew from the fire, alludes to her unique qualities of statesmanship [cf. 61].

Even more political is the 'Armada' Jewel [45–48]. The front displays a profile medallic bust of the Queen on a blue ground surrounded by the inscription painted in Roman capitals ELIZABETHA D.G. ANG. FRA. ET HIB. REGINA (Elizabeth by the Grace of God Queen of England, France and Ireland).

38 *opposite* Pendant enclosing an enamelled gold portrait medal of the Electress Sophia (1568–1622), who married Christian I of Saxony in 1582, within an openwork frame of scrolls, hanging from three chains attached to a scrolled element. Medal by Tobias Wolff (active 1567–*c.* 1606), 1589; setting by Gabriel Gipfel (active 1591–1617), Dresden. 108 × 64 mm.

39 *opposite* Gold *Gnadenpfennig* of Ernst, Duke of Bavaria (1554–1612), within an enamelled laurel crown, suspended from three chains attached to a cartouche set with a coloured stone, and hung with a pearl. 95 × 48 mm.

40 Engraving of a *Gnadenpfennig* of Karl Ludwig, Count Sulz (1560–1616), surrounded by military trophies including a helmet, sword, furled standard on lance, cuirass and pikestaff. By Valentin Maler (active in Nuremberg 1567–1603) (?), 1596.

41 Gold *Gnadenpfennig* of Wilhelm V, Duke of Bavaria (1548–1626), the enamelled gold frame with five-petalled flowers and heads of putti, surmounted by the electoral bonnet. Medal Netherlandish, by Hubert Gerhard (active 1581–1613) (?), 1587; setting after 1587. 111 × 43 mm.

42 Gold *Gnadenpfennig* of Ernst of Bavaria, Prince-Elector-Archbishop of Cologne (1554–1612). The enamelled gold openwork frame with winged half figures of androgynous youths, surmounted by the coat of arms and electoral bonnet and with a winged cherub's head at the base, hangs from three gold chains meeting at a scrolled element. Ernst owed his preferment to his brother, Wilhelm V of Bavaria. Medal by Hans Reimer (1557–1604), Munich, 1593; setting by Hans Reimer (?). 91 × 50 mm.

43, 44 Front and back of the Phoenix Jewel, a pendant with a gold portrait medal of Elizabeth I, Queen of England, in silhouette, surrounded by an enamelled crown composed of the intertwined white and red roses of York and Lancaster, signifying her descent from Henry VII who united these two factions. The portrait is inspired by a miniature of the Queen by Nicholas Hilliard dated 1572. The back displays her emblem, a radiate burning phoenix, in relief, below her crowned monogram. Medal and setting *c.* 1570–80. D 46 mm.

Renaissance Europe, 1500–1625   47

The medallic portrait on the front of the 'Armada' Jewel [45–48] is surrounded by an outer border studded with diamonds and rubies. Behind is a miniature of the Queen, protected by an enamelled cover. Her role as protectress of her kingdom is further expressed by an italic inscription inside the cover of the miniature, around a Tudor rose, HEI MIHI QUOD TANTO VIRTUS PERFUSA DECORE NON HABET ETERNOS INVIOLATA DIES (Alas, that so much virtue suffused with beauty should not last forever inviolate), and by the Ark of the English Church enamelled on the outside of the cover, inscribed SAEVAS TRANQUILLA PER UNDAS (Safe through the stormy seas), referring to her sure and steady guidance of religious affairs during difficult times. The sources of this complex imagery are as follows: the medallic bust derives from the Garter badge of 1582, the verse around the Tudor rose was composed by the court Master of Requests, Walter Haddon, published in his *Poemata* (1567), the miniature was painted by Nicholas Hilliard, and the symbol of the Ark with motto appears on a medal of the Queen of 1585. By tradition she gave this locket to Sir Thomas Heneage, Vice-Chamberlain of her household, to celebrate the victory over the Spanish Armada in 1588.

Meanwhile in Denmark, the future Christian IV was painted at the age of seven with the medallic portrait of his father, framed in enamelled scrollwork hanging from three gold chains [49]. During his reign, from 1596 to 1648, he awarded many such medallions with his own portrait to those who served him best, and at least two have survived, one signed by Nicolaus Schwabe, complete with chain, awarded by the King to the artist Peter Paul Rubens [50], and the other hanging from a chain of enamelled links.

45–48 The 'Armada' Jewel, c. 1588. Above right, the obverse, with a gold medal of Elizabeth I within a diamond- and ruby-set enamelled frame; below left, the reverse, with a miniature of the Queen by Nicholas Hilliard (1547–1619), within an enamelled frame; above left, the outside of the cover that protects the miniature, with enamelled Ark representing the Church of England sailing through stormy seas; below right, the inside of the cover, with a Tudor rose surrounded by an inscription extolling her virtues. H 70 mm.

49 *opposite* Christian IV, King of Denmark and Norway (1577–1648), as Crown Prince aged seven, painted by Hans Knieper *c.* 1585. He wears a portrait medal of his father, Frederick II of Denmark (1534–88), within an enamelled gold frame hanging from gold chains.

50 Portrait medal of Christian IV with suspension loop. Medal by Nicolaus Schwabe (Master of the Mint, Copenhagen, retired 1629), made to commemorate the King's coronation in 1596. D 38 mm. It is said to have been given (with its chain) by Christian IV to Peter Paul Rubens around 1620 – perhaps via the King's secretary, who visited the artist in 1624.

Renaissance Europe, 1500–1625 51

Miniatures

The miniature, finely painted in watercolour on vellum, one of the favourite art forms of royalty over the centuries, developed at the court of François I of France when Jean Clouet took the 'true-to-life' portrait from the pages of the illuminated manuscript and combined it with the function of the detachable coin or medallic image. From the medal the portrait miniature took its curved form and size, but it went much further in that the medium was not restricted in colour, nor limited to the profile view. As with cameos and medals, the small scale of miniatures was easily adapted for jewelled settings, so they were well suited for presentation purposes and as a new form of diplomatic gift.

The first recorded instance of miniatures being used to promote good relations between two kingdoms is in 1526, during the preliminaries to the Treaty of Amiens when Marguerite, Duchesse d'Alençon, sent Henry VIII of England portraits of her brother François I and his two sons. Early in the year the young princes had been exchanged as hostages for their father who had been imprisoned after his defeat at the battle of Pavia by the forces of the Emperor Charles V, and it was hoped that an alliance with England might result in the release of the children. According to Gasparo Spinelli, a Venetian diplomat in London, the miniatures were enclosed in round 'finely worked gold' lockets (slightly larger than the *spechi da fuoco*, 'burning glasses', sold in St Mark's Square). The cover of the François I miniature was decorated with 'two columns whose bases are on the ground and between the one and the other can be seen the sea which separates the ground on which each of them is placed: one is of white colour and the other of violet colour.' The two columns – representing the two kings – were tied together and their upper part covered by a cap of violet colour; around them was an inscription in Latin celebrating the friendship of the two rulers separated by distance and the ocean waves. The white 'antique' tablet on the

51, 52 A double-sided gold pendant with miniatures of Mary Stuart, Queen of Scots (1542–87), and her father, James V, King of Scotland (1512–42). The portraits are set within a frame of enamelled scrolls surrounded by seed pearls *en torsade*. 44 × 35 mm.

Renaissance Europe, 1500–1625   53

cover of the other, with the miniatures of the Dauphin and the Duc d'Orléans, bore a Latin inscription inviting 'a true friend' to wish to restore the children to their homeland; on the back was a chain tied with different types of knot. Spinelli thought the columns represented France and England, and the white one was for Faith, and the violet was for Love.[23]

These jewels have vanished, as have those listed in an inventory of Mary Queen of Scots, widow of François II, dating from 1561: a miniature of her father James V in a gold case shaped like an apple, and a belt composed of a chain of forty-four red and white ciphers with the portrait of her father-in-law, Henri II.[24] In a will of 1566 she bequeathed her own miniature, mounted in a diamond cross, to Margaret Carwood, her favourite bedchamber woman.[25] Later, during her captivity in England she continued to commission miniatures from France, writing in 1575 to James Beaton, her envoy, 'There are some of my friends in this country who ask for my portrait. I pray you have four of these made which must be set in gold and sent to me secretly.'[26]

The art was given a fresh impulse in the early 1560s when the Dowager Queen Catherine de Médicis, widow of Henri II, strove to diffuse the images of the royal family in France and abroad, especially in connection with marriage negotiations. She ordered a number of miniatures from the court jeweller, François Dujardin, in 1571, even indicating the exact size required, and the jewels into which they were to be inserted. These were for the Queen to hang round her neck, a mirror and tablets for the Duke and Duchess of Savoy, a hat badge and bracelet clasp respectively for the Duke and Duchess of Lorraine, all to be decorated with emblems and mottoes as directed by Catherine's son, Charles IX.[27] Evidence of the superb quality of Dujardin's jewelry comes from a surviving

53–56 *opposite and above* Four views of a locket of enamelled gold enclosing miniatures of Catherine de Médicis (cf. Ill. 20), Dowager Queen of France, in her widow's weeds, and her son, Charles IX (1550–74). The front displays the royal crown of France supported by two columns – flanked by personifications of Piety and Justice, as inscribed on the scrolling ribbon – resting on the Ten Commandments and the laws of ancient Rome. The back bears double Cs for Catherine and Charles and a royal crown, amid swags emblematic of prosperity. Miniatures attributed to François Clouet the Younger (d. 1572); setting by François Dujardin (d. 1575), *c.* 1572. H 61 mm.

Renaissance Europe, 1500–1625 55

case containing miniatures of the Dowager Queen and Charles IX ascribed to François Clouet the Younger [53–56]. The front is enamelled with the royal crown of France supported on columns resting on plinths with the Ten Commandments and the *Lex XII Tabularum* (the civil laws of ancient Rome), flanked by figures personifying Piety and Justice who hold up an olive branch, all emblematic of good government, composed by the Chancellor, Michel de l'Hôpital. On the back are the red and white crowned double C ciphers for Charles IX and his mother Catherine, surrounded by fruit and flowers in high relief.

Later in the century, Gabrielle d'Estrées at the time of her death in 1599 left no less than twenty portrait jewels of her lover, Henri IV, including 'a large diamond feather-shaped head ornament centred on a miniature of the King amidst rubies and diamonds' and 'a miniature case enamelled in grey with the King's cipher surrounded by four *fermesses* and a triangle in each corner, all set with diamonds'.[28] A *fermesse*, the letter S closed by a bar (derived from *signum*, signature), was used to signify constancy, sometimes accompanied by the Greek letter *phi*, a pun for fidelity. A design for the cover of a miniature case attributed to Etienne Delaune includes both *fermesses* and *phi*, each repeated three times [58]. A few months after Gabrielle died, Henriette d'Entragues, her successor as mistress to the King, sent her own miniature to him, and he approved the beautiful setting, since 'such a fine bird deserves a fine cage'.[29] Marie de Médicis, who married Henri IV in 1600, owned important miniature jewelry such as her

> important bracelet for the arm comprising twelve links, the device on the cover of the locket centrepiece embellished with two table-cut

57 *opposite* Portrait of a widow with a miniature of her deceased husband in a jewelled frame clasped by their small daughter, as if he were still with them. French School, *c.* 1590.

58 Alternative designs (left and right) for the cover of a miniature case, attributed to Etienne Delaune. The decoration includes the monogram AAGG, and the letter *phi* alternating with *fermesses* amidst foliage and cornucopiae.

Renaissance Europe, 1500–1625 57

59 In a locket suspended on three chains, concealed behind a gold medal, are miniatures of Duke Ludwig of Württemberg (1554–93) and his first wife, Dorothea of Baden. Stuttgart, c. 1582. 92 × 42 mm.

60 *opposite* A gold mirror back conceals at its centre, behind a cover, a miniature of the Electress Sophia of Saxony (cf. Ill. 38) on silver. The mirror back is enamelled with grotesques, flowers, animals and scrolls. South German, c. 1600. 15 × 11 cm.

diamonds, two pear pearls and a faceted ruby within a border of small diamonds. There are devices amidst diamonds on the covers of the five other lockets containing miniatures and each of the linking pieces consisting of flames and arrows tied with knots is set with a medium-size table-cut diamond, while thirty-eight small diamonds, five rubies and a sapphire embellish the Queen's coat of arms.[30]

From the court the fashion for the miniature portrait jewel was adopted by all who could afford to commission images of beloved individuals. That they kept the memory of the dead alive is made clear in a portrait of a widow with her small daughter, c. 1590 [57]. The richly jewelled frame holding a miniature of the husband and father takes centre place, hanging from the girdle of the woman's black dress, while their child, guided by the gloved hand of her mother, holds it as something sacred.

Elsewhere in Europe the miniature was enclosed in different settings – in lockets combined with a medallic portrait [59], within a lozenge-shaped mirror enamelled with grotesques [60], and in rings, the images identified by the coats of arms at the back of the bezel.[31]

Meanwhile in England the miniature had taken root and flourished as a form of national artistic expression. Henry VIII, who was the first royal enthusiast, reciprocated the gift of the Duchesse d'Alençon by sending portraits of himself and of Princess Mary, with ciphers and emblems whose meaning was explained by the envoy who delivered them to the French court. The good likeness of King Henry so pleased François I that he took off his hat, saying he knew well that face and 'I pray that God grants you a long and happy life', adding that

61, 62 *right and opposite* The Drake Jewel. The locket encloses miniatures of Queen Elizabeth – surrounded by a ruby border – and her emblem, the phoenix. The cover is set with a sardonyx cameo of a black ruler and his consort, within an enamelled and chased gold frame embellished with table-cut rubies and diamonds, hung with pearls. The jewel was presented by the Queen to Sir Francis Drake. Miniatures by Nicholas Hilliard, 1588; setting contemporary. H 117 mm.

no present could have given him greater pleasure.³² None of the miniatures commissioned first from Lucas Horenbout and then from Hans Holbein by Henry VIII has retained its original setting, although we get a glimpse of one of them from a letter to Anne Boleyn of 1527 mentioning the King's gift to her of 'my picture set in a bracelet, with the whole device which you already know'.³³ Others belonged to his daughter Mary I: 'a brouche conteyninge the Image of kinge Henry the eight with the Quene having a crowne of Diamountes over them and a rose of diamountes under them and on each side a man of Diamauntes'³⁴ and 'a tablet of golde havinge on the one side the kinges picture painted and on the same side is a rose of diamountes and Rubies cont[aining] therein five diamountes and six Rubies on the border thereof is five verie small Diamountes and one Rubie in the toppe thereof and another underneath and in the border thereof is fower very small diamountes on the other side is two men'.³⁵

As limner or miniature painter to Queen Elizabeth, Nicholas Hilliard rejuvenated and idealized her looks in a series of delicately detailed ethereal images, as required by her political programme [61], and as a goldsmith he would also have been involved in the creation of jewelled settings for them. Some were enclosed in her own jewels and accessories, such as the fan given her by Sir Francis Drake in 1587,³⁶ and an oval ruby and diamond pendant with the heraldic knot and motto of the Heneage family, FAST THOUGH UNTIED, on the cover,³⁷ for as Horace Walpole observed, 'she loved pictures of herself'.³⁸ Others were sent abroad to fellow monarchs. At home recipients such as Lord Zouche, writing to Sir Robert Cecil in 1598, were well aware that the quality of the jewel had to reflect the honour conferred: 'I wish I could have as rich a box to keep it in as I esteem the favour great'.³⁹ Thus, the

Renaissance Europe, 1500–1625   61

63 *opposite* The Drake Jewel worn by Lady Seaton, a descendant of Sir Francis Drake, attached to a double row of pearls, in her portrait by Edwin Lang, 1884.

miniature enclosed in the famous locket she presented to Sir Francis Drake during the 1580s [61, 62] is surrounded by rubies, opposite her emblem of the phoenix, paragon of every virtue: a fine sardonyx double portrait of a black ruler and his white consort is set in the cover, within a delicately enamelled gold scrolled frame interspersed with table-cut rubies and diamonds, hung with pearls. Sir Francis was portrayed displaying this important token of his Queen's regard and of his loyalty to her hanging from a long gold chain in a portrait of 1591, and it passed down through the generations: his Victorian descendant Lady Seaton wears it high on the neck in her portrait [63].

A more emblematic original setting has a pierced cover centred on a star with alternate straight and forked rays, amid scrolls, set with rubies and diamonds [64], emphasizing the message of the miniature [65], which depicts the Queen with long flowing golden locks, the eternally youthful, virginal and beautiful Stella Britannis – Star of Britain – or Beauty's Rose. The back is enamelled in colours with a symmetrical pattern of dolphins, foliage and flowers against a black ground [66]. As with her cameo and medallic portraits, Hilliard succeeded in giving visual expression to the words of a refugee asking for assistance, the French poet Georges de La Motthe (1586):

> Qui voudra figurer, d'un ouvrage parfect
> La beauté, la Vertu, l'Ornement, et les graces
> De Nature, des Dieux, de l'univers, des Graces,
> Accoure contempler la grand' ELIZABETH.

(Whoever seeks the perfect embodiment / Of the Beauty, the Virtue, the Ornament and the gracefulness / Of Nature, the Heavens, the Universe and the Graces / Has only to contemplate the great Elizabeth.)

Renaissance Europe, 1500–1625 63

On their accession in 1603 James I and Queen Anne continued to patronize Nicholas Hilliard, and increasingly Isaac Oliver, for they, like Queen Elizabeth, understood the political and dynastic importance of diffusing their royal images at home and abroad. As early as 1603 Lady Arabella Stuart saw Count Aremburg, the Spanish ambassador, present King James with miniatures of Archduke Albert and his wife the Infanta Clara Eugenia, rulers of the Netherlands, 'most excellently drawn'.[40] This new alliance with Spain, which was signed in London in 1604, was marked by exchanges not only of full-length portraits but also of miniatures in jewelled boxes. Thus Sir George Carew, the Queen's Vice-Chamberlain, presented the Constable of Castile with a pearl necklace for his wife and lockets made by the court jeweller Sir John Spilman enclosing the portraits of the royal couple. The following year, Queen Margaret of Spain reciprocated with gifts of her miniature and that of Philip III painted by Juan Pantoja de la Cruz, both set in diamond-studded lockets.[41] These no longer exist, but another case, sent by James I to the Emperor Matthias in Prague, illustrates the quality of such diplomatic gifts [4, 67–69]: the cover is set with a sardonyx cameo bust of a Roman emperor, the back with rubies and diamonds amidst chased and enamelled grotesques, flowers and leaves, and the interior is densely patterned in many colours. Now it is the value of these stones that indicates the prestige of the person portrayed rather than symbols and allegorical figures.

Introducing this new emphasis on stones is the locket given by James I in 1610 to Thomas Lyte [70–72] in return for tracing the royal pedigree back to Brute, the 'most noble founder of the Britons', through Scots, Romans, Saxons, Danes, and Charlemagne, set out in a vast genealogical table.

64–66 *opposite and this page* Three views of a case and the miniature that it encloses, of Queen Elizabeth as Stella Britannis, the Star of Britain. The openwork cover is set with table-cut rubies and diamonds centred on a star; the back is enamelled black with multicoloured symmetrical ornament of leaves and dolphins. Miniature by Nicholas Hilliard, *c.* 1600; setting contemporary. 64 × 48 mm.

Renaissance Europe, 1500–1625   65

67–69 Three views of a locket with a pearl drop that originally contained a miniature of James I of England and Ireland and VI of Scotland (cf. Ill. 72), sent by the King to the Emperor Matthias Corvinus in Prague. The interior is finely enamelled in various colours; the front is set with a sardonyx cameo of a Roman emperor, perhaps Claudius; and the back has scrolls and grotesques embellished with table-cut rubies and diamonds. French (?), *c.* 1575–90. H 80 mm. (For a closer view of the interior, see Ill. 4.)

Renaissance Europe, 1500–1625   67

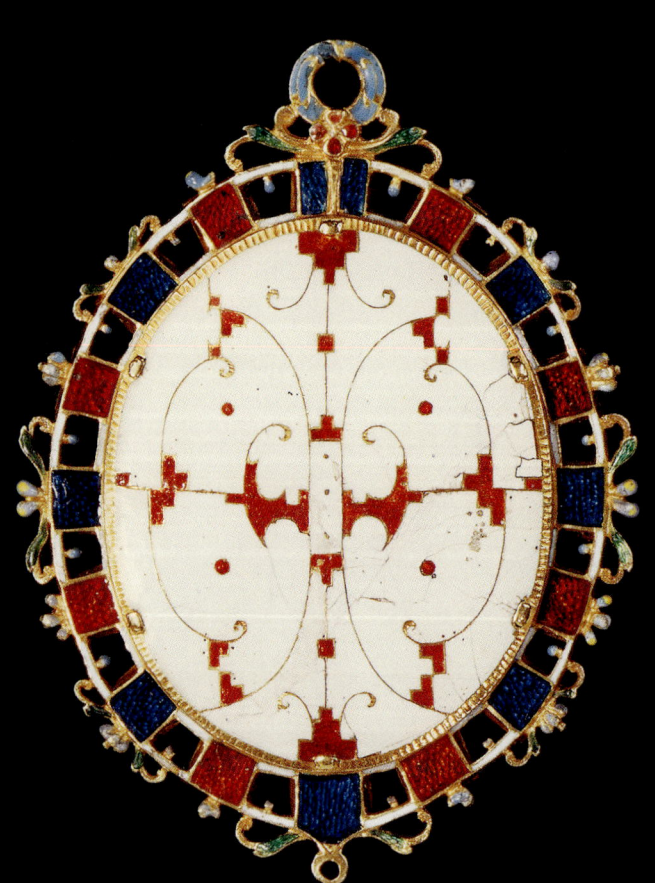

70–72 Three views of the Lyte Jewel, given by King James I of England and Ireland and VI of Scotland (1566–1625) to Thomas Lyte. The miniature portrait of the King is surrounded by table-cut diamonds. It lies under an openwork cover with the royal cipher, IR, in diamonds, and was originally hung with a trilobe diamond drop. The back is enamelled in a 'black work' pattern in red and white. Miniature by Nicholas Hilliard, 1610; setting contemporary. 65 × 48 mm.

The miniature of King James, painted by Nicholas Hilliard [72], is enclosed behind an openwork cover [70] with an outer border of sixteen diamonds surrounding the diamond monogram IR (for Iacobus Rex, King James) amidst trails of flowers and leaves enamelled in various colours; the back is enamelled red on a white ground in a 'black work' pattern [71]. More conservative is a smaller enamelled locket containing the King's miniature by Hilliard within a radiate border facing the motto and emblem of the Ark on stormy seas painted on the inside of the cover, which is a continuation of Queen Elizabeth's policy of presenting herself as the sovereign on whom the peace and safety of her subjects depended in a period of religious and political divisions [cf. 45].

Documents confirm that Hilliard was paid by King James for supplying settings for miniatures, as he had been during the reign of Queen Elizabeth.[42] These included cases for images of Henry, Prince of Wales, and his brother Charles with their sister Elizabeth, and perhaps for that of the favourite, the handsome Duke of Buckingham, which the King said he wore 'on a blue ribbon under my waistcoat next to my heart'.[43]

George Heriot, the Edinburgh goldsmith, supplied the locket that Queen Anne gave in 1610 to her maid of honour, Lady Anne Livingston, later Countess of Eglinton: it bears the diamond-studded royal cipher CAR surrounded by two *fermesses* (symbolic of constancy) and interlaced Cs [73, 74]. In her portraits by Van Somer and Marcus Gheeraerts Queen Anne wears her miniature cases hanging on a ribbon over her heart, as does Lady Anne in her portrait [75]. One of the Queen's jewelled cases was a gift from her brother, Christian IV of Denmark, during his state visit to England in 1606, when 'he took her into his cabin and slapping her familiarly on the back as when they were children he gave her his

73, 74 Two views of an enamelled gold case enclosing a miniature of Queen Anne (d. 1618), wife of James I of England and Ireland and VI of Scotland, presented by her to Lady Anne Livingston, Countess of Eglinton (see Ill. 75). The front cover has the diamond cipher CAR flanked by *fermesses*, between a royal crown and double Cs, with four diamonds in quatrefoil settings. Miniature from the circle of Nicholas Hilliard, 1610; setting by George Heriot (1563–1623) of Edinburgh. H 76 mm.

75 Lady Anne Livingston, Countess of Eglinton (d. 1632), wearing the miniature case given to her by Queen Anne (see Ills. 73, 74) on a ribbon over her heart, in a portrait by an unknown artist, c. 1612.

portrait richly set in jewels'. In August 1605 she had sent him hers with this message: 'I send herewith our portrait with the friendly and sisterly plea that you will wear the same to please us and thereby think on us with brotherly affection just as we wear your portrait not only on our dress but with the devoted memory of a sister.'[44] She seems never to have been without one of these miniatures, which were frequently being returned to George Heriot for repairs to the cases. Heriot did more than mend: he also supplied the expensive crystal covers, made new cases, two of them naturalistic – a rose, and a bay leaf, set with diamonds on both back and front – and 'a ring set with 9 diamonds, and opening on the head with the king's picture in that'.[45]

Where royalty led others followed the fashion, as is evident from Shakespeare's *Twelfth Night*, when Viola says to Olivia: 'Heere, wear this jewel for me. 'Tis my picture' (III. iv. 228). Many women would have been proud to wear Hilliard's miniature of that archetypal adventurer of the Elizabethan age, George, 3rd Earl of Cumberland; his arresting portrait dated 1589, the year after the Armada in which he had commanded the ship *Bonaventure*, is still in the original case, decorated with strapwork and hung with pearls [76, 77]. Another fine miniature case with miniatures by Hilliard is said to have been given by Queen Elizabeth to Katherine Walsingham and Sir Thomas Gresley on the occasion of their marriage [78–80]. The cover is set with a sardonyx cameo of a veiled black woman, surrounded by a band of rubies and emeralds, flanked on each side by black boys emerging from cornucopiae, firing arrows upwards; the back is finely enamelled; and the case is hung with pearls.

Lord Herbert describes how a besotted woman admirer, Lady Ayres, obtained with great difficulty a copy of his portrait by William Larkin, and then 'gave it to Mr. Isaac, the painter in Blackfriars and desired him to draw it in little after his manner which being done she caused it to be set in gold and enamelled and she wore it about her neck so low that she hid it under her breasts', infuriating her husband.[46]

Although enough miniatures survive to confirm their popularity, most often the original cases no longer exist. The cover of the locket in which Alice, Countess of Derby, enclosed her husband's miniature was thickly set with diamonds and his initials were on the back,[47] but as with almost all original settings except for a few decorated with enamels this has vanished. And though attractive and colourful, enamel is fragile: Miss Hamilton, a friend of the Duchess of Portland, on a visit to the collection at Bulstrode in 1783 observed 'Sir Walter Raleigh and his son in an old-fashioned locket which had been ornamented with jewels in a large locket black and green enamel: it had belonged to Lady Raleigh, ye ciphers of WR and E are remaining tho' ye enamel is damaged.'[48]

76, 77 Pendant enclosing a miniature of George, 3rd Earl of Cumberland (1558–1605), within a black and white zigzag border, edged with three pearls. The back is patterned with gold interlaced strapwork with blue details on a gold ground. Miniature by Nicholas Hilliard, 1589; setting contemporary. c. 47 × 38 mm.

Renaissance Europe, 1500–1625   75

78–80 Three views of the Gresley Jewel, a gold locket with pearls containing miniatures of Sir Thomas Gresley (1522–1610) and his wife, Katherine Walsingham (1559–85). The pedimented cover is set with a sardonyx cameo of a black woman, veiled, in an enamelled frame embellished with rubies and emeralds, flanked by half figures of black boys emerging from cornucopiae and firing arrows; the back is enamelled with symmetrical ornament. Miniatures by Nicholas Hilliard and setting c. 1574, the date of their marriage. H 69 mm.

Renaissance Europe, 1500–1625　77

2 The Baroque Interpretation 1625–1715

Even rarer than the portrait jewelry of the Renaissance is that of the following period, when the settings, hitherto the concern of goldsmiths, were taken over by jewellers, who enriched them with far greater quantities of stones and pearls. These gems, because of their intrinsic value, were fated to be removed, recut and reset into more up-to-date designs by the following generations, so virtually all the original 17th-century jewels have vanished. Enamel continued to be used, but in a different technique, introduced around 1625–30 at Châteaudun by Jean Toutin and at Blois by Isaac Gribelin and Christophe Morlière: a gold surface was covered with an opaque layer of white, black or pale blue enamel on which a wide range of colour was then applied, like an artist painting a canvas. Flowers and ribbon motifs, often combined with acanthus scrolls, were the dominant decorative theme for portrait jewelry settings.

81 *opposite* Detail of a portrait of the Yorkshire officer Daniel Goodricke, his sash hung with a portrait medal of King Gustavus Adolphus of Sweden (see Ill. 96).

Cameos and Intaglios

Although monarchs continued to commission their portraits from gem engravers, there is a decline in quantity and quality from the heights achieved in the previous century. In most countries this was due to religious and political divisions which were not conducive to the difficult and expensive court art of gem engraving. The instability of France, divided between the Huguenots and the Roman Catholics and by the power struggle between the crown and the nobility, is alluded to in a garnet full-front cameo portrait of Louis XIII [82, 83]. The cameo is embellished with enamelled gold features: green laurel crown, green, yellow and white cuirass with lion mask at the shoulder, and blue cloak fastened with a brooch, in a setting framed in foliate scrolls. The back is engraved with emblems and allegorical figures, all symbolically relating to the capture in 1628 of La Rochelle, stronghold of the Huguenots in revolt against the monarchy since 1625: crowned shield charged with interlaced Ls (for Louis) flanked by laurel branches held up by two putti, above a seated woman, blindfold, who holds a sword and sceptre in one hand and in the other a plaque inscribed PIETATE ET JUSTITIA (Piety and Justice). At her feet are the royal crown, sceptre and hand of Justice.

Notwithstanding the great flowering of the arts during Louis XIV's long reign, and although he took an interest in the royal collection of engraved gems and is known to have commissioned Josias Belle, the court jeweller, to frame them in varicoloured acanthus ornament, some enriched with gems, his own few surviving cameo portraits are mounted more simply. A sardonyx profile portrait dating from the early years of his reign is framed in a border of enamelled leaves [84]; another, showing him at the end of it, is surrounded by a double border of richly chased foliate gold scrolls, to be worn as a pendant.[1] An unidentified example of these rare hardstone

82, 83 Front and back of a gold medallion set with a garnet cameo *commesso* portrait of Louis XIII, King of France (1601–43), on a diapered gold ground, within an enamelled foliate border, 1628. 78 × 63 mm. The emblems on the back relate to the capture of La Rochelle from the Huguenots.

84 Gold medallion set with a sardonyx cameo portrait of the young Louis XIV, King of France (1638–1715), within an enamelled foliate border, mid-17th century. 49 × 45 mm.

images belonged to Jean Baptiste-Colbert, the all-powerful minister unreservedly trusted by Louis XIV, whom he served in many capacities from 1661.²

Across the Channel, the art received a new impulse from Charles I, who not only engaged Anthony van Dyck to paint his official image but – although his parents, James I and Queen Anne, had shown little interest in gem engraving – employed Thomas Rawlins and Thomas Simon as gem-cutters and medallists. The crises culminating in the Civil War must have restricted their activities, but several cameo portraits of the King dating from before and after his execution survive in their original ring settings [85, 86].³ Those which were worn by Stuart loyalists, who regarded him as a martyr, are set in rings inscribed with the date of his death and bear *memento mori* symbols.⁴

Whereas Rawlins followed King Charles during the Civil War, Simon supported Oliver Cromwell, who on becoming Lord Protector of the Commonwealth in 1653 appointed him to engrave his portrait as head of state, in the tradition of the Tudor and Stuart monarchy.⁵ A portrait by John Michael Wright of Betty Claypole, Cromwell's favourite child [87], shows her wearing a long chain hung with a pendant set with a cameo representing her father as the Warrior Protector, in armour and cloak, deriving from the medal commemorating his victory at Dunbar of 1650. A similar cameo portrait [88] – perhaps the same – has at the back the crowned arms of the Commonwealth (cross of St George, cross of St Andrew and Irish harp) on which Cromwell's family arms (a lion rampant) have been superimposed, and the Protector's personal authority is further emphasized by a surrounding inscription. The diamonds enriching the frame have been replaced with pastes.

German and Austrian rulers adopted shell as the medium for dynastic cameo portraits, which being easier to carve than

85, 86 Two views of a gold ring set with a cornelian cameo portrait of Charles I, King of Great Britain and Ireland (1600–1649), wreathed and wearing Roman style armour, flanked by pairs of rose-cut diamonds. Cameo attributed to Thomas Rawlins (1620–70), c. 1640; ring 1660–70. 15 × 13 mm.

87 *opposite* Mrs John Claypole (1629–58), favourite daughter of Oliver Cromwell, holding her father's cameo portrait hanging from a chain. Portrait by John Michael Wright, 1658.

88 Pendant set with a sardonyx cameo portrait of Oliver Cromwell (1599–1658), within a frame now filled with table-cut 'ruby' pastes set in collets with engrailed edges alternating with loops imitating ribbons. An inscription on the back proclaims his authority: OLIVER CROMWELL ANG: SCO: FRA: ET HIB: PRO: AN DOM 1657 (Oliver Cromwell, Protector of England, Scotland, France and Ireland, AD 1657). Cameo attributed to Thomas Simon (1618–65), 1657. Cameo 13 × 10 mm.

The Baroque Interpretation, 1625–1715

hardstone could be used for whole series of images establishing the right to occupy their thrones, mounted relatively inexpensively. Thus a mid-century group of nine portraits of the kings of Germany and the emperors Albrecht I, Charles V, Maximilian I and II, Rudolf II, Matthias, and Ferdinand I, II and III of Austria, each framed in a silver-gilt filigree border, was designed to be linked together in a chain.[6] Ferdinand III affirmed his right and that of his heirs to rule the Habsburg lands in a series of pendants mounted with turquoise, coral, and shell cameos of himself, his Spanish first wife Maria Anna and his brother, the Archduke Leopold Wilhelm, Bishop of Breslau and Governor of the Spanish Netherlands, associated with the symbols of double-headed eagle, scales of justice, sword, sceptre, imperial crown and globe [89].[7] Surrounding the portraits in this group are smaller cameos representing the twelve Habsburg predecessors of Ferdinand III, their devices and emblems, the coats of arms of Austria, Bohemia and Hungary amidst leaves and flowers enamelled in various colours with white dots, interspersed with precious and semi-precious stones.

Beside this uncompromising statement of hereditary power and the divine right to rule, in the double-sided pendant set with portrait cameos of Ferdinand III and of Leopold Wilhelm a cautionary note is struck by a concealed enamelled image of an infant blowing bubbles [90, 91]. This *memento mori* compares men's lives to bubbles – some large, some small, but all destined to break up sooner or later.[8] Similarly in a painting by Antonio de Pereda, *Allegory of the Passage of Time* [92], symbols of death – hourglass, skulls and unlit candle – contrast with the worldly power epitomized by a cameo portrait of Charles V as a Roman emperor, wreathed with laurel, wearing armour and the Order of the Golden Fleece.

89 *opposite* A pendant with cover centred on a shell cameo portrait of the Emperor Ferdinand III (1608–57), surrounded by smaller cameo portraits of his Habsburg predecessors, edged with enamelled ornament and rubies and the devices and emblems of the dynasty, mid-17th century. 68 × 55 mm.

The Baroque Interpretation, 1625–1715 87

90, 91 *opposite and right* Two elements of a double-sided locket. The exterior displays a shell cameo portrait of Archduke Leopold Wilhelm (1614–62), patron of the arts and Governor of the Spanish Netherlands, in armour, inscribed and against a blue ground, within a white and black foliate border interspersed with rubies. (A shell cameo portrait of Ferdinand III is on the front.) Concealed within the locket is an enamelled *memento mori* plaque showing a putto blowing bubbles, with a skull and hourglass. Mid-17th century. 47 × 35 mm.

The Baroque Interpretation, 1625–1715

92 In his *Allegory of the Passage of Time*, of 1654, Antonio de Pereda shows Fame holding a portrait cameo of the Emperor Charles V (cf. Ill. 6) above a globe and symbols of worldly success. These are contrasted with *memento mori* symbols on the left – hourglass, skulls, and snuffed-out candle.

His authority is reinforced by the gold cartouche frame enamelled with crescent moons, with a lion's mask at the base and an imperial eagle gripping the globe of sovereignty.

During the long reign of Ferdinand's younger son, Leopold I, the defeat of the armies of Louis XIV and the repulse of the invading Turks greatly strengthened the Emperor's political power and belief in his divine right to rule. This air of absolute authority and the unmistakable Habsburg 'look' have been captured by Daniel Vogt in his emerald portrait cameo in its rich frame of black and white acanthus scrolls alternating with rose-cut diamonds [93].

93 Silver-gilt pendant set with an emerald cameo bust of the Emperor Leopold I (1640–1705) within a frame of black and white acanthus scrolls interspersed with rose-cut diamonds. Cameo signed by Daniel Vogt (d. 1674), 1669/70; setting contemporary. 56 × 45 mm.

The Baroque Interpretation, 1625–1715

Portrait Medals

In 1662 Colbert, Minister of Louis XIV, defined the purpose of medals: 'they are an invention which the Greeks and Romans used to immortalize the heroic actions of their princes, captains and emperors. Because of the incorruptibility of the metals of which they are composed I strongly approve of them to perpetuate those of the king.' Colbert was not alone: so great was the demand for portraits of 17th-century rulers intent on establishing their authority that the role of the medallist was more important than ever. In these circumstances some outstanding exponents – G. Dupré, Jean Warin [94], François Chéron, Jean Mauger, Jérôme Roussel, Joseph Roettiers, A. Meysbusch – emerged thanks to royal patronage in France, Germany and England. The painter Pieter van Roestraeten, who appreciated the prestige of medals, includes one – perhaps his own – hanging on its chain in a *vanitas* group of de luxe objects with a skull.[9] As medals could be distributed in greater numbers than either cameos or miniatures, they played an essential role in rewarding war services and in diplomacy at the signing of peace treaties, trade agreements and the settlement of the terms of royal marriages. In Spain, for instance, gold chains with portrait medals of Philip IV and his bride Mariana of Austria were distributed to the officials involved in the negotiations of 1649; and in 1656 when Cardinal Mazarin's representative went to Madrid to arrange the marriage of Louis XIV with the Infanta Maria Teresa, his Spanish counterpart, Philip IV's minister Don Luis de Haro, wore a medallion with her portrait in his hat.[10]

From 1662 the *Registres des Présents du Roi* provides information about the recipients of medals from Louis XIV, with or without chains.[11] A great patron of this art, he awarded them to the staff of ambassadors such as Girolamo Venier of Venice, to a deputation from Tripoli, to the representatives of the Catholic

94 The young Louis XIV, King of France (1638–1715), with the medallist Jean Warin (1596–1672), portrayed by François Lemaire, *c.* 1650.

94 *The Baroque Interpretation, 1625–1715*

95 *opposite* A framed collection of simulated medals illustrating various stages of the life of Louis XIV, arranged around symbols of victory, war and sovereignty. By Antoine Benoist (1632–1717), 1704.

cantons who came to Versailles to renew the alliance between France and Switzerland, to representatives of other monarchs bringing their condolences on the deaths of the Queen, the Grand Dauphin and the Duke of Burgundy. Others were given to honour more ordinary people whose conduct had come to the attention of the King. Most were seamen: the Dunkirk sailor whose 'action d'éclat' was decisive in the battle between the great French captain Jean Bart and the Dutch navy at Texel in 1694, the mate of a ship which had captured a British man-of-war in 1703, and Captain Augier of Marseilles who put up an extraordinary fight in defence of his ship full of valuable cargo against pirates in 1712. Increasingly, it became customary to distribute medals not so much to wear but in sets which combined to illustrate the military triumphs, diplomacy and government of the King, and which were kept in cabinets.[12] The superb quality affirmed French supremacy in the arts. Medals also played a part in developing French interests in the New World: in 1710 the Marquis de Vaudreuil, Governor General in Canada, was sent forty silver medals representing the royal family to distribute among the 'sauvages', or Iroquois Indians.

Reflecting the struggle between Catholics and Protestants during the disastrous Thirty Years War are portrait medals of the hero of the Protestant cause, Gustavus Adolphus, King of Sweden. After his death on the battlefield at Lutzen, fighting the army of the Austrian Emperor, quantities of medals, pendants, necklaces and beakers were produced to commemorate his military victories, intellectual abilities and statesmanship. Some of the medals are enamelled and show him in open silhouette only: one such hangs from a black sash worn by a Yorkshire officer, Daniel Goodricke, who had enlisted with the English Volunteers to join the Swedish King's army [81, 96]. Another, struck by Sebastian Dadler, medallist at Dresden,

96 *opposite* Portrait of the Yorkshire mercenary Daniel Goodricke (1597–1657/58). From his sash hangs a portrait medal similar to that seen here of Gustavus Adolphus of Sweden, for whom he fought during the Thirty Years War. English School, 1634. (For a closer view, see Ill. 81.)

97 Portrait medal commemorating Gustavus Adolphus, King of Sweden (1594–1632), enamelled and framed in a laurel crown and forget-me-knots with pendant pearl. By Sebastian Dadler (1586–1657), after 1632; setting probably German. H 80 mm.

98 *The Baroque Interpretation, 1625–1715*

98 *opposite* Silver medallion with a portrait of Charles I, crowned and wearing the collar of the Order of the Garter, framed in laurel. By Nicholas Briot (*c.* 1579–*c.* 1646). H 57 mm.

Nuremberg and Berlin, shows him also in an enamelled open silhouette but surrounded by a green laurel crown with two forget-me-nots and a hanging pearl [97], a symbolic design adopted by other rulers.

As the monarch who engaged Van Dyck to transform his official image, Charles I also commissioned equally fine but smaller portrait medals from Nicholas Briot and his successor Thomas Rawlins as a means of rewarding political and military support to his regime [98]. They might be worn in the hat or pendant from a ribbon. (As they indicated adherence to the Stuart cause and served to keep alive the memory of the King Martyr until the restoration of Charles II in 1660, they could not be publicly displayed during the Commonwealth.) The medallic quality is high; unlike the German *Gnadenpfennige*, however, they were not further embellished with jewelled frames but bordered with laurel crowns as an integral part of the design.

Similar medallions showing Cromwell commissioned from Thomas Simon, 'Graver of the Mint and Seals', were distributed by the Parliamentarians during the Civil War and the Protectorate. As head of state, Cromwell was obliged to continue the practice not only to reward his supporters but for diplomatic presentation. Sir Bulstrode Whitelocke, the Protector's envoy to Queen Christina of Sweden, daughter of Gustavus Adolphus, in his account of the end of his mission in May 1654 described how such gifts were graduated in value according to status. After the court master of ceremony had given Sir Bulstrode the Queen's miniature framed in diamonds, he went to the envoy's two sons

> and in the Queen's name presented to each of them a chain of gold of five links, and at the end of the chain a medal of gold with the Queen's picture . . . Then he

99 Self-portrait of David Beck (1621–56), painting a portrait of Queen Christina and wearing her portrait medal, c. 1649 (engraving after Beck by Joseph-Antoine Cognet).

presented in the Queen's name, to Colonel Potley, to Dr. Whistler, to Captain Beake, and Mr. Earle, to each of them a chain of gold of four links and at the end of each chain a medal of gold of the Queen's picture . . . Then he presented in the Queen's name, to Mr. Stapleton, Mr. Ingelo, and Mr. De la Marche, to each of them a chain of gold of three links, with a medal of gold of the Queen's picture at the end of each chain . . . To Mr. Walker he presented a chain and medal of gold of three links . . . to Captain Crispe and to Mr. Swift to each of them a chain of gold of two links . . . Walker the steward and Stapleton gentleman of the horse to Whitelocke were discontented because their chains were not of four links apiece: and they and the others took exceptions because their chains were not so good and valuable as those given to Potley and Beake.

Whitelocke tried to pour oil on these troubled waters by explaining that the better chains had been awarded to Potley and Beake since one was an ancient servant of the Swedish Crown and the other commander of the Protector's guard; he also pointed out that as the Queen was not obliged to give them anything at all they should be grateful for what they had received. Notwithstanding, Stapleton announced his intention of returning his present to the master of ceremony, who explained that neither he nor the Queen was responsible for deciding who should receive the most and least valuable: this was decided by the officers of the Chamber of Accounts according to the standing of the individuals within the embassy.[13] Queen Christina, who admired Cromwell's daring rise to power and his firm leadership, sent him a double gold chain with her medal hung with pearls.[14]

100 Enamelled gold portrait medal of Christina, Queen of Sweden (1626–89). Medal by Gottfried Tabbert, mid-17th century. 40 × 33 mm.

Two examples of the chains to which 17th-century medallions were attached, proudly displayed by Elias Ashmole in his portrait by John Riley [101], have survived in the Ashmolean Museum in Oxford, which bears his name. According to Anthony Wood, Ashmole was 'the greatest virtuoso and curioso that ever was known or read of in England before his time', whose greatest achievement was his history, *The Institution, Laws & Ceremonies of the most noble Order of the Garter* (1672), and the medals attached to the chains were presented to him by foreign princes appointed to the Order, Frederick III of Denmark and the Elector of Brandenburg. Acknowledging King Frederick's gift to Count Greiffenfeld, Ashmole promised that the gold chain and medal would be bequeathed to a 'publique Musaeum' so that 'Posterity may take notice of his bounty to an English Gentleman'.[15]

The frames of *Gnadenpfennige* followed contemporary fashion. That of Friedrich Wilhelm of Saxe-Altenberg (1632), surrounded by military trophies in the traditional manner of asserting his valour in battle, is conservative in design.[16] A new note is struck by a medallion with the portrait of Duke Ernst of Saxe-Weimar on one side and on the other that of his wife Elizabeth Sophia, daughter of Duke Johann Philipp of Saxe-Altenberg (1652) [102, 103]: reflecting the emerging interest in gardens and flowers, their profiles are garlanded with a mixture of roses, tulips, irises, and five-petalled flowers and fruits with blue ribbons elegantly twisted above and below. The portrait of the young Maximilian II Emanuel of Bavaria (*c.* 1680) [104] is crowned with the head of a putto with outstretched wings and flanked by groups of fruit and flowers – as were the earlier medallions of Duchess Maria Anna (1654) and her husband Maximilian[17] – brought up to date by the addition of acanthus leaves.

101 *opposite* Elias Ashmole (1617–92), portrayed by John Riley, *c.* 1681–82. He wears on a chain a portrait medallion of Friedrich Wilhelm, Elector of Brandenburg; also displayed are a portrait medal of Karl Ludwig of Bavaria and a chain and medal presented by Frederick III, King of Denmark. (Between the latter is the George of the Order of the Garter which had belonged to Thomas Howard, 2nd Earl of Arundel.) The rich frame, with Ashmole's coat of arms and motto, was carved by Grinling Gibbons.

104 *opposite* Gnadenpfennig of the Elector Maximilian II Emanuel of Bavaria (1662–1726), in an enamelled gold frame with acanthus scrolls surmounted by a putto head. Medal by Philipp Heinrich Müller (1654–1719), Augsburg, *c.* 1680. 67 × 62 mm.

102, 103 Front and back of a *Gnadenpfennig* with portraits of Duke Ernst of Saxe-Weimar (1601–75) and his wife, Elizabeth Sophia (1619–80), within an openwork enamelled gold garland tied with blue ribbons, 1652. 128 × 48 mm.

The Baroque Interpretation, 1625–1715   105

Miniatures

Portrait cameos and medals usually served an official purpose. Miniatures too were much used in diplomacy, especially in connection with royal marriages; but they were also adopted by many private individuals, who wore them cased as handsomely as they could afford. The designs for miniature cases published by François Lefebvre (1635, 1657, 1661) [160], Gilles Légaré (1663) [152] and Thomas Le Juge (1678) diffused the latest Parisian fashions abroad, which were quickly adopted by designers such as Johann Paulus Haüer [105].

Although miniatures were painted throughout 17th-century Europe, this art seems to have been more widely patronized in England than on the Continent. The leading artists – Peter Oliver [106], David Des Granges [124], John Hoskins, Samuel Cooper and his brother Alexander [129–134, 144] – and their followers used the watercolour technique. For a brief period from his arrival in London in 1637 until the outbreak of the Civil War Jean I Petitot among others produced portraits in enamel [107–109, 153–156, 159, 161].

Since the colours fused by firing remained permanent and brilliant they did not require more than the protection of a glass cover, so the backs and borders only were embellished with enamel and gems. Unusually, the miniature of Venetia, wife of Sir Kenelm Digby, enamelled by Henri Toutin in 1637 after her death [106], is flanked by white figures holding coloured swags of fruit and flowers, echoing those framing Renaissance paintings in the chateau of Fontainebleau, surmounted by her coat of arms and a shell. The Latin inscription at the back translates 'He tries to snatch a ghost from the funeral pyre and fights a great battle with death, exhausting the skills of the artists. Everywhere he searches for thee – O, the bitterness of it – on a piece of metal.' This refers to Sir Kenelm's sorrow at the loss of the wife described by Lord Clarendon as a woman 'of extraordinary beauty and as extraordinary fame'. After his departure to France some English artists continued to use the Petitot method, but it was eclipsed by the watercolour medium until the arrival of Charles Boit in 1687.

105 *opposite* Engraving of designs for miniature cases, the central one shaped as a tortoise, its back patterned with flowers, by Johann Paulus Haüer, 1650.

106 Miniature of Venetia, Lady Digby (d. 1633), in a figurative enamelled frame. Miniature by Henri Toutin (1614–83) after Peter Oliver (1594–1648); setting by Gilles Légaré (d. 1663), 1637. 125 × 83 mm.

Of the beautiful miniatures of Charles I, his wife and their children few have retained their original settings, which could have been broken up on account of the value of the stones. One such is listed in the will of Lady Jean Wemyss of 1655: 'The king's picture which is set with 80 small diamonds' – though at that date she could have referred to Charles II, still in exile. The three images after Van Dyck of the King, Queen and future Charles II are simply bordered in the shade of blue enamel that is Jean Petitot's signature [107–109]. An oval miniature signed by Henri Toutin and dated 1636 is bordered by a curvilinear frame enamelled with flowers which echo those on the King's embroidered jacket [110].

Far more numerous are the surviving posthumous and commemorative miniatures. The most important is a large gold heart-shaped locket, embellished with pearls, enclosing a miniature with skull and crossbones below and the royal crown above, and a piece of linen stained with blood from the corpse after the King's execution of 1649 [111]. Another pendant encloses a miniature after a portrait by Sir Peter Lely within a gold filigree frame.[18] One loyal follower inserted a small miniature within the petals of an enamelled spray of flowers [112], but this was exceptional. More usually, these royal memorial miniatures were set under glass in rings with heart-shaped or oval bezels, framed and crowned in rose-cut diamonds, the back enamelled with the royal cipher and date of execution, with Latin or English inscriptions such as PREPARED BEE TO FOLLOW ME. The more cautious royalists during the Commonwealth might hide the miniatures within a hinged locket bezel, the lid left plain or decorated with a non-political symbol.[19]

107–109 *opposite* Miniatures of Charles I, Queen Henrietta Maria (1609–69) and their son, the future Charles II (1630–85), within pale blue enamelled borders. Miniatures by Jean I Petitot (1607–91) after portraits by Van Dyck, 1638–39. Each 51 × 40 mm.

110 Pendant with a miniature of Charles I after a portrait by Van Dyck, the curvilinear frame enamelled with naturalistic flowers. Miniature and frame by Henri Toutin (who added the flowers on the King's jacket), 1636. 65 × 55 mm.

111 *opposite* Gold, pearl and enamel heart-shaped memorial pendant containing a bloodstained linen relic, hair, and posthumous miniature of Charles I, the Blessed Martyr King, after Van Dyck. Heart 38 × 30 mm.

112 Multicoloured enamel spray of flowers, the petals of the central flower framing a miniature of Charles I, worn in memory of his execution, *c.* 1650. 45 × 70 mm.

Samuel Cooper produced fine miniatures of Oliver Cromwell as presents to French and Dutch men of affairs and diplomats. Another was sent to Queen Christina of Sweden accompanied by a Latin epigram by John Milton:

> Bellipotens Virgo, Septem regina trionum
> Christina, Arctoi lucida stella poli!

(O Virgin Queen of the North, expert in war, / Christina, the arctic heaven's fair shining star!) In return for it she sent him her portrait medal.[20]

As a boy and an exile during the Commonwealth Charles II was portrayed in medals and miniatures worn by Stuart supporters. One such, a slide, designed to be worn on a ribbon on the wrist or at the neck, painted with a double portrait with his father, is enamelled on the back with a pattern of flowers.[21] Other examples, finely enamelled, some with diamond crowns, or surrounded with turquoises and coloured stones, were commissioned after the restoration of 1660 [113, 114] and marriage with Catherine of Braganza. Finally, his death in 1685 was commemorated by portrait rings, of which one is shown worn by his son by Nell Gwynn, the first Duke of St Albans.[22]

A miniature of Anne Hyde, first wife of his brother, the Duke of York, and future James II, illustrates another Restoration style of setting [115, 116]: she is surrounded by an enamelled border, simulating stones, surmounted by a coronet, and her crowned cipher between palm branches is on the back. Dethroned in 1688, during the long years of exile at St-Germain in France with his second wife, Mary of Modena, James II was painted in miniature many times to meet the demand from adherents of the Stuart cause [117]. The posthumous inventory of Queen Mary's possessions lists those she

113, 114 Front and back of a gold locket with a miniature of Charles II, King of England, Scotland and Ireland, and also, it is claimed, of France (1630–85), covered by an octagonal crystal, perhaps his gift to Crown Prince Christian of Denmark. The back is inscribed in black on a blue ground and dated 1660. French (?). 32 × 22 mm.

The Baroque Interpretation, 1625–1715

117 *opposite* Gold pendant with a miniature of James II of Great Britain and Ireland and VII of Scotland (1635–1701). Miniature and setting English, *c.* 1685. 50 × 38 mm.

115, 116 *above and right* Front and back of a bracelet slide with a miniature of Anne Hyde, Duchess of York (1637–71), first wife of James II and mother of two successive Queens, Mary and Anne, in an enamelled frame surmounted by her coronet. On the back is her crowned cipher. Miniature by Richard Gibson (1615?–90), *c.* 1665; setting contemporary.

118, 119 *opposite* Front and back of an engrailed gold pendant with a miniature of Mary of Modena (1658–1718), second wife of James II, surmounted by three rose-cut diamonds; the back is enamelled with her crowned cipher. Miniature *c.* 1673; setting *c.* 1685–88.

retained for herself, including 'Two lockets for the arme, one a picture of the late King, the other of the late Princesse' – their daughter, Louise-Marie.[23] To a devoted supporter, the first Duke of Perth, who served her at St-Germain, she gave her own miniature, embellished with three rose-cut diamonds, set in silver, and enamelled with her cipher on the back [118, 119].

In England, so deep rooted had the custom of presenting miniatures as diplomatic gifts become that when William III became king in 1688 after the departure of James II, he and his wife Mary II, like all the monarchs of Europe, distributed them as badges of loyalty. Perhaps the most important survival from their reign is the large pendant, crowned, the front entirely covered with rose-cut crystals, with the miniature of King William enamelled on the back amidst enamelled scrolls [120, 121].

Since lovers took care to see that they looked their best in these portraits,[24] they also must have made sure that they were enshrined in attractive cases. Few could have been of better quality than the Grenville Jewel [122–124], the locket enclosing the miniature painted by David Des Granges of Sir Bevil Grenville, who was to be killed at the battle of Lansdown, near Bath, fighting for Charles I. Although the front of the oval case is embellished with a large sapphire, opals, table-cut rubies, diamonds and emeralds, they do not dominate the composition but blend in with the brilliant colours of the bouquet of flowers – roses, daisies – on a black ground. The back is enamelled with a complex symmetrical pattern of green, red, yellow and dark blue lozenges, quatrefoils, and octofoils outlined in white in a black cartouche on a red ground, epitomizing the heights attained by the London jewellers during the reign of Charles I.

120, 121 Back and front of a pendant surmounted by the royal crown. The back displays a miniature of William III, King of England, Scotland and Ireland (1650–1702), in armour, after Sir Godfrey Kneller, amidst enamelled foliate scrolls, while the front is covered with rose-cut rock crystals, c. 1690. 104 × 69 mm.

The Baroque Interpretation, 1625–1715

122–124 Three views of the Grenville Jewel, a locket with a pearl drop enclosing a miniature of Sir Bevil Grenville (1596–1643). The front (below) is enamelled with flowers and set with rubies, opals, emeralds and diamonds and a large sapphire, while the back is enamelled with abstract motifs. Miniature by David Des Granges (1611/13–?75) and setting c. 1635–40. 35 × 42 mm.

125, 126 Two views of a bracelet slide with a miniature perhaps of Lady Brillana Harley (1600–1643). The back is enamelled with *memento mori* motifs – pansies, skull and crossbones – linked by lover's knots and the Greek letter *phi* for fidelity. Miniature and setting English, mid-17th century. 27 × 22 mm.

Miniatures of the dead as well as the living were worn, their settings enamelled with memorial symbols and inscriptions. To commemorate his late wife, who died in 1692, John Hervey, 1st Earl of Bristol, wanted the verses on the back of her picture to recall 'the various graces God and nature had adorned her with, to remain in our family as an incentive for future daughters of it to emulate'.[25] An example of such a memorial miniature, thought to be for Lady Brillana Harley, designed to wear as a slide on a ribbon at the wrist, is enamelled at the back with *memento mori* symbols – pansies, skull and crossbones – and the Greek letter *phi*, denoting fidelity, linked to lover's knots [125, 126]. The twinned *phi* decorating the cover of the miniature case worn by the much-married Sarah Harington in her portrait painted by Cornelius Johnson is a further indication of the sentimental significance of this Greek letter [128].

For official presentation the miniature might be framed in diamonds and surmounted by a crown, as in a design by Hans Hollaender of 1635 [127]; that is annotated by Christian IV of Denmark, requiring the addition of an openwork cover with his diamond cipher. This rich type of setting was not proposed for Alexander Cooper's portraits of Christian's successor, Frederick III, his wife Sophie Amalie and their four children [129–140]: the elegant oval cases made by Paul Kurtz, the court jeweller, are simply enamelled on the back, the only ornament being the fine gold crowned ciphers and date 1656.

Further north, in Sweden, the custom of presenting royal miniatures had been adopted, some surrounded by diamonds in a bracelet slide [141] or a ring [142]. Queen Christina framed hers within a garland of enamelled marguerites highlighted with diamonds [143]. Alexander Cooper painted two fine miniatures of her successor Karl X Gustav [144] and his wife Queen Hedvig Eleonora, both surrounded by rubies.

127 Design by Hans Hollaender (fl. 1628–45) for a diamond miniature frame surmounted by the royal crown, annotated by King Christian IV of Denmark, 1635. It is inscribed 'Within, the likeness of the King's Majesty with a crystal stone [i.e. rock crystal] . . . for if this sketch shall graciously please the King's Majesty'. It was enclosed in a letter from Christian IV, where the King says that in addition he wants an openwork cover with his cipher in large diamonds (cf. Ills. 70, 72).

128 *opposite* Portrait of Sarah Harington (1565–1629) by Cornelius Johnson, 1628. She wears a miniature case decorated with the Greek letter *phi* symbolizing fidelity, twinned.

129–140 Front and back views of cases enclosing miniatures of Frederick III, King of Denmark (1609–70), Queen Sophie Amalie (1628–85) and their four children; the backs display crowned ciphers. Miniatures by Alexander Cooper (1609–60); settings by Paul Kurtz (active in Copenhagen 1655–76), 1656. Each 65 × 45 mm.

The Baroque Interpretation, 1625–1715 127

141 *left* Silver-gilt bracelet slides with miniatures of Queen Ulrika Eleonora the Elder (1656–95), wife of Charles XI of Sweden, and her mother, Dowager Queen Sophie Amalie of Denmark (cf. Ill. 130), surrounded by table-cut diamonds. Miniatures attributed to Louis Gouillon (active 1672–80), 1680; setting contemporary. Each 22 × 20 and 20 × 19 mm.

142 *above* Gold ring with a miniature of Gustavus Adolphus of Sweden under a crystal cover surrounded by table-cut diamonds, with others set on the shoulders. Miniature and setting probably Swedish, mid-17th century. 16 × 13 mm.

143 Pendant with a miniature of Queen Christina of Sweden in an enamelled frame of black and white daisies, each centred on a diamond, intertwined with diamond ribbons. Miniature by Pierre Signac (1623–84) after Sébastien Bourdon, after 1653; setting in the style of Gilles Légaré. 57 × 45 mm.

144 Miniature of Karl X Gustav, King of Sweden (1622–60), within a ruby frame. Miniature by Alexander Cooper, c. 1654; setting contemporary.

A miniature by Pierre Signac shows Hedvig Eleonora wearing King Karl's miniature [145].[26] Another miniature, probably by Signac, is of their son and successor Karl XI, surrounded by fifty table-cut emeralds bordered by black and white enamel leafy tendrils and surmounted by the royal crown [146].

Confident that his Spanish audiences understood its significance, the dramatist Pedro Calderón de la Barca in *Life is a Dream* (before 1636) makes Duke Astolfo's wearing of the miniature of another woman – Rosaura – enclosed in a locket the pretext for the Princess Estrella's decision not to become his wife, and leads him to keep his promise to marry Rosaura. In Spain as elsewhere, miniatures of the monarch rewarded loyal service and cemented diplomatic relations. The frames varied: a miniature of Philip IV after a portrait by Velásquez, enamelled on a watchcase, is surrounded by a garland of flowers in relief [147], while, according to a drawing, diamonds framed that of Charles II as a child given by his mother, the Regent, to the secretary of the Earl of Sandwich on the ratification of the Anglo-Spanish Treaty of 1667 [148].

In France, miniatures in portable settings, or *boîtes à portraits*, assumed great importance in public and private life.[27] In Charles Sorel's *Histoire Comique de Francion* (1633) the eponymous hero falls in love with a miniature of an Italian beauty, whose name, Nais, is inscribed on the lid of a locket that is 'oval and no bigger than a pocket sundial'. In Madame de Lafayette's engaging account of the magnificence and *galanterie* of French court life, *La Princesse de Clèves* (1678), by stealing the miniature – but not the case – of the virtuous princess the Duc de Nemours is making a declaration of his feelings for her, and is overwhelmed by the happiness he feels in possessing it; her husband then accuses the princess of deliberately letting her would-be lover have the portrait 'which was so dear

145 Miniature of Hedvig Eleonora, Dowager Queen of Sweden (1636–1715), wearing a miniature of her late husband, Karl X Gustav, within a diamond border. Miniature by Pierre Signac, 1664.

146 *opposite* Pendant with a miniature of Karl XI, King of Sweden (1655–97), within an emerald border edged with black and white enamelled foliate scrolls, surmounted by the royal crown. Miniature by Pierre Signac (?), *c.* 1672–75; setting Swedish, contemporary. 89 × 48 mm.

147 Watchcase with a miniature of Philip IV, King of Spain (1605–65), after a portrait by Velásquez, within a garland of flowers and ribbons. (The back is enamelled with a miniature of his wife, Queen Maria Louisa of Austria.) Watch by Edmé Burnet, Brussels, 1660; setting contemporary, in the style of Gilles Légaré. D 60 mm.

to me, and to which I was legally entitled'. The value of miniatures – whether sentimental or status – was further enhanced by the jewelled settings, such as 'a gold portrait jewel embellished with 3 large, 3 medium and 12 smaller diamonds and 3 others on the suspension loop' mentioned in the 1639 contract of marriage between Henri de Lorraine, Comte d'Harcourt and Marguerite du Cambaut, Duchesse de Puylaurent, related to Cardinal Richelieu.[28] The inventory of the jewels left by the celebrated beauty Béatrix de Cusance, Duchess of Lorraine, on her death in 1663 lists two miniatures in enamelled cases: one of the Queen of Sweden and 'a locket for a bracelet enamelled blue and containing the miniature of a young woman'.[29]

By this date the bracelet centrepiece miniature was not unusual. The posthumous inventory of Marie-Anne de Foix de Candelle in 1667 lists 'a portrait jewel encrusted with 63 diamonds, with a mixture of rose and table-cut stones clustered round the large centre stone' but also 'two lockets for a bracelet with a portrait, embellished with little diamonds'.[30] Another is recorded in the collection of Marie Charron, the rich widow of the great statesman Jean-Baptiste Colbert, sold in 1687: 'a bracelet with the portrait of the late Monseigneur Colbert embellished with four diamonds and another of the Queen similarly set'.[31] Her son, the Marquis de Seignelay, owned a miniature enamelled by Petitot in a diamond bracelet.

The Queen Mother, Anne of Austria, kept miniatures of her sons, Louis XIV and the Duc d'Orléans, in a little gold book, and another pair in diamond frames.[32] Her own portrait in court dress and that of the infant Dauphin by Henri Toutin were enclosed in an oval medallion enamelled back and front with a superbly painted collection of garden flowers dotted with black on a white ground, based on a design by François Lefebvre [149–151]. At least four miniatures surrounded by

148 *opposite* Drawing with valuation of the portrait jewel of Charles II, King of Spain (1661–1700), presented by the Queen Regent, Maria Luisa (Marie-Louise d'Orléans), to the English diplomat William Godolphin on the ratification of the Anglo-Spanish Treaty, 1667. The value was estimated at £405.

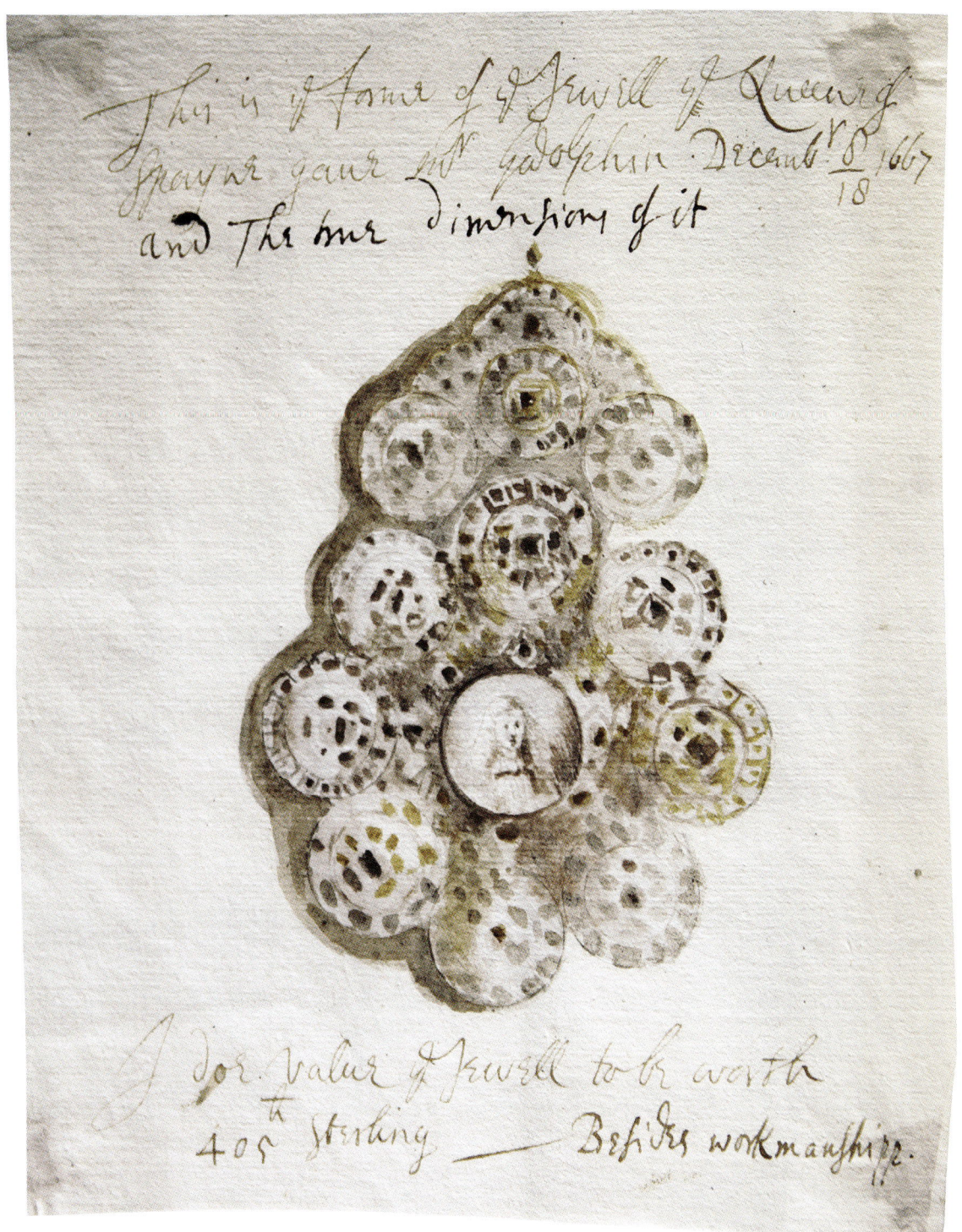

149–151 *opposite and above*
Three views of a locket containing miniatures of Anne of Austria, Queen of France (1601–66), and her son the Dauphin, the future Louis XIV, aged five. Back and front have botanical enamelling after a design by François Lefebvre (fl. 1631–c. 1676). Miniature and setting by Henri Toutin, c. 1640–42. 78 × 63 mm.

152 Title page of Gilles Légaré's *Livre des ouvrages d'orfèvrerie*, 1663, showing a characteristic floral garland.

153 *opposite* Pendant with a miniature of Cardinal Mazarin (1602–61) within an enamelled frame of black and white marguerites and leaves highlighted with diamonds. Miniature by Jean I Petitot (?) after Pierre Mignard; setting in the style of Gilles Légaré, c. 1660. 35 × 30 mm.

botanical frames in the style of Gedeon Légaré and Gilles Légaré [152] have survived. Three are enamelled in black and white only. The earliest depicts Cardinal Mazarin [153] within a border of eight flowers and trails of leaves highlighted with little diamonds. Black and white daisies and leaves frame the miniature of the Duchesse de Longueville [155]. In the border of the third, which depicts Philippe d'Orléans, younger brother of Louis XIV, by Jean I Petitot [154], the black and white flowers are interspersed with diamond ribbons. For Petitot's miniature of the notorious but beautiful Comtesse d'Olonne as Diana [156] the Légaré garland of flowers has been executed in many colours and in a technique admired by the famous 18th-century jeweller Lempereur ('by his skilful handling of these thick enamels to cover and colour he has succeeded in capturing the lightness and volume of Nature herself') and by the 18th-century owner, P.-J. Mariette, who declared that he preferred the floral border, the work of 'fairy fingers', to diamonds.[33]

At the time of her death in 1671, the Stuart princess Henriette, wife of the Duc d'Orléans, not only owned at least five miniature cases including one of the King, embellished with diamonds, rubies, emeralds and topazes,[34] but had given one of herself to her admirer, Armand de Gramont, the Comte de Guiche, 'handsome as an angel' and a courageous soldier. According to Madame de Lafayette's *Histoire de Madame Henriette d'Angleterre* this portrait, in a gold locket, saved his life in battle, for it stopped a bullet aimed at his stomach. On the death in 1689 of Henriette's daughter Marie-Louise – Queen Maria Luisa of Spain – the inventory of her superb collection of jewelry lists several miniatures in jewelled frames including one of her husband, Charles II, surrounded by 36 rose-cut diamonds with 35 more in the imperial crown above.[35]

140 *The Baroque Interpretation, 1625–1715*

154 *opposite* Pendant with a miniature of Philippe d'Orléans (1640–1701) as a boy, within a plaited rope twist border continuous in the outer frame of black and white flowers. Miniature by Jean I Petitot after a portrait by Jean Nocret; setting in the style of Gilles Légaré, *c.* 1665. Miniature 40 × 32 mm.

155 Pendant with a miniature of Anne-Geneviève de Bourbon-Condé, Duchesse de Longueville (1619–79), within a frame of black and white daisies (the suspension ring and bowknot are a later addition). Miniature by Jean I Petitot; setting in the style of Gilles Légaré, *c.* 1663. Miniature 31 × 27 mm. Famous for her love affairs and political intrigues, the Duchess was described by Madame de Maintenon as 'belle comme un ange et la plus spirituelle de son temps' – as beautiful as an angel, and the wittiest woman of her time. She retreated from the world when widowed in 1663.

156, 157 Front and back of a pendant with a miniature of the Comtesse d'Olonne (1634–1714) as Diana, within a frame of naturalistic flowers enamelled in high relief. Miniature by Jean I Petitot; setting by Gilles Légaré, c. 1660. 63 × 48 mm.

Great importance was attached to the form of these crowns. In 1698, when Queen Maria Luisa's stepsister, Elizabeth-Charlotte d'Orléans, married the Duke of Lorraine, Leopold Joseph, his gift caused adverse comment because the design of the ducal crown above his miniature was considered more like that of the Dauphin than that usually associated with the House of Lorraine and Bar.[36] The Marquise d'Armentières bequeathed in 1712 'a miniature portrait of the King mounted in gold', and significantly the woman in a print representing a jeweller holds up in her hand a miniature of the King, hanging from a bowknot [158].

Throughout his long reign from 1661 to 1715 Louis XIV was determined that his court should be sumptuous, for he believed that it was by establishing his prestige that he could secure the obedience of his people. This taste for the grand manner was expressed not only in magnificent palaces but in painting, sculpture, furniture, and all the decorative arts. It meant that every occasion – anniversaries of royal and noble families and their marriages, births and christenings, funerals, diplomatic missions, the signing of peace treaties, the arrival of important information, the offering of condolences, musical, literary and artistic achievements – had to be marked by a show of splendour that no other court could match. Gifts of *boîtes à portraits* served the purpose of demonstrating his glory perfectly for they bore his cipher and majestic image, painted in enamel by the best artists – Jean I Petitot [159], Louis de Châtillon and Jacques-Philippe Ferraud. There was also the Swedish artist Jean-Frédéric Bruckmann, whose speciality was portraits 'd'émail en relief'.[37] Moreover, when surrounded by diamonds, 'the sun shining among precious stones', the most valuable of all gems, set by the court jewellers, Jean Pittan and Laurent Le Tessier de Montarsy

158 *La Joüaillier* – the lady jeweller – has miniature pendant jewels attached to her skirt and in her hands. The large miniature in her left hand depicts Louis XIV. Engraving by Nicolas de L'Armessin, 1695.

and the latter's son Pierre [161, 162], the miniature could be worn and displayed to great effect, a more precious version of the state portraits in their gilded frames lining the walls of Baroque palaces.

A few extracts from Louis XIV's *Registre des Présents* may give some idea of how they were distributed. When portraits were enriched with diamonds, the values, which vary considerably, reflect the quantity, size and quality of the diamonds, usually in a double row of larger stones edged with smaller rose-cuts. The pattern of French foreign policy emerges from a study of these sumptuous presents. The Queen sent in 1669 to her sister, Margarita, wife of the German Emperor Leopold I, a bracelet centrepiece with her portrait surrounded by eight diamonds (7,332 *livres*); others were presented to the younger sister of the King of Poland in 1676 (9,668 *livres*) and to the Archbishop of Embrun in 1677. The King's diplomatic gifts included *boîtes* to envoys from all the courts of Europe. In Munich, at the marriage of the Grand Dauphin with Princess Marie-Anne-Christine of Bavaria in 1680 the three French witnesses to the contract were given diamond *boîtes* (total cost 16,101 *livres*) and others were presented to the Lord Chamberlain, Baron von Rechburg (6,000 *livres*), and to a lady-in-waiting, Countess Porcia (6,120 *livres*). Similarly, for the marriage in 1696 of the Duke of Burgundy with Marie-Adélaïde of Savoy a present was made to the Marquis de Dronero (14,620 *livres*) who escorted her to France. On the occasion of the signing of the Peace of Ryswick in 1697 between Spain, England, Holland, and France, both Madame Lillerot, wife of the Swedish mediator who had brought the different nations together, and the Comte de Cely, who announced the successful conclusion of the negotiations, were given diamond-encrusted portraits.

French support of the Stuarts from the restoration of Charles II was demonstrated by expensive gifts, usually of Louis XIV's portrait, to a succession of influential Englishmen such as the Duke of Buckingham in 1672 (28,000 *livres*), the Duke of Monmouth, natural son of Charles II, who was given two (15,392 and 28,000 *livres*), and the Earls of Sunderland and of Peterborough. Then after the revolution of 1688 brought William III, Stadtholder of Holland, to the English throne, the ousted James II and his court went into in exile under the protection of Louis XIV. In token of this endorsement of the Stuarts, in 1690 Louis XIV gave his miniature surrounded by 48 diamonds (21,218 *livres*) to Earl Tyrconnell, commander of King James II's army in Ireland, who had come to France asking for supplies to continue the struggle against William III. Eight years later this policy had changed: the most expensive miniature of all (40,510 *livres*) was given to the Duke of Portland, ambassador of William III, with whom, by the terms of the Treaty of Ryswick, Louis XIV had been obliged to make peace. The Duke had a huge success at Versailles with his 'brilliance, manners, polish, knowledge of the world and courtly graces' – in the words of the Duc de Saint-Simon – and the value of the gift clearly indicated the desire of Louis XIV to conciliate the supplanter of the Stuarts.

French influence in Spain was one of the great issues of the reign, leading to the War of the Spanish Succession, which only came to an end with the Treaties of Utrecht (1713) and Radstadt (1714). Devoted to Maria Luisa, the popular and clever wife of his grandson Philip V of Spain, in 1704 Louis XIV sent her a bracelet centrepiece with his miniature amidst diamonds (11,330 *livres*). After her death in 1714, in the hope that there would not be a new direction of policy, his wedding present to Philip's second wife, Elizabeth Farnese,

159 Pendant with a miniature of Louis XIV, wearing a tunic and cloak, within an enamelled frame of flowers and foliage tied with a bowknot at the top. Miniature by Jean I Petitot, c. 1670; setting contemporary. 28 × 25 mm.

was jewelry, of which the most expensive was his portrait. This she received as she journeyed from Parma across France towards Madrid, from the Duc de Saint-Aignan. The value was so high (48,376 *livres*) on account of the size of the diamonds, '4 gros brillants', illustrating how anxious Louis XIV was to enlist her support.[38]

From his birth in 1643, towards the end of the Thirty Years War, Louis XIV was involved in no less than seven different wars. To seek glory in war was in accordance with the spirit of the time, and he took on the role of soldier king, fighting bravely in battle, planning campaigns, in pursuit of French interests. Those who distinguished themselves in battle and allies who rendered valuable service could expect to receive the honour of his portrait. In 1673 during the Dutch war he presented it to the Prince de Montbéliard, and in 1678 during the Flanders campaign others were given to the Earl of Oxford, sent by Charles II, and to Colonel Churchill, future Duke of Marlborough, representing the Duke of York (6,900 *livres*).

Although many miniatures of Louis XIV have survived, because of the value of the diamonds most of the frames have been broken up and the settings left empty or filled with paste substitutes. In one recently acquired by the Louvre [161, 162] these valuable stones remain as a witness to the generosity, power and grandeur of the monarch they surround like the sun, his emblem, and clearly reveal the political significance of such an object as a gift. At the same time, the miniatures have changed hands so often that the original circumstances of the gift have been lost. Exceptionally, not only does the miniature given by Louis XIV to the Bolognese scholar Carlo Cesare Malvasia in 1681 survive in its diamond frame but its history is documented. The portrait, which is attributed to Jean I Petitot, is surrounded by a silver frame set with

160 Engraving by François Lefebvre of a design for a frame with diamond fleurs-de-lis for a miniature of Louis XIV, 1661. At the bottom is a view of the Ile de la Cité in Paris.

The Baroque Interpretation, 1625–1715 149

161, 162 *Boîte à portrait* of Louis XIV, shown in court dress, the miniature surrounded and crowned by two rows of rose-cut diamonds. On the enamelled back is the King's crowned cipher. Miniature by Jean I Petitot (?) after a portrait by Pierre Mignard; setting by Pierre Le Tessier de Montarsy (d. 1710) or his father Laurent (d. 1684), *c.* 1680–85. 72 × 46 mm.

163, 164 *above and opposite* Back and front of a portrait badge of Peter the Great, Emperor of Russia (1672–1725). The pendant is surmounted by the Russian crown. On the back is engraved the double-headed eagle clutching sceptre and orb, and St George killing the dragon. The same motif is used in enamel for the element from which the pendant is suspended. The jewel was presented to Arnould Dix, the Emperor's instructor in shipbuilding, 1713.

68 diamonds of various cuts and sizes surmounted by the French royal crown with fleur-de-lis and the back is enamelled with the royal cipher in white, black and crimson amidst floral motifs. Although it is now contained in a large oval case bordered with laurel and a solid silver crown of leaves encircles the diamonds, it remains to exemplify the work of the court jeweller Pierre Le Tessier de Montarsy, who charged 4,439 *livres* for it. The King sent this gift with a letter of thanks to Malvasia who dedicated his book, *Felsina pittrice*, to him, and after the first was stolen by bandits on the journey from Paris to Bologna ordered this to replace it, referring to it as 'the portrait I am sending you as a token of my regard'.[39] Malvasia bequeathed it, 'the most precious thing that I have in this world', to the Archconfraternity of Santa Maria della Vita in Bologna, and it survives in the adjacent museum. Equally well documented is the miniature, also attributed to Jean I Petitot and Pierre Le Tessier de Montarsy (2,648 *livres*), given to the representative of the Netherlands, Anthonie Heinsius, who offered his condolences on the death of Queen Marie-Thérèse of France in 1683. Although the diamonds were removed long ago the foil with which they were backed to enhance their brilliance remains in some settings, as does the original case.[40]

It was now, after his visits to the courts of Europe in 1697–98, that Peter I, called 'the Great', introduced to Russia the custom of awarding the sovereign's portrait. His envoy to Vienna, Prokop Bogdanovich Voznitsyn, and the Scotsman General Richard Gordon, the first to receive this honour, were followed by officers who fought in the war against Sweden. Another, given in 1713 to Arnould Dix, Peter's tutor in shipbuilding, reflects the Tsar's desire to create a modern navy [163, 164].[41]

3 Eighteenth-Century Absolutism, Elegance and Sentiment 1715–1800

The political importance of the diffusion of portraits in this age of absolutism was defined by Prince von Kaunitz, Chancellor of the Austro-Hungarian Empire, when recommending his own to a Russian visitor: 'in your country, Monsieur, people will be pleased to know the face of one of the most famous men, the best horseman, the best minister governing this monarchy for fifty years, a man who knows everything, understands everything.'[1] Official and private images were now predominantly painted in miniature. The settings, which at first reflect Rococo taste and from the 1770s Neoclassical styles, are illustrated in various published ornamental designs.

165 *opposite* Detail of a portrait of Alexandra, Countess Branicka, wearing a jewelled badge with a miniature of her natural mother, the Empress Catherine the Great, surmounted by the imperial crown. (For the complete portrait, see Ill. 229.)

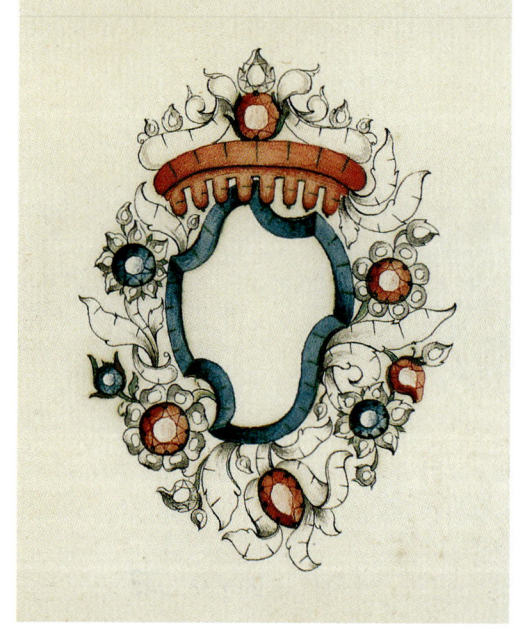

166, 167 Mid-18th-century frames for portrait jewels: an Italian design of a narrow scrolled border set with rose-cut diamonds and coloured stones, and a German design, by Christian Taute, for an asymmetrical ruby and sapphire foliate border beneath a canopy.

156 *Eighteenth-Century Absolutism, Elegance and Sentiment, 1715–1800*

168–170 A Spanish royal frame with lion, castle and crown, by the French jeweller Augustin Duflos, and two Italian designs: a double portrait bordered by an asymmetrical leafy frame, and a frame of leaves and berries attached to a pearl bracelet.

Eighteenth-Century Absolutism, Elegance and Sentiment, 1715–1800

Cameos and Intaglios

Few engraved gem portraits of men and women from the first half of the 18th century survive, and their rarity is reflected in the limited number of references to them in wills, inventories and jewellers' ledgers. However, by mid-century there was a revival of interest, and the cradle of the art of gem engraving, Italy, continued to take the lead. The prestige of the sitters is indicated by the use of precious coloured stones – emeralds, sapphires, rubies – and further enhanced by diamond frames. The will of the last Medici princess, the Electress Palatine Anna Maria Ludovica, lists 'An octagonal portrait jewel with sapphire intaglio bust of the Grand Duke Giovanni Gastone embellished with five large faceted diamonds, transparent set, and some smaller'. There were also two others, both cornelian intaglio portraits – again of her brother, Grand Duke Gian Gastone, and of her husband, the Elector Palatine Johann Wilhelm, respectively embellished with agates and garnets and with agates and emeralds.[2]

In France, the engraver François-Julien Barrier specialized in portraits. One of these, set in a ring, was sent by Voltaire to a lady accompanied by the following verse:

Barrier grava ces traits destinés pour vos yeux
Avec quelque plaisir daignez les reconnoître
Les vôtres dans mon Coeur furent gravés bien mieux
Mais ce fut par un plus grand maître.

(Barrier engraved this portrait [of Voltaire] for you; / Deign to recognize the features with some pleasure. / Your features were engraved on my heart much better, / But there the work was done by a greater master [i.e. Love].)

By mid-century Jacques Guay had emerged as the best of the French engravers, encouraged by the arbiter of the arts in France, the Marquise de Pompadour, favourite of Louis XV [173]. Her inventory records her large collection of cameos and intaglios, beautifully engraved by Guay and then

171, 172 Bracelet centrepieces with frames of emerald laurel leaves tied with diamond ribbons, set with sardonyx cameo heads of two kings of France. One represents Louis XV (1710–74), wreathed; the other Henri IV (1553–1610). Cameo of Louis XV by Jacques Guay (1715–93), cameo of Henri IV earlier; settings by Pierre-André Jacquemin (d. 1773), c. 1750. They were made for Madame de Pompadour, who was painted wearing the portrait of Louis XV (see Ill. 173).

Eighteenth-Century Absolutism, Elegance and Sentiment, 1715–1800   159

173 The Marquise de Pompadour (1728–64), portrayed at her toilette by François Boucher in 1750, displays the cameo portrait of Louis XV (Ill. 171) on her wrist.

set in rings or bracelet centrepieces by her jeweller, Pierre-André Jacquemin. A woman of superb taste, she surrounded these miniature works of art with the glitter and colour of precious stones. Her smaller portraits of the King were bordered with white brilliant-cut diamonds and set in rings. In bracelet clasps a larger portrait, again of the King, and another of Henri IV, founder of the Bourbon dynasty, were framed within crowns of emerald laurel leaves tied with diamond ribbons, echoing those that both are wearing [171, 172]. Henri IV was considered such a good king, 'si français de coeur et d'esprit' (so French in heart and mind), that, as representing 'le Bonheur de la France', his Bourbon descendants Louis XV and Louis XVI wished to be associated with him. These portrait jewels of her royal lover and his ancestor demonstrated the Marquise's power as Queen of France in all but name. This is the significance of the cameo of Louis XV which is so very prominently displayed on her wrist in François Boucher's famous painting of Madame de Pompadour at her toilette [173].

Guay is likely to have executed the sardonyx cameo portrait of the King set in a bracelet centrepiece for the Baroness Starhemberg, lady-in-waiting to Marie-Josèphe de Saxe at the time of her marriage to Louis XV's son, the Dauphin, in 1747.[3] This most tactful Princess was disappointed when, arriving in France, she found there was no portrait of her father-in-law among the collection of jewels awaiting her. Later, in 1758, both she and the Dauphin were portrayed in a fine sardonyx framed in a moulded gold border, tied with ribbons and surmounted by a bowknot.[4] In her posthumous inventory of 1767 there were at least two rings set with engraved gem portraits – an onyx cameo of her father, Friedrich August III, Elector of Saxony and King of Poland, and an emerald of Henri IV, surrounded by diamonds.[5]

174 Gold ring set with a sardonyx double portrait of Louis XVI, King of France (1754–93), and Queen Marie-Antoinette (1755–93), within a diamond border surmounted by a crown, c. 1770. 13 × 11 mm.

The grandchildren of Louis XV – Louis XVI who succeeded in 1774, and his brother the Comte d'Artois – were only rarely portrayed in gems, whether for setting into the lids of snuff boxes or in jewelry.[6] However, double portraits of Louis XVI and Queen Marie-Antoinette were mounted in rings with royal crown above [174] and that of the Comte d'Artois was set for his wife in a ring in 1776 by Ange-Joseph Aubert, the court jeweller.[7] A sardonyx bust of Marie-Antoinette, one of the masterpieces of Jacques Guay, is set in a fine snuff box by A.-J.-M. Vachette chased with a laurel crown and with the lilies and crown of France [175]. There were a few others. One was sold by the jeweller Jean Gaillard in 1772 to the Duchesse de Villeroy: 'A ring with a cornelian portrait of Henri IV surrounded by brilliants, mounted in the antique style'; Aubert in 1769 sold to Monsieur de Pair 'A ring with swivel bezel set with portraits of the King and of Henri IV in a setting of roses',

175 Gold snuff box, the lid set with a cameo portrait of Queen Marie-Antoinette surmounted by a crown and surrounded by lilies and laurel. Cameo by Jacques Guay; box by Adrien-Jean-Maximilien Vachette (1753–1839), c. 1780. 47 × 36 mm.

176 Gold brooch with a ceramic-like paste cameo bust of Maria I, Queen of Portugal (1734–1816), wreathed in laurel, the royal blue frame crowned and set with diamond stars. Portuguese, *c.* 1785. H 50 mm.

and in 1782 to the Marquis de Monconseil 'A ring with the portrait of the King of Poland surrounded by small brilliants continuous round the hoop'; and another was bought by the Marquis de Vernouillet. Representing the new generation of the family of engravers was Jean-Henri Simon, who was appointed to the Duc d'Orléans in 1775. After 1789 his portraits of the leading figures of the Revolution, Marat and Le Pelletier, were reproduced in glass, as were intaglio portraits of the Duchesse d'Orléans and their children: the latter were set in a steel chatelaine terminating in a seal inscribed with the revolutionary name adopted by the Duke – Philippe-Égalité.[8]

As an alternative to cameos, images in relief of Louis XV and Louis XVI were created in ivory on a red ground or in porcelain, also covered with crystal and surrounded by rose-cut diamonds. A ceramic-like paste, invented by Brigadier Bartolomeu da Costa for portraits of Maria I, Queen of Portugal, in 1785, was used for pendants, bracelets, rings and brooches [176]. Pearls were also used for portraiture in relief. Inspired by the continuity of papal history, anonymous goldsmiths created no less than 240 medallions enclosing an image of St Peter and of each of his successors, ending with Clement XII [177]: the profiles, pontifical robes and tiaras are executed in freshwater pearls of different sizes and coloured stones, standing out against a dark ground. These *tours de force* of portrait jewelry were presented to Louis XV, who gave them to the Cabinet des Médailles. Rarest of all were portraits in relief entirely composed of small diamonds. There was one of Louis XVI on a blue enamel ground,[9] and the Guild of the Paris Goldsmiths presented another to Christian VII of Denmark when he visited the city in 1768 [178].

In England, the outstanding gem engraver of the first part of the century, Lorenz Natter, portrayed various illustrious

177 *opposite* Gold medallion enclosing a profile portrait bust of Pope Clement XII (1652–1740), the face and hair composed of seed pearls, the tiara and pontifical robes in pearls and various gems. 1730–40. D 40 mm. This is the last in a series of images of the popes: each bust was modelled in wax and then covered with minute seed pearls and other gems and applied to a black marble or slate ground. A short Latin biographical note is inscribed in gold on the reverse sides.

178 Gold medallion with a diamond portrait cameo of Christian VII, King of Denmark (1749–1808), on a blue ground. Paris, 1768.

people, but none seems to have survived as jewelry embellished with precious stones. The most important example that remains intact in the original setting is a sardonyx bust by an unknown engraver said to be of Anne, the Princess Royal [179], daughter of George II, who married William IV of Nassau in 1734: it is mounted in a medallion framed within a diamond and ruby garland tied with a bow. Other portrait cameos and intaglios for seals demonstrating loyalty to the Hanoverian monarchs – George I, George II, George III – were usually worn in the plainest of designs, based on ancient Roman models, following the advice of the French scholar P.-J. Mariette: 'without ornament, imitating ancient rings which are almost always of a single material and extremely simple'.

The Prince of Wales, the future George IV, bought 'a pair of portraits of the late and present kings of Prussia mounted in a very large Roman setting swivel ring', but he also liked more de luxe settings. His extravagance is reflected in 'A curious matchless ring of sardonyx elegantly engraved in the natural colours with a striking likeness of the bust of the Rt Hon. Charles James Fox neatly mounted in gold and set round with fine large brilliants of the first water', bought for £105 from Benjamin Laver in 1785. In addition to this declaration of support of the leader of the reformist Whig political party, the Prince went on to buy other expensive portrait rings: 'a brilliant ring of the head of the King of Prussia' from Thomas Gray in 1786, and another diamond ring with his own portrait in 1787.[10] Always in advance of fashion, he showed his enthusiasm for Scottish national dress by commissioning a cameo portrait bust of himself wearing a Highland bonnet with plume [180]. After the death of Prince Charles Edward Stuart in 1788 Jacobitism ceased to be a political threat, and

179 *opposite* Pendant with a cameo portrait perhaps of Anne, Princess Royal (1709–59), within a diamond and ruby garland of flowers and leaves tied with a ribbon. Cameo and setting English, *c.* 1730. 50 × 40 mm.

180 Gold medallion enclosing a cameo portrait of George, Prince of Wales (the future George IV, 1762–1830), in Highland dress, within a chain border. Cameo and setting English, *c.* 1790. Cameo H 25 mm. The Prince gave this medallion to his morganatic wife, Mrs Fitzherbert.

Eighteenth-Century Absolutism, Elegance and Sentiment, 1715–1800

181 *opposite* John Drummond, 5th Duke of Perth (1679–1757), in armour, his cloak fastened with a cameo portrait brooch of James III, the Old Pretender, for whose cause he endured exile, and the loss of his fortune. Portrait by John Alexander, 1735.

in 1790 the Prince and his two brothers attended Mrs Sturt's masquerade in Highland dress.[11] The cameo [180], which portrays him as he must have appeared then, was a gift to Mrs Fitzherbert, his morganatic wife.

Several portrait cameos in the collection of his mother, Queen Charlotte, were mounted as jewels: 'a brooch in the shape of a caduceus of brilliants with a fine cameo head of William III in the centre' and a 'cameo portrait set with cluster diamonds as a locket'.[12] The royal family wore cameo portraits of George III, and so did his subjects, as a means of demonstrating loyalty. This was the intention of the patriotic Marchioness of Salisbury, who according to the *Lady's Magazine* appeared at court to celebrate the King's birthday on 4 June 1803 'in a blue and silver dress festooned with oak leaves: headdress a profusion of diamonds in front. We observed a cameo of His Majesty on a large ruby to which was suspended a very large and beautiful pearl.'

Similarly political are the earlier rings and medallions for Stuart supporters set with cameos and intaglio portraits of James III, Stuart Pretender to the throne, living in exile in Rome. They were defiantly displayed by loyal Jacobites such as the 5th Duke of Perth, who was painted by John Alexander in 1735 with a cameo portrait of James III in the brooch fastening the cloak over his armour [181]. In the next generation, both before and after his defeat at Culloden in 1745 Prince Charles Edward Stuart distributed others of himself, and of his father, some with mottoes such as JAMES III (of England) VIII (of Scotland), GOD SAVE YE KING, and symbols. In one of the most important (dating from his marriage in 1772) the cameo is encircled by a blue Garter inscribed with the motto HONI SOIT QUI MAL Y PENSE, within a diamond border beneath the royal crown of England [182].

Eighteenth-Century Absolutism, Elegance and Sentiment, 1715–1800   171

182 *opposite* Brooch set with an onyx cameo head of Prince Charles Edward Stuart, the Young Pretender (1720–88), within a Garter frame with motto, surmounted by a royal crown and surrounded by brilliant-cut diamonds. Cameo Italian; setting Scottish or English, *c.* 1772.

183 Portrait badge with a sapphire intaglio head of Stanislaus Augustus, King of Poland (1732–98), surmounted by a royal crown and bordered with diamonds. Intaglio by Jan Regulski (1732–98); setting by Jean Martin (d. 1795), 1786. 31 × 26 mm. The jewel was made for presentation to the Russian Chancellor, Alexander Bezborodko.

Stanislaus Augustus, the last King of Poland, commissioned portraits from the French gem engraver Romain Jeuffroy[13] and from the Polish engraver Jan Regulski. In 1786 Regulski's intaglio bust engraved on a Ceylon sapphire was mounted into a medallion by the court jeweller Jean Martin in Warsaw and surrounded with diamonds removed from the King's shoe and knee buckles, for presentation to the Russian Chancellor, Alexander Bezborodko [183]. The Polish King had high hopes for his meeting with Bezborodko and the Empress Catherine II – 'the Great' – and the value and beauty of this gift expresses his desire to reach an agreement and his consciousness of his royal status. As for the Russian Empress, no woman sovereign since Queen Elizabeth I of England had distributed more images of herself. An avid collector of engraved gems, she also commissioned hardstone cameo and intaglio portraits from Johann Caspar Jaeger, richly set in diamonds [184], principally in rings but also in medallions, sometimes surmounted by the imperial crown [187]. The portrait jewels of this most autocratic of all rulers, commanding the resources of an immense empire, express the power of an absolute monarchy.

184 Pendant with an emerald intaglio head of Catherine II, the Great, Empress of Russia (1729–96), wearing a laurel wreath and pearl head ornament, within a frame of circular-cut diamonds with suspension loop. Intaglio by Johann Caspar Jaeger (active in St Petersburg 1772–80); setting later. The jewel was given by the Empress to Count Orlov.

185 Ring set with an agate cameo head of Catherine the Great within a diamond border. Cameo and setting St Petersburg, c. 1782–90. 28 × 25 mm.

Eighteenth-Century Absolutism, Elegance and Sentiment, 1715–1800 175

186 Pendant set with an agate cameo head of Catherine the Great within a brilliant-cut diamond border. Cameo and setting St Petersburg, c. 1782–90. 32 × 29 mm.

187 *opposite* Pendant set with an agate cameo portrait of Catherine the Great within a brilliant-cut diamond border edged with smaller diamonds, surmounted by an imperial crown, attached to a diamond chain. Cameo by Johann Caspar Jaeger, c. 1774–80, based on a medal of 1774 commemorating peace with Turkey; setting St Petersburg, contemporary. Medallion 43 × 26 mm

Portrait Medals

Medals commemorating military and naval victories and outstanding events in the reign of monarchs were struck in quantities and awarded either in sets or individually, with or without chains, to be worn like a decoration. Their political significance is clearly demonstrated by the frontispiece to G.-R. Fleurimont's *Médailles du regne de Louis XV*, in which a portrait medal of the King is associated with symbols of sovereignty [188]. Framed in laurel and attached to the pyramid of immortality which rises high into the clouds, it is crowned by Glory and supported by Fame who praises the King as hero of the universe, a scene admired by the personification of France; the passage of Time is halted; the King's achievements are inscribed on a shield attached to a palm tree; and infants scatter medals across the globe.

In 1718, according to the *Registre des Présents du Roi*, Giberto, a naval officer from Monte Carlo, was given a gold medal portraying the Regent, Philippe d'Orléans, on one side and on the other the infant Louis XV, in recognition of the support he had given to French traders in the Middle East. In the same year, the twenty-four-year-old Voltaire was given another for his play *Oedipus*, and Charles Boit, miniature painter, 'a medal with gold chain awarded in recognition of his achievement in creating an extraordinarily large portrait of the King in enamel'. Those thus honoured took immense pride in their awards, as Martin van Meytens, court painter to the Empress Maria Theresa, demonstrates in his self-portrait dating from the 1740s [2, 189]: he is holding up her miniature, which is in a decorative frame, and the medal of her husband, the Emperor Franz I, hangs from the chain round his neck.

The custom of medallic awards continued: in 1755, for instance, the secretary of the Earl of Albemarle received from Louis XV a gold medal with chain, valued at 1,580 *livres*. In

188 Frontispiece to G.-R. Fleurimont, *Médailles du regne de Louis XV*, 1748, by François Le Moine.

LA Pyramide qui s'éleve dans les Nües, est le Simbole de l'Immortalité. Un Genie y attache le Buste en Medaillon de LOUIS XV. LA GLOIRE le Couronne, et la RENOMÉE qui le soutient annonce le Heros a l'Univers. A la Base de la Pyramide Divers Genies arrestent le TEMPS, e s'éforcent de l'enchaisner. sur le devant la FRANCE contemple avec admiration ce Spectacte, Tandis que son GENIE ecrit les FASTES du Prince sur un Bouclier suspendu en Trophée à un Palmier, et que d'autres Enfans s'amusent a rependre des Medailles sur le Globle de la Terre.

1757 the Marquis de l'Hôpital presented to Count Woronzow, Chancellor of the Empress Elizabeth, a medal cabinet with 150 gold medals, valued at 29,986 *livres*, it being understood that as the Russian court was a byword for magnificence, gifts from France had to be the best and richest available.

Medals might be attached to ribbons and hung round the neck, but since the image was often surrounded by an integral decorative border and was considered sufficiently prestigious in itself, it is unusual to find examples of medals in jewelled settings.[14] An exception was the 'magnifico e nobil dono' – the magnificent and noble gift – which Christian VI, the art-loving King of Denmark, sent to the engraver, art dealer and connoisseur Antonio Maria Zanetti, which is illustrated at the end of the catalogue of his collection, *Le gemme antiche di Anton-Maria Zanetti*, published by A. F. Gori in 1750 [190]. The gold medal is surmounted by the royal crown and surrounded by diamonds; the King is portrayed on the front, and the back shows Minerva holding up a laurel wreath. Gori applauded this 'extremely rare example of the virtues of wisdom and generosity'.

From the 1720s, as snuff boxes became the most usual royal gift, more and more medals were inserted in the lids, as in a tortoiseshell box bearing a medal of Charles I, indicative of loyalty to the House of Stuart and the Pretender, James III, in Rome [191]. In *Le Mercure* the enterprising M. Granchez, owner of 'Au Petit Dunkerque', in January 1775 advertised 'Bonheur de la France' snuff boxes with portrait medals of Louis XVI and his ancestor, Henri IV, and in January 1776 others, at various prices, of the King's brother, the Comte d'Artois, by C.-F. Trébuchet.[15] Two rulers who were awarded the rare title of 'Great' by their subjects are commemorated by similar boxes. The first, signed by the Swiss medallist Jean-Melchior

189 Self-portrait of Martin van Meytens (1695–1770), 1740s. He shows himself holding a framed miniature portrait of the Empress Maria Theresa and wearing the medal of her husband, the Emperor Franz I, awarded him as her court painter in Vienna. (For a closer view, see Ill. 2.)

Eighteenth-Century Absolutism, Elegance and Sentiment, 1715–1800   181

190 *opposite* Engraving of a portrait medal of Christian VI, King of Denmark (1699–1746), crowned and surrounded by diamonds, awarded to Anton Maria Zanetti of Venice, *c*. 1740. The engraving appears in the catalogue of Zanetti's gems, published in 1750.

Morikofer, alludes to the military genius who laid the foundation of the Prussian empire [192]: it is set with a silver medal of Frederick II – Frederick the Great – wearing a cloak embroidered with crowns over armour, with his title, FRIDERICUS MAGNUS REX BORUSSORUM, and on the back a figure of Victory inscribing 'Saeculum Friderici' (the Age of Frederick) in a book supported by Father Time. Inserted in the lid of the second box is a medal of Catherine the Great of Russia [193], fully armed in the character of the goddess Minerva, executed by Johann Georg Waechter for her coronation and distributed to those who had taken her side in the palace revolution which brought her to the throne.

In England, the recovery of George III from the first bout of his illness in 1789 was celebrated by his subjects at various gatherings where they showed their loyalty by wearing his portrait medal – most plainly set, but others within pearl and even diamond borders.

191 Tortoiseshell snuff box made for a supporter of the Stuarts, the lid set with a memorial portrait medal of Charles I, King of Great Britain and Ireland, with Garter motto and star. Medal by Thomas Rawlins (fl. 1620–70) after Van Dyck; setting *c*. 1720. 75 × 57 mm.

Eighteenth-Century Absolutism, Elegance and Sentiment, 1715–1800   183

192 Silver box set with a silver medal of Frederick II, the Great, King of Prussia (1712–86). By Jean-Melchior Morikofer (1706–61), 1759. 50 × 10 mm.

193 *opposite* Gold snuff box, the lid set with the coronation portrait medal of Catherine the Great as Minerva, inscribed in Russian translating 'By God's grace Catherine II Empress and Autocrat of all the Russias. Behold thy salvation'. Medal by Johann Georg Waechter (1726–1800), 1762; box by Jean-Pierre Ador, 1774. D 82 mm.

Miniatures and Silhouettes

While miniatures awarded by the monarch or other person of high rank were marks of favour and prestige, when exchanged between private individuals they were regarded as precious tokens of love and friendship. As Araminte in the play by Marivaux, *Les Fausses Confidences* (first performed in 1737), declared to her suitor, Dorante: 'Give you my portrait? But that would be the same as saying I love you!'

The strong feelings aroused by the possession of a miniature inspired poets, playwrights and novelists. Jean-Jacques Rousseau's novel *La Nouvelle Helöise* (1761) contains many passionate words describing the effect of a miniature on Julie's lover, Saint-Preux, who exclaims 'my eyes are ravished with your heavenly beauties' [195]. A disputed miniature, almost culminating in a duel, was the theme of a comedy by Lady Craven, *The Miniature Picture*, performed at the Drury Lane Theatre in London in 1780. In real life, according to Madame de Genlis, her future husband, Monsieur de Puisieux, a prisoner of war in England, fell in love with her miniature, set in a box which her father, also imprisoned, carried with him everywhere.[16] Designed to be held lovingly in the hand, these miniatures were worn with as much pride and pleasure as were those given by sovereigns as a mark of distinction.

The smallest miniatures were set in rings, enriched with pearls and precious stones, such as that bequeathed in 1749 to Monsieur de Croismart by the Marquise de Vassé – 'the large portrait of my brother hanging in my room and a ring set with a miniature of the same framed in brilliants'[17] – and others were bought from the court jeweller, Aubert:

> 1756, to the Duchesse de Cossé-Brissac: 'a ring set with a portrait of the Marquis de Brissac within an emerald and diamond border on a gold hoop'

1768, to M. Murat: 'an important portrait ring with a large portrait surrounded by 43 diamonds with 5 others at each shoulder with another picture underneath, both under crystal'

1770, to the Marquis de Barbantane: 'a ring with the portrait of the Duchesse de Bourbon, set in antique style, with rose diamonds on the shoulders and round the hoop composed of 63 rose diamonds'

1775, to Queen Marie-Antoinette: 'a ring set with the portrait of the Princesse de Lamballe within a rose diamond border and shoulders in antique style'

More simple was – again from Aubert – Madame de Laval's 'plain gold ring with a portrait under crystal'. In 1778 Gravier, jeweller 'A la Descente du Pont Neuf', undertook for Monsieur de Portelance 'a diamond ring made to fit the portrait of Madame; the same for that of Mademoiselle, but the size of a monogram ring'.[18] There were orders for royal miniature rings: in 1763 the miniaturist Cazaubon supplied five of Louis XV for presentation, and, also presumably for an intimate of the royal family, portraits of his daughters, Adélaïde, Sophie and Louise, all three to be enclosed in the same ring.[19] In 1769 both Monsieur de Pair and the Marquis de Vernouillet bought from Aubert rings with swivel bezels set with portraits of Louis XV and Henri IV 'both within a rose diamond frame', and in 1776 the Duchesse de Civrac showed her support for Louis XVI with 'a ring set with the King's portrait within a border of 25 brilliants with a so-called antique style setting and a crystal'.

Most miniatures were enclosed in medallions *de col*, to hang from the neck [194]. Listed as *boîtes à portraits*, as in the preceding period, they were offered as diplomatic gifts – to

194 *opposite* The Comtesse de Flahaut (1761–1836) with her son Charles: he holds a miniature of his aunt and godmother, the Comtesse d'Angivillers. After the portrait by A. Labille-Guiard, 1785.

195 Saint-Preux rejoices in the possession of the miniature of his lover, Julie: engraving after Jean-Michel Moreau from the 1793 edition of *La Nouvelle Héloïse* by Jean-Jacques Rousseau.

190 *Eighteenth-Century Absolutism, Elegance and Sentiment, 1715–1800*

196 *opposite* Miniatures of the brothers Joseph (1740–1810) and Etienne (1745–99) de Montgolfier, the first aerostats, framed in laurel and ribbons tied with a bow in a gilt metal setting. Miniatures attributed to André Pujos (1738?–88), 1783; setting contemporary. Each 34 × 29 mm.

those involved in the negotiations for royal marriages (including the bride), to those standing in for the King and Queen as godparents at christenings, and as tokens of affection between various members of the family. The settings, now enriched with diamonds, of various sizes and some of the first water, were supplied from 1714 by the jeweller Claude-Dominique Rondé, and thereafter by his successors Jean Gaillard and Ange-Joseph Aubert. By far the most splendid (costing 129,852 *livres*) was given in 1720 to the Marchese Scotti, ambassador from the Duchy of Parma at the marriage of the Regent's daughter, Mademoiselle de Valois; the light from 42 brilliant and 15 rose-cut diamonds blazed like the sun around the portrait of the young King by Jean-Baptiste Massé.

The motifs of the borders evolved from scrolls to the more decorative garlands, laurel crowns and rosettes, and ribbons with a bowknot above [196]. In the new classical taste the miniature of the future Louis XVI painted by Pierre-Adolphe Hall, sent to the Archduchess Marie-Antoinette before their marriage in 1770, was in a 'cadre à la grecque' – a Greek-style frame – set with 70 'gros brillants'. Unusually, instead of the customary crown the miniature of Louis XV sent to the Sardinian minister of foreign affairs at the time of the marriage of Princess Marie-Thérèse of Savoy with the Comte d'Artois in 1773 had 'large palm branches, flowers and ribbons, set with 688 diamonds'.

In his correspondence with Sophie Voland, Denis Diderot, leading figure of the Enlightenment, reveals the significance of the medallion to lovers. As soon as she suggests placing her sister's miniature with his 'to feel us both with you, to see her with us and me with her', he consents, but conditionally: 'If your sister agrees to our request and you have both our portraits, take care, Sophie, and do not look at her more tenderly than at me. Do not look at her more often.'[20]

Although the size varied, the shapes were almost uniformly oval. (There were exceptions: in 1786 Countess Esterházy ordered from the Parisian jeweller Guidi the more symbolic heart, in plain gold, polished inside and out, and containing two miniatures.) Designed to hang, the medallions were crowned with a bowknot, or a trefoil, covering the suspension loop.[21] Hair in a plait might surround the miniature or might be placed behind, arranged in a sheaf or some other token. Cristals like windows covered the miniature. The Comte de Noailles in 1791 ordered 'a large double-sided gold medallion with the picture of the Count on one side and a blue ribbon on the other, both with crystal covers'.[22] The frames might be enriched with diamonds or pearls, and gold, sometimes beaded. One of the most moving of all medallions, depicting the Comte de Beaujolais at the age of eleven during the Revolution, by Jean-Urbain Guérin, is quite plain, but a later inscription at the back, composed by his mother, the Duchesse d'Orléans, expresses her love for him – 'so deserving of her love for at all times his heart and hers beat as one' – and sadness at his death.[23]

The popularity of the miniature bracelet, so prominently displayed in portraits, is confirmed by the number recorded in the *Registre des Présents*, in jewellers' accounts, and in wills and inventories. According to the *Registre* four such bracelets enclosing portraits of Louis XV surrounded by diamonds were sent to Vienna for the ladies attending the Archduchess Marie-Antoinette at the time of her marriage with the Dauphin. One year later, the miniature by Pierre-Adolphe Hall of the Comte de Provence in a bracelet for Marie-Joséphine of Savoy made a very good impression on his bride, who wrote, 'the image of the young prince depicted there aroused in me more than one agreeable emotion'.[24] In 1775 when Princess Clothilde of

France married the Prince of Piedmont, during the embassy ball she gave Countess Viri, wife of the Sardinian ambassador in Paris, '2 bracelets from Solle set with 36 diamonds, one with the portrait of the King painted by [J.-D.] Welper, the other with that of the Princess of Piedmont by [R.] Ducreux'. Most of those given by Louis XVI represented the Queen as well: Countess Braschi, niece of Pope Pius VI, who brought his gift of a christening robe for the Dauphin in 1782, received 'two bracelets and a medallion, with portraits of the King, the Queen and the Dauphin by [Louis-Marie] Sicardi, each surrounded by 20 brilliants'.

Attached to rows of pearls – the most expensive being 'rondes, blanches et parfaites' and the cheapest made from various artificial substances – these centrepieces for pairs of bracelets might be miniatures of mother and father or a brother and sister. Madame Hérault de Marville in 1753 bequeathed 'two bracelets with portraits, one of my father, the other of my sister'.[25] Mothers liked seeing their children on their wrists: thus in 1756 the Duchesse de Cossé-Brissac left '2 bracelets with portraits depicting the Comte de Cossé-Brissac and the Marquis de Cossé-Brissac (my children), each surrounded by 2 rows of 42 diamonds, on bracelets consisting of 9 rows of little imitation white pearls'.[26] Two such portraits might be mounted on a swivel, 'tournant'. Instead of another portrait the corresponding centrepiece might enclose a cipher or hair (the pair to the miniature of the Duc de Bourgogne which the widowed Princess Marie-Josèphe de Saxe wore, for instance, enclosed the hair of her late husband, the Dauphin).[27] Some were bordered by plain gold rings, but others were more de luxe with frames of lover's knots, flowers and ribbons, as illustrated in the designs in J.-H. Pouget's *Traité des Pierres précieuses* (1762).

197 *L'Amant regretté*: engraving after P. Davesne by Antoine-François Dennel, *c.* 1770. The feelings of the lady gazing at her absent lover's miniature are emphasized by the frame of ivy leaves symbolic of enduring attachment.

While most miniatures were set in rings, medallions and bracelet centrepieces, there were other alternatives – particularly the *tabatière* or snuff box given by the monarch and also by private individuals. At first miniatures were placed inside, exposing them within a few days to the damaging effects of the black tobacco dust: to avoid this, in the 1720s a rich *fermier général* or tax farmer, Monsieur Le Riche de La Popelinière, hit on the idea of inserting them on the cover. Similarly they adorned other jewelled accessories: *carnets* [199, 200], *carnets de bal* (dance cards) [198], *nécessaires* (portable needlework or cosmetic cases), souvenirs, note cases, watches, even sets of buttons [202]. A story was told about a gentleman who arrived late for a ball because he was kept waiting by the tailor he had engaged to sew on a set of buttons representing French beauties, and he then took a long time deciding which was to be placed closest to his heart.[28] An indefatigable huntsman, the Prince de Condé, wore the miniature of his small son Louis-Henri-Antoine de Bourbon, Duc d'Enghien, beside his watch, set in an enamelled gold frame attached to leather straps terminating in tassels made of the child's hair [201].

For people who preferred not to display miniatures, the jewellers concealed them in *tabatières à secret* [203–205], rings and lockets which opened when pressure was put on a secret spring. A famous example was the diamond and cornelian ring always worn by Madame du Châtelet, in which she hid the miniature of her lover at the time – first Monsieur de Richelieu, then Voltaire, and finally his successor, Monsieur de Saint-Lambert. On being told of this betrayal Voltaire reacted with a philosophical shrug: 'to each his turn. So goes the world.'[29] Several miniatures ordered from Aubert were concealed under ciphers, such as that for the Marquis de Spinola in 1773.

198 *Carnet de bal* with a miniature of Queen Marie-Antoinette, inscribed in diamond letters D'AMITIÉ. Miniature by Louis-Marie Sicardi (1746–1825), 1783; setting contemporary, Paris.

201 *opposite* Medallion with a miniature of the infant Louis-Henri-Antoine de Bourbon, Duc d'Enghien (1772–1804), in an enamelled border. Attached to green leather straps terminating in tassels of his hair, it was worn by his father, the Prince de Condé, when hunting. Miniature and setting French, *c.* 1775. 26 × 35 mm.

199, 200 Gold *carnet* of Japanese *hiramaki-e* lacquer enclosing miniatures under glass of the Dauphin and Marie-Josèphe de Saxe and his six surviving sisters, the Mesdames de France. Given by one of them, Madame Adélaïde, to her lady-in-waiting, the Comtesse de Narbonne, in 1750. *Carnet* by Antoine Leschaudel. H 145 mm.

196 *Eighteenth-Century Absolutism, Elegance and Sentiment, 1715–1800*

202 Part of a set of silver buttons set with miniatures of famous French political and artistic personalities (their names engraved on the back) within paste frames, 1790.

203–205 *Tabatière à secret* with a concealed slide framing miniatures of Voltaire (1699–1778) and his mistress, Madame du Châtelet (1706–49). Miniatures by Hubert Drouais (1699–1767); box by J. C. Neuber, Dresden, 1775. 44 × 34 mm (Voltaire), 46 × 36 mm (Madame du Châtelet). The miniatures of the famous couple were inserted later, replacing those originally in the box.

This was 'a monogram ring, the letters composed of 72 rose diamonds applied on a blue composition ground within a border of 28 brilliants, made in the antique style with room for a portrait inside'. More symbolically, the ring with a mechanism hiding the miniature made for the Prince de Monaco in 1775 was guarded by the god Silence, signifying discretion, painted *en grisaille* on the bezel within a diamond border. Similarly in 1769 for Madame de Berville: 'a bracelet with the monogram LBD within a diamond garland and a portrait hidden inside'. The miniature Marie-Antoinette gave her friend, the Princesse de Lamballe, hidden in a rose, could only be seen when released by a spring, hidden in the stem: this the Princess wore as a brooch pinned to her *fichu*.[30]

Other miniatures which might have a political purpose were concealed in *tabatières*, *nécessaires à portrait*, and *écritoires* (portable desks), of which one of the most famous, in lacquer, was sent by the Empress Maria Theresa in 1759 as a mark of gratitude to the Marquise de Pompadour for using her political influence to bring about the Franco–Austrian alliance during the Seven Years War.[31] Whereas this gift contained the miniature of the Empress alone, surrounded by diamonds, in others there were two miniatures, depicting her and her husband Franz I, with whom she ruled as co-regent. Significantly, the snuff box made by Franz von Mack which she sent in 1775 to the Archduke Charles Alexander of Lorraine, widower of her sister Maria Anna and Governor of the Austrian Netherlands, makes an even stronger political statement [206, 207]: thirteen miniatures painted by Antonio Bencini, the court miniaturist, on the lid, sides and base of the box, all framed in diamond borders, depicting her four surviving sons and six daughters and herself, flanked by the Archduke Charles and his wife, affirm the strength of the dynasty she had established.

206, 207 *opposite* View and base of the grand dynastic Habsburg snuff box, with the entwined initials of the widowed Empress Maria Theresa (1717–80) and her husband, Franz I, and miniatures of her ten surviving children, within diamond borders. Her miniature at the base is flanked by those of the Archduke Charles Alexander of Lorraine (1712–80) and his late wife Maria Anna (1718–44), Maria Theresa's sister. Charles Alexander, to whom the Empress sent this gift, was doubly her brother-in-law, since he was the brother of her late husband, Franz I. Miniatures by Antonio Bencini; box by Franz von Mack, Vienna, 1773.

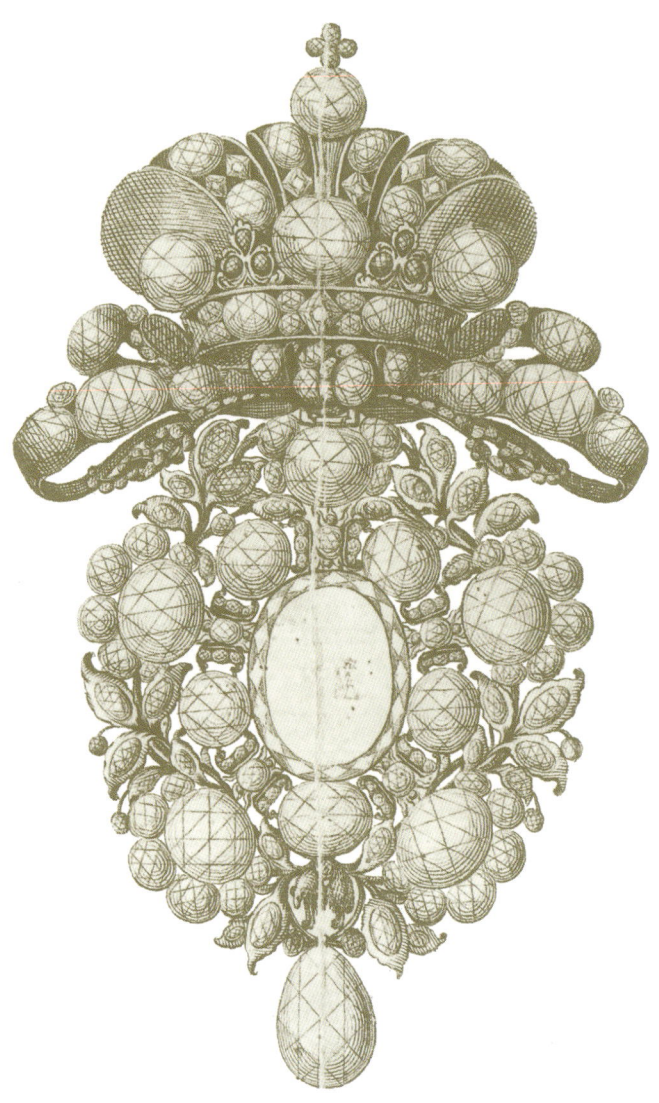

208 Engraved design for a frame for a miniature surrounded by laurel and the badge of the Order of the Golden Fleece, and surmounted by the imperial crown, all set with rose-cut diamonds. German, mid-18th century.

The Habsburg succession was assured through her eldest son, Joseph II, who had assumed his father's position as co-regent, and then by his brother, Leopold, with the two younger brothers, Maximilian and Ferdinand, in reserve. The marriages of three daughters to the rulers of France, Naples and Parma had consolidated the alliances between those courts and Vienna not only for the present, but for the future. Thirty-five years earlier, in 1740, the young Empress's right as a woman to succeed her own father had been disputed, and the fortunes of the Habsburg empire were at a low ebb. The gift of the multiple portrait box can therefore be regarded as a triumphant assertion of her achievement, both as a mother and as a monarch. Similarly triumphant is the setting designed for a single imperial miniature [208].

Striking a quite different note, the eye miniature, originating in France, was considered more personal because it was so expressive of the feelings [208]. Horace Walpole, in a letter to Lady Ossory of 27 October 1785, disapproved: 'when human folly, or rather French folly can go so far, it would be trifling to instance much further silliness – but do you know Madam, that it is the fashion now, is it not, to have portraits but of an eye? They say, "Lord, don't you know it? A Frenchman is come over to paint eyes here."' Most people disagreed with him, and the eye, mirror of the soul, so easily recognized by close friends, was adopted enthusiastically by Richard Cosway and his rival, George Engleheart, for their fashionable clients.[32] Occasionally, the loving gaze is accompanied by mottoes and verses inscribed on the reverse such as 'Happy who sees without being seen / Accept the heart and the portrait of her who loves you and will be faithful'.

The many references in 18th-century English literature confirm the widespread custom of wearing miniatures as

204 Eighteenth-Century Absolutism, Elegance and Sentiment, 1715–1800

209 Brooch set with a miniature of a blue left eye weeping a diamond tear, within a pearl border. Miniature and silver-gilt setting English, late 18th century. 21 × 30 mm.

210, 211 Back and front of a gold locket with royal crown and pearl drop. The front displays a miniature of George II, King of Great Britain and Ireland (1683–1760), within a diamond and ruby frame. On the back his hair is set under the royal cipher and bordered by star and buckled Garter with motto. Miniature in the style of G. A. Wolffgang (1703–45); setting contemporary.

tokens of love between men and women, parents and children, as a mark of esteem between sovereign and subject, and as a badge of political loyalty. The heroine of Samuel Richardson's novel *Clarissa Harlowe* (1778) bequeathed her miniature painted by an Italian 'to bestow on the man whom I would one day be most inclined to favour'. When Miss Sterling, the spoilt heiress about to marry a baronet in George Colman's satire *The Clandestine Marriage* (1766), shows off her new jewels to a friend, she asks 'What d'ye think of these bracelets? I shall have a miniature of my father, set round with diamonds, to one, and Sir John's to the other.' In Henry Fielding's novel *Amelia* (1752) the theft of the virtuous heroine's miniature, 'set in gold with three little diamonds', by Captain Atkinson leads to its return after a deathbed confession, then to her pawning it to buy supper for her husband, culminating in the repentance of the criminal who had defrauded the couple of their property.

Away from fiction, the poet Richard Hayley wrote his first verses to a Miss Read who had painted his miniature in Van Dyck costume for his mother's bracelet. Tysoe Paul Hancock left the miniature of his wife, Philadelphia – sister of the Rev. George Austen and aunt of Jane Austen – by John Smart, set in a diamond ring, to his daughter, Betsy, hoping she would never part with it, as 'I intend it to remind her of her mother's virtues as well as her person'.[33] In 1755, the wife of Admiral Edward Boscawen sent him her miniature as he set sail for America with the message 'a very sincere friend of yours, who though a lady, I recommend very strongly to your memory and affection because I durst answer for her that she will give you the first place in hers. I don't know that she will make you any professions of her particular regard, but if you'll consult her looks you'll plainly read it there.'[34]

In England, the Hanoverian monarchs, especially George II [210, 211], adopted the miniature jewel as a reward for friendship and loyal service. George III and his wife Queen Charlotte, who married in 1761, also set great store by miniatures for personal and official purposes. One centrepiece of the pair of pearl bracelets he sent for their engagement enclosed his miniature, the other bore his crowned diamond cipher and his hair, both framed in diamond borders. The miniature is on Queen Charlotte's wrist in the sketch made by Sir Joshua Reynolds of the marriage, and again in portraits by Zoffany [212], Benjamin West, and Beechey. In a Gainsborough portrait she wears a miniature of the King set in a large medallion, perhaps that which according to the *Lady's Magazine* Charlotte wore on her birthday, 18 January 1798, hung round her neck with a diamond chain. This could have been in the frame that was sold with her jewels after her death in 1818, 'set with 24 large and fine white brilliants and numerous smaller ditto, suspended from a diamond bow, with fine white brilliant in the centre'.[35] For his birthday on 4 June 1764 she gave the King miniatures of the princes, George and Frederick, as babies, painted 'from life' by Francis Sykes, in a diamond ring.[36] The King and Queen gave miniatures of themselves and their children [213] to various people. The Duchess of Ancaster as Mistress of the Robes was very close to the Queen: she had 'her Majesty's picture set in a kind of frame of diamonds and the crown in diamonds at the top: the Duchess wore it one side as the Queen wears his Majesty's'.[37] In 1784 'the Queen told Lady Weymouth to tye a string round my Aunt Delany's neck and at the end of the string was the king's picture set in gold and diamonds'.[38] In 1794 the King, who had awarded a pension to the Corsican patriot General Pasquale Paoli, also gave him 'a gold chain with my picture set in diamonds for him to wear on all

212 *opposite* Queen Charlotte (1744–1818), in a portrait attributed to Johann Zoffany, 1771. She is wearing a miniature of her husband, George III, as the centrepiece of her bracelet, a betrothal present.

210 *Eighteenth-Century Absolutism, Elegance and Sentiment,* 1715–1800

213 *opposite* Gold watch, the case chased and enamelled with a double portrait miniature of George, Prince of Wales (1762–1830), and his brother, Frederick, Duke of York (1763–1827), in Van Dyck costume, after Johann Zoffany. Miniature and case by G. M. Moser (1707–83) for A. Heckhel, Vienna, *c.* 1765–67. D 58 mm.

public occasions'.³⁹ A godson, James, 3rd Earl of Courtown, received, possibly on his marriage in 1791, a locket with miniature backed with blue glass scattered with stars and a crowned monogram GR in diamonds, to be worn on a chatelaine from the waist, beside a seal; another example was given to Lord and Lady Harcourt [214, 215]. Others of royal provenance are inscribed with the King's name, enclose locks of his hair, and are decorated with symbols such as St George and the Dragon.⁴⁰

A group of miniatures recall the various love affairs of the royal children. As a young man, the Prince of Wales, who was always falling in and out of love, demonstrated his current preference by the gift of his miniature [216, 217]. A Miss Lloyd informed the Dowager Lady Spencer in 1792 that Mrs Fitzherbert 'now wears the Prince of Wales's picture hanging at her breast which she never has done till lately. The diamonds about it are immensely fine and large beyond the Duke of York's which the Duchess wears.'⁴¹ Always looking for something new, the couple exchanged lockets – one octagonal, the other oval – enclosing miniatures of their right eyes, commissioned in 1785 and 1786 from Richard Cosway.⁴² In 1799, after a reconciliation, he gave her another set in a gold locket hanging from a bracelet inscribed REJOINDRE OU MOURIR (Come together or die). More tender and romantic feelings are evoked by a miniature of his sister, Princess Augusta, enclosed in the original locket with lover's knots framing the cipher A(ugusta) S(pencer) in front and the date 1799 on the back. It is kept in the Royal Collection with a card recording its importance in her life: 'Her Royal Highness / Princess Augusta / daughter of George III / married Sir Brent Spencer / 1799. Miniature (taken from the neck of Sir Brent Spencer / after death) of HRH Princess / Augusta, daughter of George III / whom he married in 1799'.

214, 215 *opposite* Two views of a chatelaine hung with a key, seal tassels and trinkets and a locket with royal cipher on a blue ground scattered with diamond sparks, outlined in diamonds, enclosing a miniature of George III after Thomas Gainsborough. Miniature and setting English, *c.* 1781. Locket 51 × 39 mm.

216, 217 Front and back views of a gold locket with a miniature of George, Prince of Wales, the back with his crowned seed pearl cipher on a ground of his hair. Miniature by Richard Cosway (1742–1821), *c.* 1786; setting contemporary. H 50 mm. The Prince gave this locket to Mrs Fitzherbert.

Eighteenth-Century Absolutism, Elegance and Sentiment, 1715–1800 213

Political statements were made by miniatures, as well as by cameos and intaglios in rings. While those people upholding the established order paraded the images of the Hanoverian monarchs, those opposed showed their admiration of the political agitator John Wilkes with rings of his miniature, some inscribed FRIENDSHIP WITHOUT INTEREST.[43] Jacobites supporting the cause of the Stuarts wore the miniature of Charles I and Henrietta Maria and the Old Pretender, James III, in rings and pendants, framed in acanthus, crowned and jewelled.[44] From mid-century the portrait of James's son, Prince Charles Edward, the Young Pretender, dominated Jacobite iconography. The smaller miniatures were worn as scarf or neck pins, while the larger ones could be set in a diamond frame with a bowknot, or associated with the Jacobite symbols of white roses and thistles together or individually. One of the most important survivals, now in the collection of the Duke of Buccleuch, is a locket ring enclosing Prince Charles's miniature in armour with the cover set with a turquoise cameo crown and the sides of the bezel and hoop inscribed BY EVERY CLAIM TIS YOURS and RD AD NUPTIAS 1772, alluding to the Prince's marriage with Princess Louisa of Stolberg, and her right to the English throne. The identity of the donor, RD, is not known.[45] Whereas the small size made a ring easy to conceal, a bracelet centrepiece was less so. The Princesse de Talmont, an ardent French Jacobite and Catholic, wishing to avoid trouble, placed the miniature of Prince Charles Edward in her bracelet on a swivel with an image of Christ; when asked to explain the connection, a quick-witted friend quoted the Gospel: 'My kingdom is not of this world.'[46]

Enamelled or painted on vellum or ivory, for rings, lockets, watches,[47] medallions, bracelets and accessories, the miniatures might be covered with crystal and bordered by enamel [218] –

218 Pendant with a miniature of James Drummond, 3rd Duke of Perth (1713–46), surrounded by a gold laurel crown within a dark blue enamelled frame embellished with diamond laurel branches and surmounted by his diamond cipher, P. The Duke was wounded at Culloden, and died on board the ship that rescued him. Miniature by Jean-André Rouquet (1701–58), c. 1740. H 45 mm.

green, white, royal blue – or diamonds, pearls, and coloured stones, both precious and semi-precious. Some frames combined the colour of enamelled flowers with the sparkle of tiny diamonds in the centres. Messages, such as THINK ON THY FATHER AND BEHOLD HIS FACE,[48] were inscribed on those worn in memory of deceased friends and relations. Rank was indicated by coronets [219] and by coats of arms on the backs [221]. Hair, identified by the cipher, was either enclosed with the miniature or, in the case of bracelets, plaited into bands. Dr Samuel Johnson, writing in *The Idler* (1759), questioned the fashion of wives wearing pictures of their husbands on their wrists, for 'if the joy of life is variety is it in the interest of the husband to want a place on the bracelet – the tenderest love requires to be rekindled by absence and fidelity itself will be wearied with transferring her eye only from the same man to the same picture.' An innovation was reported by Sophie von La Roche, a visitor to London, when a woman of great taste, the wife of the famous Warren Hastings who had made a large fortune in India, said she intended to 'set a new fashion of wearing men's portraits in the buckle of a belt'.[49]

Around 1777, some fashionable gentlemen began wearing their watches in pairs: the second was a *fausse montre* or dummy, with a dial for compass or barometer or a miniature instead of a movement [222, 223]. In 1791 Rundell, Bridge and Rundell sent Thomas Eccleston, a Lancashire gentleman, alternative designs to choose from: 'we have sketched on the other side designs of setting your picture round with brilliants for a *fausse montre*. No. 1 represents a circle of large brilliants set transparent with blue and white enamelled borders each side of the diamonds – £120. No. 2 is a brilliant circle of smaller diamonds and may be set with or without enamel borders – £90, or with smaller diamonds 35 or 40 guineas.

219 Pendant with a miniature of the Countess of Coventry (1733–60) – the greatest beauty of her generation – within a ruby border with emerald and diamond earl's coronet. Her name and title are inscribed on the back. Miniature by Penelope Carwardine (1730–1801) after Quentin de La Tour, 1757; setting contemporary. 44 × 36 mm.

Eighteenth-Century Absolutism, Elegance and Sentiment, 1715–1800 215

220, 221 Front and back views of a pendant with a miniature of General Henry Seymour-Conway (1719–95) in an enamelled floral border with ribbons at the top. On the back are the Seymour-Conway arms in a Rococo cartouche. Miniature by Christian Friedrich Zincke (1683–1767), c. 1750; setting English, contemporary. 46 × 37 mm.

222, 223 Two views of a gold *fausse montre* enclosing a miniature of a lady dressed in white within a green and white enamelled border of husks and rosettes. On the back is her hair under a glass cover. Miniature by Abraham Daniel (*c.* 1760–1806), *c.* 1780; setting English, contemporary. H 50 mm.

224, 225 *below and right* A pair of bright-cut gold bracelet clasps with silhouettes of the 4th Duke of Atholl (1755–1830) and his wife (d. 1790). Silhouettes by John Miers (1758–1821), *c.* 1780–90; setting contemporary.

226 *opposite* Portrait of the Infanta Maria Giuseppa de Bourbon (1744–1801) by Anton Raphael Mengs, after 1768. She has a miniature of her mother, Queen Maria Amalia, on the pearl bracelet on her wrist, and she holds up the pair, with the miniature of her father, Charles III.

At the back of the *fausse montre* we usually introduce a blue composition and in the centre of that a medallion with a hair plait or knot and sometimes a cipher on the hair of diamonds.'[50]

From the 1770s, silhouettes were a fashionable alternative to the portrait miniature, and being cheaper were very popular. Using black paper and a pair of scissors, they could be made by family or friends, or cut by professionals. John Miers, who excelled at this branch of portraiture, had many clients, including the 4th Duke of Atholl [224, 225]. These well individualized stark black profiles which stood out against ivory behind glass or crystal covers were set in severe round or oval frames with bright-cut gold borders, sometimes embellished with pearls or gems. Like miniatures, they might have a lock of hair at the back of the frame with a cipher. They too were worn in rings, lockets, scarf pins, and as bracelet centrepieces and clasps.

Elsewhere in Europe miniatures were just as much a part of jewelry as in France and England. The 1743 inventory of the Florentine-born Electress Palatine Anna Maria Ludovica lists the enamelled and painted portraits of numerous relations set in bracelet centrepieces, single and in pairs, surrounded by diamonds, including one of her late husband, Johann Wilhelm, wearing his electoral bonnet, set in a medallion within '11 big faceted diamonds and 11 smaller in different sizes'.[51] The Infanta Maria Giuseppa, daughter of Charles III and Queen Maria Amalia of Spain, was painted by Anton Raphael Mengs with the miniature of her mother on her wrist, and that of her father held up in her hand [226]. Six members of the family of Bourbon-Sicily, Ferdinand IV and his wife Maria Carolina and their four children, were set in a box embellished with marcasite and inscribed NOS PENSEES SONT A VOUS (We are thinking of you).[52] For her mother, Queen Maria Luisa, wife of Charles IV, the Infanta Maria Isabella, married in 1802 to the future

218 *Eighteenth-Century Absolutism, Elegance and Sentiment, 1715–1800*

220 *Eighteenth-Century Absolutism, Elegance and Sentiment, 1715–1800*

227 *opposite* Pendant with a miniature of Friedrich August II of Saxony (1696–1753), surrounded by diamond and enamel laurel branches tied with ribbons and surmounted by a diamond crown – a wedding present to his bride, Archduchess Maria Josepha of Austria. Miniature by Georg Friedrich Dinglinger (1668–1728), 1719; setting by the Dinglinger workshop; bow and crown *c.* 1740–50. 76 × 38 mm.

Francesco I of the Two Sicilies, inscribed her miniature: 'The image that you see expressed in this small ivory, Mother, is me: look upon me in it. You bear me stamped on your heart.'[53] Good mother she may have been, but the Queen was not a faithful wife, and a former lover showed Lady Holland his 'honours' which included 'a ring with secret springs and amorous devices . . . which was not to be examined'.[54] These miniatures *à secret* also appealed to the Venetian adventurer Giacomo Casanova: for two of his conquests, in 1753–54, he concealed them beneath devotional imagery. Thus, the Annunciation was represented on a medallion given to the nun MM, and a St Catherine in a ring for CC, which he describes: 'In the bezel one could only see the Saint, but an almost imperceptible blue dot on the white enamel that surrounded it activated a spring that made my portrait appear, an effect achieved by pressing the blue dot with a pin.'[55]

Whereas the Venetian jeweller who made these tokens is anonymous, the name of Georg Friedrich Dinglinger, goldsmith to the court of Saxony, is famous, and rightly so. He devoted his great talents to enamelling the miniature which Friedrich August II of Saxony gave his bride, Maria Josepha, daughter of the Emperor Joseph I of Austria, in 1719, and to enhancing it with a magnificent diamond setting [227].

The splendours of Dresden were eclipsed by those of St Petersburg. Peter the Great, who was the first tsar to adopt the Western custom of awarding his miniature, was followed by his successors, notably his daughter Anna and the Empress Catherine the Great.[56] Since the gift of the Empress Catherine's miniature, like that of her engraved gem portrait and medal, was a mark of the very highest approval, whether small or large, set in a ring, pin [228], bracelet clasp or medallion, it was prominently displayed, and the owner, radiant with pride and pleasure, would show it everybody [165, 229]. To a favourite visitor, the Prince de Ligne, she joked: 'since you told me that you would either sell, gamble or lose any diamonds I would give you, here are no more than 100 roubles' worth bordering my portrait in a ring.'

There was a long-established custom of removing the diamonds surrounding a presentation portrait. Princess Dashkov, after a meeting in 1783 at court in St Petersburg with Gustav III of Sweden, noted: 'As a sign of friendship he handed me a ring with his portrait embellished with large diamonds. I could hardly wait to remove the diamonds from the portrait of the King of Sweden and replace them with little pearls, and give the diamonds to my niece.'[57] When this occurred, some families still remembered the royal provenance of the diamonds. It was in this spirit that the will of the 4th Earl of Hardwicke in 1873 stipulated that the stones taken from snuff boxes, rings and medallions given him by Queen Victoria and the Emperors of Russia and Prussia and reset in fashionable jewels were to remain in the family as heirlooms.[58]

228 Pin with an oval miniature of the Empress Catherine the Great surrounded by brilliant-cut diamonds, under a rock crystal cover. Miniature and setting St Petersburg, late 18th century. 23 × 17 mm.

229 Portrait of Alexandra, Countess Branicka (1754–1838), natural daughter and lady-in-waiting to the Empress Catherine the Great, by Richard Brompton, 1781. She is wearing a jewelled badge with a miniature of the Empress, surmounted by the imperial crown.

Eighteenth-Century Absolutism, Elegance and Sentiment, 1715–1800   223

4 Dynastic Pride and Private Affection from Napoleon to World War I 1800–1916

Contemporary memoirs and literature show that the jewelled portable portrait continued to have an important place in both public and private lives in the first half of the 19th century. By 1900, however, in spite of the enthusiasm for photography (which soon eclipsed the miniature), there were fewer royal presentation portraits, and in a more prosaic age less demand for jewels of sentiment. As before, the settings of examples that have survived reflect current fashions in jewelry design.

230 *opposite* Cameos of the Emperor Napoleon are displayed by his wife, the Empress Josephine, in her portrait by Andrea Appiani (see Ill. 231). One in the centre of her belt shows him as a young man, while another, in the centre of her tiara, flanked by Victories bearing crowns, depicts him as emperor.

231 *opposite* Portrait of the Empress Josephine (1763–1814) as Queen of Italy by Andrea Appiani, 1807. She wears a ruby, diamond, pearl and cameo parure, with cameos of Napoleon in her belt and in her tiara (for a closer view, see Ill. 230).

Cameos and Intaglios

Napoleon liked to present himself as the successor of Alexander the Great and the Emperor Augustus, and like them he associated his cameo and intaglio portrait with his regime, thus stimulating the last flowering of the art of gem engraving in Rome. There the leading artists, Nicola Morelli, Giuseppe Girometti, Gaspare Capparoni, Giuseppe Cerbara and Luigi Pichler represented every phase of his astonishing career – the lean and intense young consul, the heroic and victorious general, and the mighty emperor – in gems, which, set in a variety of objects, rings and pendants were distributed to his family, the marshals of his army, his closest supporters at home, and foreign diplomats. François-Regnault Nitot, his jeweller, received such a box, with Napoleon wreathed like a Roman emperor, to which his emblem of eagle with thunderbolt was later added [232]. His secretary, the Duc de Bassano, used a seal engraved with an intaglio head of Napoleon at the base of a jasper handle. In accordance with classical taste, most were set in gold outlined with a fillet of royal blue enamel and decorated with his emblems – star, bee, eagle with thunderbolt. Set in this manner in the centre of a jewelled tiara, his portrait bust is worn by his mother, Madame Laetizia Bonaparte, in a portrait by Baron Gerard.[1]

Napoleon encouraged his first wife, the Empress Josephine, to patronize contemporary gem engravers, and she with her excellent taste led the fashion for wearing cameos in jewelry. Andrea Appiani painted her as Queen of Italy in 1807 [230, 231] wearing a pearl and ruby tiara centred on a cameo portrait of Napoleon wreathed with laurel, flanked by winged figures of Victories; another, showing him as a young man, bare-headed, is set in the belt at her high waist. In a drawing by J.-B. Wicar, Joachim Murat (married to Napoleon's sister Caroline) is depicted with his Roman-style

233, 234 *opposite* Front and back of a gold pendant set with an onyx cameo of the Emperor Napoleon *habillé* with diamond laurel crown and drapery and gold cipher N and symbolic bees. The back displays a chased gold eagle and thunderbolt on a lapis lazuli ground. Cameo by Nicola Morelli (1771–1831), Rome, *c.* 1804–14; *habillé* setting contemporary, probably Roman. 40 × 32 mm. The pendant was sent by the exiled Emperor to William Fraser in India.

232 Tortoiseshell box set with an agate cameo head of Napoleon I (1769–1821) as emperor, wreathed, between branches of oak and laurel, later surmounted by his symbolic eagle and thunderbolt. Given by the Emperor to his court jeweller, François-Regnault Nitot, it bears the mark of Pierre-André Montauban (fl. 1800–1825), *c.* 1810. 77 × 47 mm.

cloak fastened with a cameo portrait of Napoleon.[2] The rarest are *habillé*, that is enriched with diamonds, set in the laurel crowning his head and in the cloak over his shoulder: one such was set in a ring for the Princesse de Moscova, wife of Marshal Ney; another, in a locket, was given to a Scottish admirer, William Fraser, who sent Napoleon books and delicacies from India to alleviate the tedium of life as an exile on the island of St Helena [233, 234].

A portrait cameo of Josephine by Teresa Talani, presented to the wife of General Bertrand, most faithful of Napoleon's friends, is simply framed in gold outlined in blue enamel,[3] but Josephine's imperial status is indicated by the frame of green enamel laurel leaves and pearl berries surrounding her cameo bust in a pendant [235]. Another, by Giovanni Beltrami of Cremona, encircled by a gold wire frame with pearls, has an inscription on the back celebrating Josephine as patron of the arts.[4]

Josephine's son, Eugène de Beauharnais, who was appointed Viceroy of Italy, commissioned from the same engraver portraits of himself and his wife Augusta for his mother and for official presentation.[5] His sister, Queen Hortense of Holland, is depicted on an octagonal sapphire cameo playing the lyre, alluding to her musical talents. It was inherited by her son, Napoleon III, who had it set with diamonds and pearls on the cover of a locket he gave his wife, the Empress Eugénie [237]. This was the only jewel the Empress took with her when she fled from Paris after the fall of the Second Empire in 1870, and on her arrival in England she presented it as a token of gratitude to Lady Burgoyne, in whose yacht she had crossed the Channel.

There are cameo portraits of Joachim Murat,[6] and in her terracotta statue by Joseph Chinard Julie Bonaparte wears a

Dynastic Pride and Private Affection from Napoleon to World War I, 1800–1916

235 Pendant set with an onyx cameo of the Empress Josephine wearing a tiara edged with pearls, surrounded by green enamel laurel leaves with pearl berries tied with ribbons. Cameo Roman; setting probably French, *c.* 1800. 46 × 28 mm.

236 Hortense de Beauharnais, Queen of Holland (1783–1837), playing the lyre: engraving after a portrait by Jean-Baptiste Isabey. This image of the Queen served as the model for her sapphire cameo, later set by her son, Napoleon III, for his wife, the Empress Eugénie (*right*).

237 Gold locket, the cover set with an octagonal sapphire cameo of Queen Hortense of Holland playing the lyre, surrounded by diamonds, within a diamond and pearl laurel border. The locket was created for the Empress Eugénie. Cameo Italian, *c.* 1808; setting French, *c.* 1860. 15 × 13 mm.

Dynastic Pride and Private Affection from Napoleon to World War I, 1800–1916 231

238 *opposite* Terracotta bust of Julie (1771–1845), wife of Joseph Bonaparte, King of Spain, executed from life by Joseph Chinard in Lyons in 1808. She wears a tiara with cameo portraits of her husband and their daughters, Zénaïde and Charlotte.

tiara set with a cameo bust of her husband, Napoleon's brother Joseph, King of Spain, flanked by those of their children [238]. For Madame Laetizia Bonaparte her stepbrother, Cardinal Fesch, commissioned from Nicola Morelli a parure of earrings and necklace with chains linking medallions set with cameo portraits of her husband and all her children surrounding that of Napoleon: recorded in 1807 by Giovanni Antonio Guattani in *Memorie enciclopediche romane*, unfortunately it has vanished.[7] However, a gold chain with links set with cameo portraits of Napoleon and his brothers and sisters, also engraved by Morelli, survives as an expression of the imperial family theme, albeit on a smaller scale.[8]

At home in Paris, Jean-Henri Simon, who had engraved portraits of the Revolutionary leaders Marat and Le Pelletier, was now engaged by Napoleon throughout his reign to produce portraits of himself and his family, chiefly for snuff boxes and rings. Simon's son, Jean-Marie-Amable-Henri Simon, continued the family tradition by engraving portraits of the restored Bourbons and the family of Louis-Philippe, but none of those intaglios was given more than a plain gold frame.[9]

Following his uncle's example, Napoleon III also commissioned cameo portraits of himself, more as objects for exhibition than as jewelry; however, a small brooch set with his portrait facing that of the Empress Eugénie was obviously worn by someone close to them.[10] Members of the Second Empire nobility such as the Duchesse de Cambacérès now reaffirmed their Bonaparte credentials by wearing cameo portraits of Napoleon I newly mounted in contemporary designs.

The pattern for imperial cameo portraiture established by Napoleon was adopted by the Emperor of Austria, Franz II, the father of the Empress Marie-Louise. Giovanni Beltrami, formerly patronized by Eugène de Beauharnais, portrayed the Emperor in old age, wreathed and draped like a Roman emperor [239, 240]. His widow, the Empress Carolina Augusta, commissioned the setting in his memory. His motto, IUSTITIA REGNORUM FUNDAMENTUM (Empires are founded upon justice), surrounds the cameo, with at the base a black cross flanked by olive leaves and weeping willow, within a gold scrolled border surmounted by the imperial Austro-Hungarian crown. The inscription behind, MEINE LIEBE VERMACHE ICH MEINEN UNTERTHANEN. ICH HOFFE DASS ICH FÜR SIE BEY GOTT WERDE BETEN KÖNNEN · TEST.14 § 1.MÄRZ.1835 (I bequeath my love to my subjects. I hope to pray for them before God. 1 March 1835), asserts his conviction that by divine right the authority to rule his people resided in his person. On the outer rim his widow added IHRE MAJESTÄT DIE KAISERINN CAROLINA AUGUSTA LIESS DIESES BILDNISS IHRES UNSTERBLICHEN GEMAHLS FÜR DAS K. K. MÜNZ UND ANTIKEN-KABINET ARBEITEN UND ÜBERGAB ES DEN 14. APR. 1840 (Her Majesty the Empress Carolina Augusta had this portrait of her immortal spouse made for the Imperial-Royal Cabinet of Coins and Antiquities and presented it on 14 April 1840).

No English monarch since Queen Elizabeth liked portraits of themselves more than George, Prince of Wales, later Prince Regent and from 1821 George IV. The long struggle against the French which ended with the victory of Waterloo in 1815 fostered the spirit of patriotism, which being centred on the monarch provided the pretext for the commissioning of cameo portraits of himself, usually wreathed in laurel like a Roman emperor. Some were by the Roman engraver Benedetto Pistrucci, who arrived in London in 1814 and was appointed Chief Medallist of the Royal Mint.[11] The intaglios were usually set in austere Roman-style signets, though a few

239, 240 Front and back of a gold memorial pendant with an onyx cameo portrait of Franz II, Emperor of Austria, surmounted by the imperial crown and surrounded by his motto; at the base is a cross flanked by sprays of olive and weeping willow. The back of the cameo is incised with the Emperor's initial and the dates of his birth and death – 12 February 1768–2 March 1835; on the frame is a message from the Emperor dated the day before his death, and on the rim an inscription by his widow, the Empress Carolina Augusta. Cameo by Giovanni Beltrami (1777–1854); setting by Joseph Damhart, Vienna, 1840. 105 × 70 mm.

Dynastic Pride and Private Affection from Napoleon to World War I, 1800–1916 235

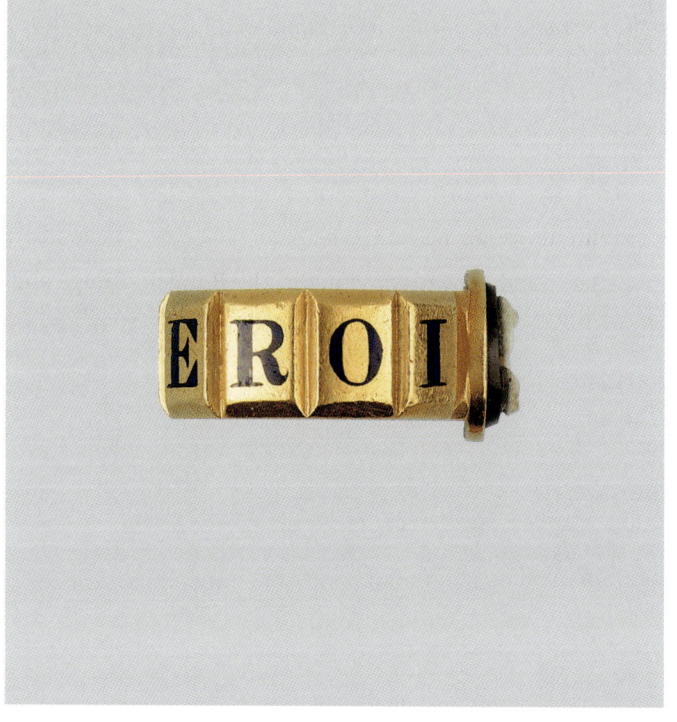

241 *above* Gold ring with an onyx cameo of George IV, King of Great Britain and Ireland (1762–1830), wreathed like a Roman emperor, given at his coronation in 1821 to his brother, the Duke of Cumberland. Cameo perhaps by Benedetto Pistrucci (1783–1855); setting by Rundell, Bridge and Rundell, London, 1821.

242, 243 *above right and right* Two views of a gold ring with an onyx cameo head of George IV, the band divided into nine sections inscribed VIVE LE ROI in blue enamel. One of several distributed at the coronation in 1821, it was given to the 6th Duke of Devonshire. By Rundell, Bridge and Rundell, 1821.

were rather heavily chased. These royal cameo or intaglio portraits were either surrounded[12] and crowned by diamonds or framed within patriotic motifs of wreaths of laurel and oak, or else set in bracelets and brooches with the Garter motto HONI SOIT QUI MAL Y PENSE inscribed on a dark blue ground. Rings distributed at the time of the coronation in 1821 [241–243] were usually inscribed GEORGIUS IV DEI GRATIA BRIT REX MDCCCXXI on the back. A variant was a broad hoop with the King's cameo head and the motto VIVE LE ROI. A most important setting, emblematic of the three kingdoms of England, Scotland and Ireland, was 'A very fine remarkably large sardonyx cameo with the device of His Majesty's bust with a dove, figures of Britannia and Neptune in front, and on the reverse Aurora and her horses and chariot and the sign Leo surrounded with laurel, all in cameo of the finest workmanship'; it was mounted with 'very fine large brilliants and richly chased gold compartments set with rubies, brilliants and sapphires, emeralds etc. in devices of roses, thistles, harps and with brilliant collets on the border' and cost £1,336.[13]

A dynastic cameo representing all four King Georges – I, II, III and IV – set in 'a very elegant and richly chased Snuff box with device of the four Georges raised on onyx Brilliant ornaments and Crown' was supplied by Rundell, Bridge and Rundell on 21 October 1821, probably for George IV to give to one of his brothers or sisters.[14] They too were portrayed in cameos and intaglios, some of them commemorative, such as the brooch with the Duke of York's bust encircled by a diamond and black enamel snake, symbolic of eternity [244]. Another British royal memorial jewel is a bracelet with clasp decorated with *cannetille* and *grainti* technique set with a cameo head of Princess Charlotte, daughter of George IV, depicted as a Roman princess [245].

244 Gold memorial brooch set with an onyx cameo bust of Frederick, Duke of York (1763–1827), surrounded by a snake swallowing its tail, enamelled black with a scattering of diamonds. Cameo and setting 1827. 55 × 44 mm.

Dynastic Pride and Private Affection from Napoleon to World War I, 1800–1916 237

During her long reign Queen Victoria's portrait was diffused through many different media, of which the rarest are the cameos. This reflects the decline of the art: even the great Benedetto Pistrucci, who portrayed Prince Albert in a cameo at the time of his marriage to the Queen in 1840,[15] complained of the lack of commissions in the last phase of his life. An unusual example, in which a cameo by Paul Lebas after Thomas Sully's portrait of the Queen is combined with enamelled gold like a Renaissance *commesso*, was shown at the Great Exhibition of 1851 by the Parisian jeweller Félix Dafrique [246]: it is framed in a border with white and red roses representing the Houses of York and Lancaster, united by Victoria's Tudor ancestors. Others are set in the badges of the two Orders she established. Since the purpose of the Order of Victoria and Albert was to perpetuate the memory of Prince Albert, her consort, who had died the previous year, the badge is set with their cameo portraits side by side, encircled by diamonds and crowned [247]. The Order of the Star of India was instituted in 1861 to reward the Indian rulers and those who had stood by the British Crown during the Indian 'Mutiny' of 1857 [248]: in her cameo portrait, Victoria wears the 'Gothic crown' as in William Wyon's coin of 1857, within a frame inscribed in diamonds HEAVEN'S LIGHT OUR GUIDE, surmounted by a five-pointed diamond star probably made by Garrards, the court jeweller.[16]

There was not a royal monopoly. As in the 18th century, private individuals also commissioned their cameo portraits. Calling on the Duchess of Wellington on St Patrick's Day, 1818, the novelist Maria Edgeworth observed a jeweller who had arrived with some bracelets, one of which had the clasp set with a cameo portrait of the Duke – which was then corrected on the advice of the Duchess.

245 *opposite* Gold mesh bracelet with an onyx cameo head of Princess Charlotte (1796–1817) in the *cannetille* and *grainti* centrepiece, which can also be worn as a brooch. Cameo and setting English, *c.* 1820. Centrepiece 34 × 29 mm.

246 Brooch with a shell cameo *commesso* bust of Victoria, Queen of Great Britain and Ireland (1819–1901), wearing a regal circlet set with diamond sparks and emeralds, and enamelled gold robes of state. The design is based on the portrait by Thomas Sully that shows the Queen ascending to her throne in the House of Lords. The setting combines the red roses of Lancaster and the white roses of York. Cameo by Paul Lebas (fl. 1851–76); mounted by Félix Dafrique (fl. 1829–70) for the Great Exhibition of 1851. H 61 mm.

247 Badge of the Order of Victoria and Albert: onyx cameo portraits of the Queen and her consort are surrounded with diamonds and surmounted by an enamelled, diamond, ruby and emerald crown. Cameo by Tommaso Saulini (1793–1864), Rome; setting by Garrards, London, 1860s. 85 × 44 mm.

248 Gold badge of the Order of the Star of India, with an onyx cameo portrait bust of Queen Victoria surrounded by a diamond inscription and surmounted by a star. Cameo after the 'Gothic crown' coin by William Wyon, 1857; setting by Garrards (?). 215 × 165 mm.

Dynastic Pride and Private Affection from Napoleon to World War I, 1800–1916 241

The hardstone cameo portrait was soon eclipsed by those carved from shell, which being soft made it easier to obtain good likenesses much less expensively. In Rome a whole industry of cameo portrait-cutters, led by Giovanni Dies and by Tommaso and Luigi Saulini of 96 via del Babuino, served the visitors arriving in ever increasing numbers to the city. Shell cameos might be set in medallions to wear as pendants, or in groups for bracelets, sometimes enamelled, but usually – as for the hardstone portrait of the 7th Duke of Beaufort [250] – in the archaeological style, decorated with corded wire, filigree and beading. Significantly, Americans as well as Europeans were now commissioning these shell cameo portraits when in Rome.[17] In Paris in 1843 Mrs William Bingham, the American wife of a banker, ordered from the jeweller Jules Fossin 'a gold swivel medallion hanging as a Sévigné from a large bow knot' to enclose a pair of portraits.[18] Moreover, to meet the demand for portraits shell-cutters were established in New York, and the sculptor Augustus Saint-Gaudens began his career in 1861 as a thirteen-year-old apprentice to one of them, Louis Avet. His most ambitious creation was for a bracelet set with portraits of Anna Watson Stuart and her banker husband with their four children, each in a gold medallion surrounded by seed pearls. Mrs Watson wears it in her portrait by Daniel Huntington [249].[19]

The Roman pontiffs continued the long tradition of giving their portrait jewels to high-ranking dignitaries and zealous servants of the Church. The most splendid were *habillé* with diamonds, a speciality of the Roman jeweller Capazzi. Thus in a swivel ring not only are the cap and stole of Pope Pius VII highlighted with diamonds, but the back of the setting is pavé-set with diamonds patterned with the coat of

249 *opposite* Anna Watson Stuart, wearing a bracelet with shell cameo portraits of herself, her husband and their four children, by the young Augustus Saint-Gaudens (1848–1907), set in gold medallions surrounded by seed pearls. Detail of her portrait by Daniel Huntington, 1862.

250 Gold archaeological style pendant set with an onyx cameo portrait of the 7th Duke of Beaufort (1792–1853), 'an excellent landlord', with 'a countenance whose features were set in a truly noble mould' (*Gentleman's Magazine*). Cameo by Luigi Saulini (1818–83), *c.* 1860; setting contemporary. H 99 mm.

Dynastic Pride and Private Affection from Napoleon to World War I, 1800–1916   243

arms (a mountain) of his family, the Chiaramonti.[20] Even more elaborate is a double-sided pendant with cameo *habillé* depicting the Pope giving thanks to Our Lady of Sorrows on his return to the Vatican after years of exile [251, 252], the frame inscribed DOMINUM REFUGIUM MEUM ET LIBERATOR MEUS (The Lord is my refuge and my deliverer); on the back are the papal cross, the word PAX (Peace), the Chiaramonti mountain, and three small cameo heads of blindfolded blackamoors, another family emblem. In Rome in 1818, the Polish Countess Potocka attracted much attention when publicly displaying this pendant – or one very like it – over her bodice.[21] Years later, in 1849, when a republic was set up in Rome, the Princesse de Ligne, the devout wife of a Belgian diplomat, described how Pius IX, obliged to take refuge in the Kingdom of Naples and Sicily, was still able to give her 'a gold-mounted cameo, which greatly moved me'.[22] Hardstone and shell cameo portraits of Pius IX and Leo XIII are set in simpler gold mounts, the most ambitious being in the archaeological style.[23]

In Russia, Tsarina Maria Feodorovna, a talented gem-engraver herself, was painted in her widow's weeds with the cameo portrait of her husband Paul I simply rimmed in gold [253]; this she continued to wear for the next twenty-five years. Both her sons, Alexander I and Nicholas I [254], were portrayed by the leading artists of the day in gems for setting in rings, brooches and pendants, given as marks of distinction.[24] Under Nicholas I and his successors the imperial family and the nobility patronized the shell cameo-cutters Tommaso and Luigi Saulini, and their portraits were usually mounted in archaeological style brooches or bracelets.[25] Since shell eclipsed hardstone cameo portraiture, a hardstone cameo of the Grand Duke Vladimir, which is still in a heart-shaped brooch, can be considered a rarity.[26]

251, 252 Front and back of a pendant with a cameo *habillé* of Pope Pius VII (1740–1823) praying at the altar of the Virgin of Sorrows. The back is pavé-set with diamonds with papal symbols and the mountain of the Chiaramonti, the Pope's family; another family emblem is the blindfolded blackamoor heads. Cameo and setting Roman, *c.* 1818. 44 × 32 mm.

Dynastic Pride and Private Affection from Napoleon to World War I, 1800–1916 245

Сія книжка ИМПЕРАТОРА АЛЕК=
САНДРА I^{го.} пожалована ИМПЕРА-
ТОРОМЪ НИКОЛАЕМЪ I^{мъ.} Д: Т: С: Кн:
Алекс: Ник: ГОЛИЦЫНУ.

ПОРТРЕТЪ ИМПЕРАТРИЦЫ МАРІИ
пожалованъ ЕЯ ВЕЛИЧЕ-
СТВОМЪ ЕМУ ЖЕ.

253 *opposite* Miniature of Maria Feodorovna (1759–1828), Dowager Empress of Russia, veiled and displaying a cameo portrait of her husband Paul I (assassinated in 1801) which she herself engraved. Maria Feodorovna was admired by her people as 'a Sister of Charity enthroned as Empress', and her death was thought to mark the disappearance of 'Old Russia'. Miniature by Franz Gerhard von Kügelgen (1722–1820), presented by the Empress to her son Alexander I and subsequently mounted on a book cover. H of oval 70 mm.

254 Gold brooch set with an onyx cameo portrait of Nicholas I, Emperor of Russia (1796–1855), surrounded by diamonds. Cameo by Alexis Klepikou (1803–52), *c.* 1840; setting contemporary. 22 × 16 mm.

Dynastic Pride and Private Affection from Napoleon to World War I, 1800–1916   247

255 Neo-Renaissance style pendant set with an onyx cameo bust of Giuseppe Mazzini (1805–72), given by the radical politician Peter Alfred Taylor to his wife Clementia to celebrate their fortieth wedding anniversary. It is suspended from a gold chain with plaited wire links interspersed with pearls and coloured gems. Cameo by De Felici; setting by Accarisi & Nipote, Florence, 1882. Pendant 99 × 60 mm.

In Rome, the leading jeweller, Augusto Castellani, anxious to save the ancient art of hardstone gem-engraving, continued to commission cameos and intaglios for setting in the historicist jewelled frames associated with his name. Although the subjects and figures were usually derived from mythology and classical history, Castellani did make settings for the occasional portrait, such as that of the American Ellen Walters [256].[27] One of the firm's many imitators, Accarisi of Florence, set an onyx cameo portrait signed by De Felici of Giuseppe Mazzini, one of the leaders of the movement for the unification of Italy, in the pendant to a Renaissance Revival necklace worn by Mrs Peter Alfred Taylor, wife of the radical English politician, from 1847 Chairman of the Society of Friends of Italy. Although Mazzini had died ten years previously, the couple chose his image in 1882 for this jewel marking the fortieth anniversary of their marriage [255].

256 Gold brooch with a shell cameo portrait of Ellen Walters (1822–62) in a plain archaeological style setting, commissioned in Rome in 1862 after her death earlier that year by her widower, William Thompson Walters of Baltimore (founder of the Walters Art Gallery). Cameo by Tommaso Saulini, after a marble bust by W. H. Rinehart of 1862; setting by Castellani, Rome, c. 1862. H 67 mm.

257 *opposite* Gold snuff box, the lid set with a portrait medal of George IV, bordered by oak leaves. Medal by Thomas I Wyon (1767–1830), box by Alexander Strachan (fl. 1799–1850), sold by Rundell, Bridge and Rundell, 1821–22. D 85 mm. This box was presented by the King to Simón Bolívar, 'El Libertador', in South America.

Portrait Medals

For political reasons monarchs continued to have medals cast or struck with portraits of themselves to commemorate the outstanding events of their reigns, notably coronations, marriages and deaths. In Great Britain the victories of Lord Nelson and the Duke of Wellington, and the achievements of illustrious subjects such as the acquisition of the Parthenon marbles by Lord Elgin, were also marked by medals.[28] Many were commissioned by the Prince Regent – the future George IV – but only a few of those converted into jewelry survive. Invoices of the latter's purchases from Rundell, Bridge and Rundell provide clues to their use. In May 1820, to mark his accession, he bought 'A fine gold medal of His Majesty George IV [i.e. himself] with the King's profile on one side, the reverse with a wreath of oak, and national devices, with loop and inscription £52.10 plus 12 shillings: large solid gold chain to ditto £49.10',[29] and in July another accession medal, but silver, for his sister, Princess Augusta.[30] Others were set in rings[31] and in pendants in jewelled frames,[32] but most were inserted in the lids of boxes for presentation [257].

William IV, who succeeded his brother in 1831, commissioned a coronation medal with his portrait which was set in a Garter bracelet inscribed with the motto NEC TIMERE NEC TIMIDE (Neither rashly nor timidly) in black letter; another bracelet was set with two coronation medals – his and that of his wife, Queen Adelaide.[33] The reign of his successor, Queen Victoria, was marked by medallic bangles, rings and pins commemorating her coronation in 1837, her Diamond Jubilee in 1897,[34] and her death in 1901. There were also medallic mementoes of her personal life: rings presented to those attending her marriage with Prince Albert in 1840 [259], double cravat pins commemorating the birth of the Prince of Wales in 1841,[35] and brooches mounted with medallic

259 Gold ring, the bezel set with miniature portrait medals of Prince Albert and Queen Victoria within blue enamel borders, surmounted by a turquoise and diamond forget-me-not – one of six dozen given to mark their wedding in 1840. By Rundell, Bridge and Rundell. D 15 mm.

portraits of the royal couple and their six eldest children.[36] Loyalty to Queen Victoria was expressed by the chain of office made by the sculptor Alfred Gilbert for the President of the Royal Institute of Painters in Water Colours [258]: it is centred on a medallic portrait of the Queen – also by Gilbert – below a crown. Gilbert's medals were also worn as jewelry by private individuals.[37]

In Britain a very large series of war service medals were awarded, first during the Napoleonic Wars and subsequently during campaigns to secure British interests in India, Afghanistan, the Crimea, Egypt, Africa and the Arctic. As was the case with medals awarded for saving life, special merit, long service and good conduct, however, they were worn on ribbons and not converted into jewelry.

Across the Channel, Napoleon employed Romain Vincent Jeuffroy and Bertrand Andrieu to portray himself and members of his family in medals, to be worn as jewels [261, 262] or set in the lids of boxes and accessories.[38] In Russia the death of Alexander I in 1825 and the coronation of his brother Nicholas I were commemorated by a group of jewelry which

258 *opposite* Silver wire chain of office terminating in a crowned medallic portrait of Queen Victoria, made by Alfred Gilbert (1854–1934) for the President of the Royal Institute of Painters in Water Colours, *c.* 1890–97.

Dynastic Pride and Private Affection from Napoleon to World War I, 1800–1916   253

260 Gold snuff box, the lid centred on a coronation portrait medal of the Emperor Nicholas I within a laurel crown. Medal by Vladimir Ephraimovich Alexeiev (1784–1832), 1826; setting by Johann Wilhelm Keibel (fl. 1809–41), St Petersburg, c. 1840. 101 × 68 × 28 mm.

261, 262 Front and back of a gold pendant with the marriage medal of Napoleon and the Empress Marie-Louise on the front and their infant son, the King of Rome, behind, surmounted by an eagle clasping a thunderbolt. Medal by Bertrand Andrieu (1761–1822) with André Galle (1761–1844), Paris, 1811. 32 × 16 mm.

264 Gold bracelet enclosing a double portrait medal of Christian VIII, King of Denmark (1786–1848), and Queen Caroline Amalia marking their anointing at his coronation in 1840, and made for her. Medal by C. Christensen (1806–45), 1840; mount by Emil Ferdinand Dahl, Copenhagen.

263 *opposite* Plaster bust of the widowed Caroline Amalia, Queen of Denmark (1796–1886), wearing a portrait medal of her husband, Christian VIII, after his death in 1848.

included rings and gold snuff boxes.[39] Set in the lid of one of this series is a medallic portrait of Tsar Nicholas [260] within a laurel crown inscribed in Russian translating 'By God's Grace Nicholas I Emperor and Autocrat of all the Russias', with on the reverse the inscription translating 'The Pledge of Felicity of All and Everyone Crowned in Moscow in 1826'; behind is a cornelian cameo portrait of his late brother Tsar Alexander within a black enamel border with an inscription translating 'Our Angel in Heaven'. Another coronation ceremony was marked in this way by a bracelet set with the 'anointing' medal of the Danish King Christian VIII and his Queen on his accession in 1840 [264]. The widowed Queen Caroline Amalia wears his medal round her neck in her portrait bust [263].

The long German medallic portrait tradition was maintained in Prussia, where in 1862 Queen Augusta, as a farewell present to Baroness Bloomfield, married to a diplomat, 'took

Dynastic Pride and Private Affection from Napoleon to World War I, 1800–1916 257

off a gold pin she was wearing with a medal of the King and herself saying "Now mind you never forget me, my dear, and whenever you have an opportunity come and see me: I have been so happy to see you again.'"[40] This double medallic portrait was also set as the centrepiece of a gold bracelet with wide band.[41] Medals of King Wilhelm IV were mounted as the centrepieces of black enamel bangles worn in his memory by members of noble families after his death in 1861: there was one in the collection of the Princes of Thurn und Taxis.[42] A Hohenzollern dynastic brooch was composed of three medals by Emile Weigand representing King Wilhelm's successors, the Emperor Wilhelm I, the Emperor Friedrich and the Emperor Wilhelm II, divided by two arrows set with rose diamonds.[43] More elaborate is the pendant designed by Ludwig Paar of Karlsruhe in 1881 as a frame for the double portrait of the Grand Duke Friedrich and Grand Duchess Louise of Baden, daughter of the Emperor Wilhelm I, which marked the twenty-fifth anniversary of his accession and their marriage [266].

Essentially private were the marriage medals which were in use *c.* 1850–1905, bearing the portraits of the couple with their names, titles and date of the ceremony. Given to the bride, the bridegroom, close relations, and occasionally to the best man and bridesmaids, most were in silver but a few were in gold, to be worn as pendants at the neck or attached to a bracelet. During the last decades of the century, the art of the medallist took on a new lease of life in France with the emergence of Louis Oscar Roty, Emile Vernier [265] and Frédéric Vernon. However, although their medals and plaquettes made attractive jewels, especially brooches, those adopted for this purpose were not so much the excellent portraits of individuals as poetic evocations of contemporary events, characters from literature, genre, religion and mythology.

265 Gilt bronze marriage medal of Prince Roland Bonaparte (1858–1924) and Marie-Félix Blanc (1859–82), surmounted by the Napoleonic crown. (Other examples are surmounted by the symbolic eagle and thunderbolt.) Medal by Emile Vernier (1852–1927), 1880. 55 × 28 mm.

258 *Dynastic Pride and Private Affection from Napoleon to World War I, 1800–1916*

266 Gold neo-Renaissance style pendant enclosing a medal of Grand Duke Friedrich of Baden (1826–1907) and Grand Duchess Louise (1838–1923), marking the twenty-fifth anniversary of his accession and their marriage. Of gold, enamel, lapis lazuli and pearls, it incorporates flanking chimerae and the grand-ducal crown. Medal by R. Mayer (d. 1916); setting by Ludwig Paar, Karlsruhe, 1881. 162 × 77 mm.

267 *opposite* Gold snuff box set with a miniature of the Emperor Napoleon, bordered with symbolic bees and stars, given to Jean-Baptiste Duvoisin, Bishop of Nantes. Miniature by Jean-Baptiste-Jacques Augustin (1759–1832). 90 × 65 mm.

Miniatures and Photographs

Napoleon's image was diffused not only in cameos and intaglios and in medals but also in miniatures, painted by the great Jean-Baptiste Isabey, by Daniel Saint and by Jean-Baptiste-Jacques Augustin [267]. The majority, surrounded by classical ornament of palmettes, anthemion or acanthus scrolls, were set in the lids of snuff boxes – round, oval or rectangular, gold, chased and enamelled royal blue, or gold-mounted tortoiseshell. Comte Clary, summoned to Paris in 1810 for Napoleon's marriage to the Archduchess Marie-Louise, described in a letter to his wife how the Grand Chamberlain, the Comte de Montesquiou, had invited him to dinner, and before the meal

> gave me on behalf of the Emperor a box. I did not dare to look at it, and put it in my pocket... Even after my departure I did not dare open the case for fear that my man would kill me: thus I arrived my treasure always in my pocket at Monsieur de Champigny's. There, I took my time and hidden behind someone I opened the case in my hat.

He then described it:

> The box was splendid, much more magnificent than I could have expected and admirably made. He is a great ruler, the Prince who gave it to me!... On the lid one sees his portrait, marvellously painted by Saint, very flattering but a good likeness. Inside the cover there is an eagle and a border of arabesques and bees in blue enamel that are the prettiest things in the world.[44]

Those closest to Napoleon were given miniatures to wear as jewels, like the badge of an order of chivalry. The Empress Josephine's pride in his great achievements is expressed in Isabey's portrait of her painted in Strasbourg in 1805, where she displays his miniature in a brooch pinned to her red velvet

gown.⁴⁵ Miniatures of her grandchildren set in medallions and in the centrepieces of bracelets enclosing locks of their hair demonstrated her love for her family. Wonderfully elegant and bejewelled, she herself was painted many times in miniatures for rings [268] and snuff boxes for presentation. Her dresser, Mademoiselle Avrillion, recorded what Josephine's miniature meant to her: 'This treasure of which I am the devoted custodian will remain with me until the day I die. I am always proud to wear it whenever I am with my friends. They all want to look at it, and the portrait leads naturally on to conversation about the admirable qualities of the original.'⁴⁶

Napoleon marked the consent of the Emperor of Austria to his second marriage by giving the Archduchess Marie-Louise his miniature set in a medallion framed in fourteen huge diamonds, which she then wore at the wedding ceremony. During their years together he gave her others, including one framed in pearls to wear as the centrepiece of a pearl bracelet. The court jeweller, Nitot, surrounded her miniature with stones whose initials spelt out the message 'Louise je t'aime' (Louise, I love you) for the lid of a snuff box. Further acrostic messages framed a pair of bracelets in brilliants and coloured stones enclosing the portraits and hair of the Emperor and their son, the King of Rome. The cherubic features of the child, painted in enamel, were surrounded by eight coloured stones with initials spelling out the name 'Napoleon' mounted on a band of plaited locks of hair.⁴⁷ Of those of herself, one is set in an oval pendant framed in a narrow dark blue enamel border decorated with four leaves,⁴⁸ while others are set in the lids of snuff boxes [269]. After Napoleon's fall, in the following phase of her life as Archduchess of Parma Marie-Louise was similarly attached to

268 Gold ring with a miniature head of the Empress Josephine, within a pearl and diamond border, given to her son, Eugène de Beauharnais, for his wife, Amalia Augusta of Bavaria. Miniature by Jean-Baptiste Isabey (1767–1855), c. 1804. 27 × 22 mm.

269 Gold snuff box with a miniature of the Empress Marie-Louise (1791–1847). Miniature by Abraham Constantin (1784–1855) after the portrait by François Gérard showing her with her son, the King of Rome; box by François-Regnault Nitot (1779–1853), c. 1812. 90 × 65 mm.

264 *Dynastic Pride and Private Affection from Napoleon to World War I, 1800–1916*

270 *opposite* Gold brooch with a miniature of Caroline Murat, Queen of Naples (1782–1839), in an acrostic border: the initials of the stones alternating with pearls spell 'souvenir'. Miniature by Jean-Baptiste-Jacques Augustin, *c.* 1807; setting contemporary.

miniatures of her morganatic husband, Count Neipegg, and their children. Among the other jewels of sentiment listed in her will she bequeathed a gold medallion containing an eye miniature of 'General Neipegg which hangs from the chain which is always round my neck'.

Other members of the Bonaparte family shared the taste for miniatures. A miniature of Augusta of Bavaria, wife of Eugène de Beauharnais, Viceroy of Italy, surrounded by three rows of diamonds, was mounted on a wide pearl bracelet. Devoted to her and their five children, Eugène carried all their miniatures in his watch chain. Similarly, Joachim Murat, Napoleon's brother-in-law, wrote to his daughter Laetizia in August 1812, 'I'm waiting for the miniature of Achille; yours and your mama's are always with me – they are my talismans.'[49] A brilliant cavalry officer, he kept them close to him throughout all the Napoleonic campaigns and when, three years later, he died courageously before a firing squad, he was holding these miniatures which had previously adorned the hilt of his sword.[50] A miniature of his wife, Napoleon's sister Caroline, in a brooch, is surrounded by an acrostic message, 'souvenir', the coloured stones interspersed with pearls [270]. Not all her miniatures were for everyone to look at: on 19 September 1807 she bought from Breguet a watch with 'a secret portrait in its base'.[51] An exception to the more usual rings, bracelets and brooches is a pendant with a miniature of Laetizia Bonaparte, her mother, encircled by pearls and attached to a chain necklace.[52]

The demand for miniatures of loved ones was not exclusive to the imperial family. Even Isabey, favourite painter of the Empress Josephine [268], occasionally found time to execute private commissions independent of their political significance. His miniature of a child – now unknown except for the name ERNEST inscribed on the back of the setting – has an irresistible charm which must have delighted the parents [271–273]. It is set between diamond bowknots in the centre of a necklace, the child's hair enclosed in the clasp at the back of the neck. Others reflect the number of separations and deaths resulting from the circumstances of the Revolutionary and Napoleonic Wars. One victim of his political involvement was the young Comte de La Bedoyère, who in the will drawn up just before his execution in August 1815 reveals his attachment to the miniatures of his wife Georgine and their infant son Georges: 'I wish that the portrait of my dear Georgine which I will have with me at the moment of my death should go to my son, and I beg my dear mother to accept the portrait of my little angel and to transfer to him all the love she has shown me.' The great novelist Balzac tells Madame Hanska in 1835 how much he longs for her portrait: 'Oh, how much longer must I wait for your dear portrait? If by chance you are thinking of having it set, then have it placed between two enamelled plaques, the whole no thicker than a 5 franc coin, as I want to wear it over my heart. When I feel it there it will be my talisman, from which I will draw strength and courage.'

Strong passions were aroused by miniatures. On 25 May 1846 the actress Rachel ordered from Jules Fossin a miniature of her lover, Count Walewski, set in the clasp of a bracelet and surrounded by stones whose initials spelt out his name, Alexandre: A(methyst) L(apis) E(merald) X(yloide) A(methyst) N(atrolite) D(iamond) R(uby) E(merald). However, on learning that on 4 June he had married the Florentine Marianne de Ricci, without informing her, her rage knew no bounds and she refused to collect the bracelet and never looked at the miniature again.[53]

271–273 Three details of a diamond bowknot necklace with a miniature bust of a child, Ernest; his name is on the back of the centrepiece, while the clasp encloses a lock of his dark hair. Miniature by Jean-Baptiste Isabey; necklace first quarter of the 19th century. D of centrepiece 18 mm.

From around 1829 'épingles à la Ninon', or stick pins centred on a miniature in an oval medallion surrounded by a border either set with stones or richly chased, were intended to replace the fashion for bracelets. (In that they were unsuccessful.) This trend continued and oval brooches, always favoured for fastening cashmere shawls and scarves, became even more popular and much bigger. By 1840, as Alphonse Karr reported in *Les Guêpes*,

> More than ever before women are wearing paintings as brooches at their throat – some unbelievably large – and many show off family portraits in this way. . . . Recently I paid a visit to a lady and while waiting for her in her drawing room heard her maid ask, 'Will Madame wear her grandfather or her little dog?' This parade of ancestors is awkward for much of the new aristocracy . . . I also think it an odd custom to cover one's bosom at balls and parties with portraits of the dead: it gives women a slight suggestion of a catafalque, which is not very appealing.[54]

Whereas a swivel brooch or pendant could hardly contain more than two miniatures, as many as eight might be displayed on the bands of bracelets.

The restored Bourbon monarchs continued the custom of giving their miniatures as rewards to their supporters and to members of the family. Marie-Caroline, Duchesse de Berry, mother of the heir to the throne, the Duc de Bordeaux, was a particular enthusiast. She always wore a pair of bracelets, each with miniatures of her closest relations. Those on one wrist represented the living, those on the other the dead, such as Queen Marie-Antoinette, inscribed 'Portrait of my very dear aunt Marie-Antoinette, Queen of France'. So when there was a death in the family the miniature was removed and set among the dead.⁵⁵ She commissioned *c.* 1826 a spectacular letter box for her sister, Luisa Carlotta Maria Isabella de Bourbon [276], with miniatures mounted on two sides: on one side her brother-in-law, the Duc d'Angoulême, flanked by images of his wife and of herself, and on the other her children, the Duc de Bordeaux and Louise de France, flanking her father-in-law – their grandfather – Charles X. All are surmounted with crowns and coronets and surrounded by fleurs-de-lis and coats of arms. Her own miniature, by Salomon-Guillaume Counis, showing her wearing her widow's weeds after the assassination of her husband in 1820, is set in a brooch within a varicoloured gold branch of roses with thorns alluding to the trials of this life, interspersed with coloured stones spelling out an acrostic message [274]. In the matching acrostic brooch with the miniature of her husband [275] there are no symbolic thorns but only a garland of varicoloured gold flowers, celebrating his short life. More solemn is a bracelet of blued steel with his miniature flanked by his initials, CB, fleurs-de-lis and flames, so small it might have been worn in his memory by his daughter Louise.⁵⁶

Succeeding Charles X in 1830, Louis-Philippe, Duc d'Orléans, and his wife Marie-Amélie, who had a large family, were even more enthusiastic about miniatures. At the time of their engagement in 1816 she sent him her miniature set in a heart-shaped medallion enclosing some of her hair, with the inscription 'This belongs to you' and bordered with forget-me-nots [277]. A malachite and gilt-bronze musical box is set with miniatures of the entire family in 1822: Louis-Philippe, his sister Adélaïde, his wife Marie-Amélie and, garlanded with roses, their eight children.⁵⁷ Throughout the successive phases of their lives other miniatures were painted of the parents and their children.

276 *opposite* Letter box in elm and fruitwood mounted in ormolu with symbols of the Bourbon monarchy and miniatures of members of the family, commissioned by Marie-Caroline, Duchesse de Berry, as a gift for her sister, Luisa Carlotta Maria Isabella de Bourbon. On this side are images of her brother-in-law, the Duc d'Angoulême, flanked by his wife and Marie-Caroline herself. Miniatures by Emilie de Lorme; box by Alphonse Giroux (1775–1848), *c*. 1826. 305 × 420 mm.

274, 275 A pair of varicoloured gold brooches set with miniatures of the Duc de Berry (1778–1820) and his widow, Marie-Caroline (1798–1870), framed within garlands of flowers – hers of roses with thorns – interspersed with stones spelling out acrostic messages. Miniatures by Salomon-Guillaume Counis (1789–1859), *c*. 1820; settings contemporary. 35 × 27 mm (Duchesse), 34 × 25 mm (Duc).

270 *Dynastic Pride and Private Affection from Napoleon to World War I, 1800–1916*

277 *opposite* Gold heart medallion centred on a miniature of Marie-Amélie of Bourbon-Sicily (1782–1866), radiating strips of her hair and outlined by a border of forget-me-nots, sent to her fiancé, the future King Louis-Philippe of France. Miniature by Giuseppe Tresca (?), Naples or Palermo, 1816. 41 × 34 mm.

278 A pensive lady hiding a pendant with a miniature of her beloved in her *décolleté*: print by Alexandre Legrand (1822–1901), 1840s.

Some were set in bracelets, single and in pairs, with a miniature on the clasp only, others combining portraits of as many as six children set in the band of hinged plaques and in brooches [279, 280].[58] Princess Adélaïde showed her preference for her favourite nephew, the Prince de Joinville, by wearing a miniature of his eye, 'so attractive, . . . blue with black lashes', in a medallion round her neck.[59] Always attached to these souvenirs of her family, the widowed Queen Marie-Amélie was painted by Ary Scheffer towards the end of her life, in exile in London, her collar fastened by a brooch set with the miniature of Louis-Philippe surrounded with pearls or diamonds.[60]

When the Orléans princes and princesses grew up they too ordered similar portrait jewels of their respective wives, husbands and children – the eldest, the Duc d'Orléans, ordering a bracelet in 1837 in which the portrait was hidden under a cover.[61] In 1857, while in exile, the Orléans princes gave a miniature of their deceased sister, Louise, Queen of the Belgians, to her daughter, Princess Charlotte, as a present on her marriage to the Archduke Maximilian of Austria, the ill-fated future ruler of Mexico [295]. C. F. Hancock, the London jeweller, framed it in a medallion enamelled and interspersed with diamonds in a Holbeinesque design inspired by the Devonshire Parure, which had brought fame to the firm the previous year [281].

The custom continued during the Second Empire. Both Napoleon III and the Empress Eugénie distributed gold boxes with their miniatures surrounded by diamonds [284]. Two of the very first commissions from the Empress to Jules Fossin were for brooches with miniatures. One, 'surrounded with diamonds, surmounted by a rose diamond imperial crown with red enamel cap, ruby and rose diamond ribbons', could have been intended as the badge of her lady-in-waiting.

279, 280 Front and back of a gold brooch set with enamelled miniatures of Louis-Philippe, King of the French (1773–1850), and his son, the Duc d'Orléans (1810–40). The crowned strapwork frame encloses three putti holding phylacteries of enamelled flowers with rose diamond stamens. Brooch signed by Latreille of Bordeaux, c. 1830–40. H 95 mm.

281 Chromolithograph of the Devonshire Parure, created by C. F. Hancock of London from eighty-eight cameos and intaglios and hundreds of diamonds from the ancestral collection of the 6th Duke of Devonshire, in a Holbeinesque enamelled setting. Made for Countess Granville, married to the Duke's nephew, to wear at the coronation of the Emperor Alexander II in Moscow in 1856, it set an immediate fashion.

282, 283 Front and back of a gold locket on an adjustable gold chain with diamond-set slide, hung with a lozenge-shaped diamond drop, in the style of the Devonshire Parure by C. F. Hancock (*opposite*). The front contains an enamelled miniature of William IV, King of Great Britain and Ireland (1765–1837), within the petals of a Tudor rose, bordered by a Holbeinesque royal blue frame set with diamonds amidst flowerheads and scrolls. The back displays a miniature of his wife, Queen Adelaide (1792–1849), also within a Tudor rose. The locket setting, and the black-letter inscription THE LAST GIFT OF MY BELOVED GRANDFATHER KING WILLIAM THE FOURTH, were added by Wilhelmina, Countess Munster. Miniature of William IV by Charles Jagger (*c.* 1770–1827), of Queen Adelaide by William Essex (1784–1869); locket *c.* 1856.

Dynastic Pride and Private Affection from Napoleon to World War I, 1800–1916

284 *below* Gold box with a miniature of the Emperor Napoleon III (1808–73) in military uniform, wearing a sash and the cross of the Legion of Honour. Miniature by Gabriel-Aristide Passot (1797–1875) after a portrait by F. X. Winterhalter; box by Maurice Meyer (1838–75), mid-19th century. 95 × 60 × 28 mm.

285 *above* Gold bracelet composed of hinged plaques with miniatures of (from left to right) Napoleon III's cousin Prince Jérome Bonaparte (1784–1860), the Empress Eugénie (1826–1920), Napoleon III, and Jérome's children Mathilde and Jérome. Miniatures by Philippe Prochietto, known as Prochet (1825–90), of Geneva; setting by Mellerio of Paris (?), after 1854. 35 × 220 mm.

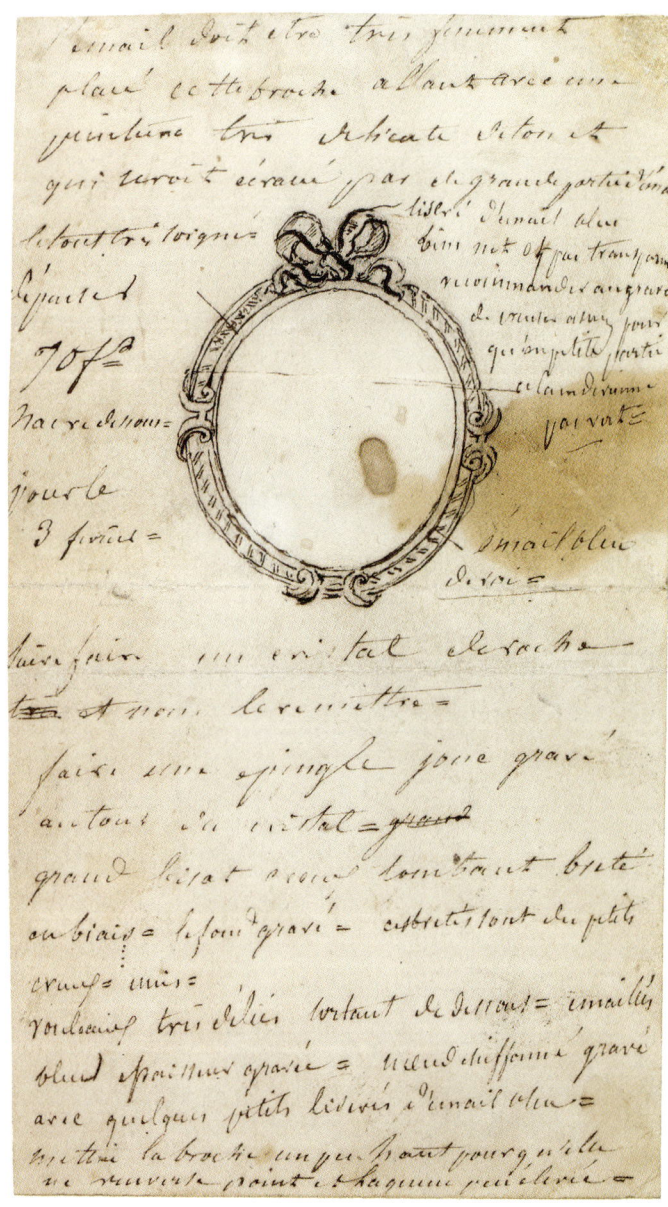

286 Drawing for the frame of a brooch to contain a miniature. It is annotated in detail, pointing out that the frame must be delicately enamelled so as to harmonize with the portrait. By Jules Fossin (1808–69), c. 1840.

The other, 'bordered by diamond rays with four emeralds surmounted by a green enamel trefoil within a diamond surround', could have been for herself, as the trefoil recalled her first gift from Napoleon III and she is known to have worn his portrait by Paul de Pommeraye in a brooch, just as the wives of Napoleon I had worn his. More dynastic is the wide hinged bracelet displaying not only the imperial couple but their Bonaparte uncle, Prince Jerome, and his son and daughter [285].

The frames varied in design. There were symbolic snakes, ivy, decorative garlands of flowers, ribbons and strapwork, chased in gold, enamelled and embellished with precious stones. The care and attention lavished on them is demonstrated by the detailed annotations surrounding a design by Jules Fossin [286]. One of the most elaborate enamelled garlands was created for the Duc d'Aumale by Emile Froment-Meurice in 1870 for the miniature of his Italian duchess as a two-year-old in 1824 [287]. A memorial to her, it was composed of leafy branches symbolic of the various phases of her life: 'sprays of orange blossom, branches of vine and holly recalling the lands where the Princess spent her life – Sicily her birthplace, France, and then England where she died'. Applied to an easel, it was placed on a marble base with a plaque recording her dates of birth and death.

Some years later another great Parisian jeweller, René Lalique, created a necklace for Emile Zola's mistress, Jeanne Rozerot: from a chain of enamelled ivy leaves hangs a pendant framing the profiles of their two young children, Denise and Jacques [288]. It encapsulates the elderly Zola's passion for the young Jeanne, and their devotion to their 'chers beaux mignons', their lovely little darlings. Meeting these children helped the angry and humiliated Madame Zola come to

287 *left* Miniature of the Duchesse d'Aumale (1822–69) as a child of two, within an enamelled gold frame of orange blossom, vine and holly, symbolic of the countries in which she spent her life. It is mounted on a stand for the bedroom of the widower. Frame by Emile Froment-Meurice (1837–1913), 1870. Miniature D 32 mm.

288 *above* Jeanne Rozerot (1867–1914) wearing a necklace with a pendant enclosing enamelled miniatures of Denise and Jacques, her children by Emile Zola. Necklace and miniatures by René Lalique (1860–1945). The photograph is from a negative in the possession of Jacques' grandson, Dr François Emile-Zola.

289, 290 A pair of diamond bracelets with miniatures of Ludwig I, King of Bavaria (1786–1868), patron of the arts, and his wife, Queen Therese (1792–1854), after their portraits by Joseph Stieler, c. 1850.

terms with her husband's infidelity and in 1904, as his widow, she had them legally named Emile-Zola.

The fashion for miniatures was universal. In Bavaria King Ludwig I and his wife had theirs – both arrayed in full court dress – mounted within diamond frames for centre-pieces [289, 290]; the bands of the bracelets were also executed in diamonds. Although not so expensive, a hinged bracelet proudly displayed by the Russian-born Queen Anna of the Netherlands made a resounding political statement [291]. The miniature of her husband Willem II is on the clasp, and each of the hinged links is inscribed with the name of one of the battles in which from 1811 to 1815 the King fought as aide-de-camp to the Duke of Wellington in the campaign against Napoleon.

291 Gold bracelet with a miniature of Willem II, King of the Netherlands (1792–1849); names of battles in which he fought against Napoleon in 1811–15 are inscribed on the links of the band. The bracelet was worn by his Russian wife, Queen Anna. Miniature by Jean-Baptiste-Joseph Duchesne (1770–1856), 1825.

In England, both as regent and as king, George IV bestowed miniatures on his mother, Queen Charlotte, the princesses, and on ladies who had long served the court. He explained the significance of his portrait in a note of 3 November 1813 accompanying a snuff box for Queen Charlotte:

> Having received the glorious intelligence [Napoleon's overthrow at the battle of Leipzig] perhaps you will indulge me in a little piece of superstition which is in accepting of this trifle putting it in your pocket and taking a piece of snuff out of it before you retire to rest as it bears upon it the effigy of one who I hope you will now think is no disgrace to you, to his family or to his country, and who as far as his mite could go has contributed to his utmost in and of and towards the accomplishment of all the great and splendid events and success with which it has pleased divine Providence to bless and to crown our joint, combined and allied exertions and arms.[62]

In 1816 the Dowager Countess of Ilchester was proud to receive such a jewel, 'a magnificent present from the Regent – his own picture superbly set with diamonds. He gave it to me on Princess Mary's birthday, saying I feel myself much obliged to you.'[63] The rare miniatures by Henry Bone which were used for this and others of varying size were set within crowned diamond frames with the royal cipher on the back similarly set. This was the beginning of the Royal Family Order, which was and still is limited to ladies of the royal family and ladies of the highest rank, like the Mistress of the Robes. George IV gave it to Lady Conyngham, and later Lord Melbourne recalled that only two other non-royal ladies had received the honour: Lady Cowper and Lady Aboyne. As the victorious head of state the Regent also awarded his miniature, richly set, to foreign allies such as the famous Matvei Ivanovich Platov, leader of the Russian Cossacks, who visited London in 1814 [292].

The tragic death of Charlotte, Princess of Wales, in childbirth in 1817 was marked by national mourning and the creation of miniature jewels worn by those closest to her. From Rundell, Bridge and Rundell her father ordered 'A chased gold brooch with picture of Her Royal Highness the Princess Charlotte with celestial crown, rosebud etc.' and a memorial ring, the picture encircled by a snake.[64] Her husband Leopold, future King of the Belgians, gave one of these memorial miniatures to Lady Jersey within a locket with hair, the front enamelled black surmounted by a ruby and diamond coronet and her initials, PC, the back inscribed SHE WAS HAPPY / AH, DO NOT PITY HER.[65] Significantly, Leopold kept for himself another miniature of the Princess as a memento of their brief but happy married life. It was inscribed in Italian, translating 'Blessed be the day, the month and the very hour / Fidelity and love 16 Dec. 1816', alluding to his joyful birthday celebrations then at Claremont in Surrey. After his death in 1865, Leopold II, his son, gave the miniature to Queen Victoria, who as a disconsolate widow would have understood how much it had meant to her uncle.[66]

Miniatures of William IV and his wife Queen Adelaide were set in the centre of Tudor roses, as clasps for bracelets, in rings, and in an important locket created for their granddaughter, Wilhelmina, Countess Munster [282, 283]. Their successor, Queen Victoria, from her early childhood and well into her widowhood distributed more miniatures of herself, her husband Prince Albert and their children than any other type of portrait. Miniatures of her handsome husband recorded the happiness of their early married life. The earliest, 'which is quite speaking and my delight', painted by William Ross

292 *opposite* Matvei Ivanovich Platov, Commander of the Cossacks (1751–1818), appears in his portrait by Thomas Phillips wearing a miniature of the Prince Regent presented to him in London by the Prince in 1814. The setting, with surrounding diamonds and crown, is similar to that of George IV by Henry Bone (*above*).

293 Presentation miniature of George IV, King of Great Britain and Ireland (1762–1830), with diamond and enamel crown and frame. Miniature by Henry Bone (1735–1844), 1820; setting probably by Rundell, Bridge and Rundell, 1821.

294 A miniature of Prince Albert (1819–61) wearing medieval armour, surrounded by the Garter collar on a bracelet with the knots and roses of the collar of the Order. Miniature by William Essex; bracelet by Garrards, 1844. Miniature 30 × 25 mm.

in 1839, was at once worn in a bracelet: their eldest daughter, Princess Victoria, holds it in her miniature of 1844.[67] From 1840 until her death the Queen wore another, attached to a bracelet or as a brooch, showing the Prince in profile surrounded by diamonds, 'a most exquisite likeness'; the colours are faded, indicating that this was her favourite.[68] Less personal and more symbolic of their royal status is a miniature of Albert wearing armour like a medieval knight, surrounded by the Garter collar, attached to a bracelet by Garrards reproducing the knots and roses of the collar of the Order [294].[69] Always, from her accession until her death, Queen Victoria wore a miniature of herself, surrounded by diamonds, hanging from a crimson ribbon bow.

Miniatures for other pendants, rings and bracelets were painted by William Ross and William Essex after her portrait in her coronation robes by A. E. Chalon and another by F. X. Winterhalter. She gave them as wedding presents to her family and to the children of those who served her: in 1877 Mary Anson, daughter of the Secretary of the Prince Consort, received a locket enclosing likenesses of the royal couple, and in 1890 when Miss Dorothy Tennant married the explorer H. M. Stanley she wore, hanging from a diamond necklace, the Queen's miniature framed in diamonds with a lock of her hair at the back. The long succession of ladies-in-waiting all received gold bracelets with her miniature on the clasp, the back inscribed with an affectionate message.

Others, usually enamelled, were also sent to favourite relations such as Louise, Queen of the Belgians [cf. 295], the wife of Victoria's uncle, Leopold I; Clementine, wife of the Duke of Saxe-Coburg; and Victoire, Duchesse de Nemours; and one was given to Stephanie of Hohenzollern-Sigmaringen during her brief visit to England on her way to Lisbon for her marriage with

290 *Dynastic Pride and Private Affection from Napoleon to World War I, 1800–1916*

295 *opposite* Bracelet in neo-Renaissance style, enamelled and embellished with diamonds, with a miniature of Louise, Queen of the Belgians (1812–50), given by her brothers and sisters as a wedding present to her daughter Charlotte in 1857. The miniature is a copy of one by William Ross of 1840; the bracelet is by C. F. Hancock. H 71 mm.

296 Gold and jewelled bracelet with a miniature of Queen Victoria given to the Queen's cousin, Stephanie, future Queen of Portugal, in London on her way from Germany to Lisbon in 1858. Miniature by John Simpson (1811–71), mid-19th century; setting contemporary. 55 × 48 mm.

Pedro V in 1858 [296]. To the Duchesse d'Aumale the Queen gave a slide which could be worn at the neck or on the wrist, the miniature framed in brilliants and coral, the back inscribed SOUVENIR D'AMITIE VICTORIA R. / 26 AVRIL 1859, the date of the Duchess's birthday.[70] A bracelet with a miniature picture gallery of her children, similar to those worn by their grandmother, the Duchess of Kent [297, 298], was given to their governess, Lady Lyttleton, on her retirement in 1850. The number of children represented varied according to the date of these gifts.[71]

Other monarchs, such as the King and Queen of Hanover, might receive the traditional gift of Victoria's portrait in a snuff box, surrounded by diamonds. She gave one to the French ambassador, Count Walewski, as a souvenir of the Peace Treaty. When the Queen was asked if Countess Walewski might make the portrait into a bracelet, she said she would much prefer it on the arm of Madame than in the pocket of her husband. Queen Victoria liked to remember her dead with miniatures: after 1863 she wore that of Prince Albert set in a large diamond cross, and that of her second daughter, Princess Alice, from 1878.

Queen Victoria shared a liking for eye miniatures with her subjects and other monarchs [299]: for Christmas 1863 her present to Princess Beatrice was a bracelet with locket enclosing a miniature of Prince Albert's eye combined with a lock of the Queen's hair.[72] Another, set in an engraved locket with Prince Albert's cipher and crown, was sent to the Duchess of Saxe-Coburg-Mecklenburg in 1845, and in 1847 Louise, Queen of the Belgians, received the Queen's eye set in an engraved gold heart, followed the next year by that of the Princess Royal, also in a gold locket. For commemorative and presentation purposes the British royal family went on commissioning miniatures well into the 20th century, principally for setting in bracelets and brooches.

297, 298 A pair of hinged gold bracelets, each containing seven miniatures of the grandchildren of the Duchess of Kent, given to her on her sixtieth birthday by Queen Victoria and Prince Albert. Miniatures by William Ross (1794–1860) with Guglielmo Faija (1803–after 1861), 1846; setting contemporary. L 20 cm.

The many literary references to miniatures, set in lockets, bracelets and rings, reflect their popularity in the first half of the 19th century. In Lady Caroline Lamb's novel *Glenarvon* (1816) Buchanan gallops beneath Calatha's window, 'his hands decorated with rings, a gold chain and half concealed picture hung round his neck'. A fashionable jeweller is described by Lady Blessington in her *Confessions of an Elderly Gentleman* (1836) showing the heroine the diamond and sapphire centrepiece of a bracelet belonging to a parure and then touching 'a secret spring when the gold plate at the back flying open discovered a small enamel miniature of Mr. Vernon'. Juliet, in love with the eponymous hero of *Fitzgeorge* (1828), looks at his miniature, enshrined in gold and pearls, 'sighed over it, wept over it, and pressed to her bosom ... miniature portraits are made for lovers, they soften the features, they bring the resemblance into so condensed a form that only one pair of eyes can gaze on it at once'. Balzac in *Splendeurs et misères des courtisanes* (1838) has Esther Gosbeck write to Lucien de Rubempré for the last time: 'I have in front of me the lovely

299 Bracelet of hair, the centrepiece set with a miniature of the eye of Princess Augusta of Leuchtenberg (1788–1851) within a frame of gold leaves, *c.* 1820–30. Centrepiece 47 × 37 mm.

294 *Dynastic Pride and Private Affection from Napoleon to World War I, 1800–1916*

miniature which Madame de Mirbel did of you. The ivory panel often consoled me for your absence, I look at it with intoxication as I write my last thoughts, depict my last heartbeats for you.' In Kate Chopin's story *The Locket* (1897) the jewel is regarded as a talisman by the young soldier Edmond, who had been given 'her most precious earthly possession' by Octavie when they parted. It was 'an old fashioned golden locket bearing miniatures of her father and mother with their names and the date of their marriage'.

Outside fiction, in real life, women wore miniatures of beloved individuals, many fated to be killed in the long Napoleonic wars [301, 302]. The statesman Lord Castlereagh, heir to the Marquis of Londonderry, sent his wife Emily the picture given him by the King of Naples surrounded by diamonds: 'Dearest Em, I send you an ugly face and some pretty diamonds which will become yours rather than his Sicilian Majesties.' She removed the miniature and in its place put a picture of her handsome husband, which she wore hanging across her breast on all great occasions.[73] In the 20th century the wife of the 7th Marquis of Londonderry wore his miniature in the same setting, as the centrepiece to a gold bracelet [300].

Personal friendships, love affairs, marriage, parenthood were all marked by gifts of miniatures, and the openness with which British women displayed them surprised foreigners. Lady Oxford caused a scandal by parading Lord Byron's picture in the front of her girdle when walking about Naples in 1815.[74] Another lady, more discreet, wore his eye miniature mounted in a medallion, rimmed in diamonds [304]. Popular admiration for military and naval heroes – Nelson after Trafalgar, and the Duke of Wellington after Waterloo – and for politicians such as Charles James Fox was demonstrated by jewels enclosing their miniatures, usually with the palm and laurel of victory.

300 A miniature of the 7th Marquess of Londonderry (1878–1949), set in a diamond frame which formerly held the miniature of his ancestor, Lord Castlereagh, 2nd Marquess of Londonderry (1769–1822), made into the centrepiece of a gold bracelet. The 7th Marquess's decorations were awarded for his distinguished war service, political career, and involvement in national institutions.

301, 302 Front and back of a gold memorial locket enclosing a miniature of Captain the Hon. William George Crofton of the Coldstream Guards, who rather than surrender died at his post in the Peninsular War in April 1814. The miniature was painted on a visit home, just before he returned to the campaign. On the back of the locket, strands of his hair are arranged as palms of victory around the seed pearl border of a scene of a tomb in a landscape with a dove returning to its nest, on an opalescent glass ground. Miniature by Horace Hone (1754/56–1815) and setting 1814. H 72.

298   *Dynastic Pride and Private Affection from Napoleon to World War I, 1800–1916*

303 *opposite* The Duchess of Hamilton (1817–88), painted by Sir Francis Grant with a bracelet displaying a miniature of her husband, the 11th Duke of Hamilton, or of their son.

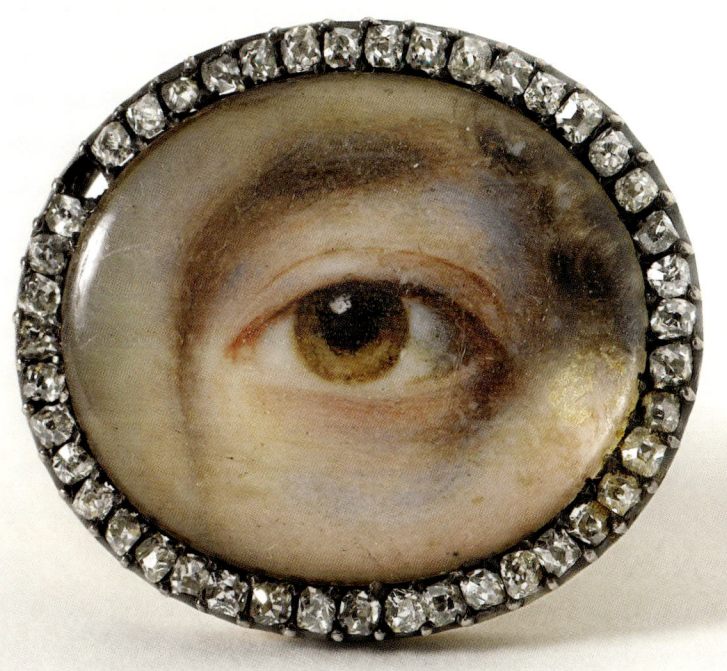

304 A miniature of the eye of Lord Byron (1788–1824) within a diamond frame. Another poet, Samuel Taylor Coleridge, admired Byron's clear and luminous eyes, 'the open portals of the sun, – things of light and for light'. 22 × 26 mm.

Trompe-l'oeil portraits combined the cameo and the painted miniature, making the sitter look like an ancient Greek or Roman. One such impressed Cornelie van Wassenaer, lady-in-waiting to the Russian-born Queen Anna of the Netherlands, visiting St Petersburg in 1824–25, who noticed Countess Yulia Pahlen, engaged to Count Samoilov [305]: 'She wears his present of a magnificent sea-green cashmere shawl, a bracelet with his portrait as an antique bust *en grisaille* like a cameo on the clasp.'[75]

As far as the Russian monarchy was concerned, miniatures in rings, medallions, badges and snuff boxes remained the usual imperial awards [306, 307, 309], at least until the reign of Alexander II [308]. An English visitor, the Marchioness of Londonderry, was immensely flattered to receive the portrait of the reigning Empress in 1837, wearing it prominently on her right arm so that all could see this mark of the very highest distinction.[76] An interesting development was the presentation of dynastic portrait badges set with miniatures of two or three tsars. Rings gradually became rarer, until finally in the reign of Nicholas II only four recipients are recorded. Instead, the sovereign's portrait either in the lid of a snuff box or set in a fine frame to place on a table was the more usual gift. As a matter of course miniatures were given to the immediate members of the imperial family to mark engagements, marriages and other events [310–312].

An innovation introduced by Carl Fabergé in 1908 was the column table portrait, with the crowned miniature surrounded by diamonds attached to the centre: only five are known [313]. Surmounted by the crowned imperial eagle, the fluted gold column with laurel leaves had a political significance in itself, representing as unshakeable the royal virtues of fortitude, strength and constancy.[77] Miniatures also decorate some of the spectacular Easter eggs by Fabergé for the imperial family.

305 *opposite* Countess Yulia Pavlovna Samoilova (1803–75): the centrepiece of her gold bracelet holds an enamelled simulated cameo portrait of her husband, Count Samoilov. Portrait by Charles-Benoît Mitoir, *c.* 1825.

306 *opposite* Count Alexei Andreievich Arakcheev (1769–1834), Russian general and statesman, is shown wearing a miniature of the Emperor Alexander I in his portrait by George Dawe, painted for the Military Gallery of the Winter Palace in St Petersburg, 1824.

307 Gold box with a miniature of Alexander I, Emperor of Russia (1777–1825), in uniform with sash and star of the Order of St Andrew, within a wrought gold floral and foliate border. The box was presented to the 1st Lord Granville, British ambassador to St Petersburg in 1804–5. Miniature by Domenico Bossi (1767–1858); box by Samuel Otto Keibel (1768–1809), St Petersburg, *c.* 1801–5. 98 × 83 mm.

Dynastic Pride and Private Affection from Napoleon to World War I, 1800–1916   303

308 Medallion set with a miniature of Alexander II, Emperor of Russia (1818–81), in uniform wearing decorations and the sash of the Order of St Andrew, within a rose-cut diamond border. St Petersburg, c. 1870–80. 31 × 25 mm.

309 *opposite* Count Fedor Logginovich van Heyden (1821–1900), Governor-General of Finland 1881–98. He is proudly portrayed by Fredrik Ahlstedt wearing portrait badges of the Emperors Alexander II and Alexander III and military orders.

310 A miniature of Maria Feodorovna, Empress of Russia (1847–1928), wearing a *kokochnik* tiara with veil and the blue sash of the Order of St Andrew, in a pearl and red enamel heart-shaped engine-turned gold frame – a gift to her sister, Princess Thyra of Denmark, Duchess of Cumberland, at Christmas 1905. Miniature by Johannes Zehngraf (1857–1908), St Petersburg, 1890; frame by Mikhail Perkhin (1860–1903), workmaster for Carl Fabergé, St Petersburg. H 75 mm.

311 Brooch with miniatures of Nicholas II, Emperor of Russia (1868–1918), and the Empress Alexandra Feodorovna (1872–1918) framed in diamonds, linked by a diamond ribbon and a sapphire, a gift to mark their wedding in 1894. Setting by Michael Perkhin, workmaster for Carl Fabergé. 35 × 39 mm.

312 Miniatures of Elena Vladimirovna, Grand Duchess of Russia (1882–1957), and Prince Nicholas of Greece (1872–1938) are set on either side of Cupid's arrow terminating in myrtle leaves, alluding to their marriage, on this cigarette case enamelled with green and mauve stripes. Miniatures by Johannes Zehngraf; case by Mikhail Perkhin, workmaster for Carl Fabergé, 1902. L 99 mm.

308 *Dynastic Pride and Private Affection from Napoleon to World War I, 1800–1916*

313 *opposite* Column table portrait with a miniature of Nicholas II, Emperor of Russia, presented to Count August zu Eulenberg, Grand Marshal of the Imperial German Court. Miniature by Vasili Zuiev (1870–c. 1917); column by Henrik Wigström (1862–1923), workmaster for Carl Fabergé, 1910.

Some were hidden within as surprises: a trefoil with the miniatures of Tsar Nicholas II and the Tsarina with their eldest daughter within heart-shaped diamond frames (1897); three others surmounted by the imperial crown within the 'Lilies of the Valley' egg (1899) [314]; and a grisaille of all five children within the 'Mosaic' egg (1914). Other miniatures were placed outside on the shell: seven – parents and children – on the 'Fifteenth Anniversary' egg (1911), and two – the Tsar and his son – concealed under gold covers enamelled with a medallion of the cross and a medal of the Order of St George (1916) [315].

The photograph, favoured for a good likeness and expression, was set in fashionable jewelry very soon after its invention in 1839. An early example, 'for a small daguerreotype mounted in a pin' recorded in the ledger for 1843 of Jules Fossin, was for a Monsieur Mignon. From the 1860s clients were buying 'a star-shaped rose diamond ring', bracelets, and lockets for photographs in designs similar to those for miniatures [316, 317]. The photograph was soon adopted by royalty. In 1853 Queen Victoria gave Lady Caroline Barrington a gold bracelet 'in the centre the photographs of the Princes Arthur and Leopold'; to her maid of honour, Miss Stopford, 'An engraved gold bracelet containing photographs of the Princesses Alice and Helen'; and to Princess Mary of Cambridge 'A gold and platina bracelet containing a photograph of Prince Leopold'. In 1858 the Queen attached a photograph of their eldest daughter, Victoria, to a miniature of Prince Albert painted in 1840, enclosed in a gold locket decorated with forget-me-nots and pansies with a four-leaf clover to commemorate the Prince's escape from a carriage injury; this was attached to a bracelet.[78] Just before he died Prince Albert designed a bracelet in memory of his mother-in-law, the Duchess of Kent, whose hand-coloured photograph is surrounded by a pearl snake [318].[79]

314 The 'Lilies of the Valley' egg, with three miniatures that emerge as a surprise, showing Nicholas II in military uniform and his two eldest children, the Grand Duchesses Tatiana and Olga. It was a gift to his wife, the Empress Alexandra Feodorovna, at Easter in 1898. Miniatures by Johannes Zehngraf; egg by Mikhail Perkhin, workmaster for Carl Fabergé. H 20 cm.

315 The 'Order of St George' egg, presented by Nicholas II to his mother, the Dowager Empress Maria Fedorovna, at Easter in 1916. On this side, a miniature of the Emperor is revealed under a medallion of the cross; on the other, a miniature of his son, the Tsarevich, is concealed under a medal of the Order of St George. Miniaturists unknown; workmaster unknown, for Carl Fabergé. H without the stand 84 mm.

316, 317 Front and back of a jewel enclosing a photograph of the Prince de Joinville (1818–1900) with a lock of his hair, given to his mistress, the actress Rachel; the attached flacon bears her initial, R, and the motto TOUT OU RIEN (All or nothing). Photograph and setting Paris, c. 1841.

318 Memorial bracelet of Queen Victoria's mother, the Duchess of Kent (d. 1861), the centrepiece displaying her tinted photograph surrounded by a seed pearl snake swallowing its tail, emblematic of eternity, mounted on a velvet band. This was the last gift to Queen Victoria from Prince Albert. Designed by Prince Albert; maker unknown, London, 1861. D of centrepiece 20 mm.

319 Silver medallion with a photograph of Queen Victoria as a widow, within a crown of thorns, inscribed to the Duchesse d'Aumale on the Queen's forty-first birthday, 26 April 1863. 18 × 15 mm.

After Prince Albert's own death in February 1862, Queen Victoria ordered from Garrards in May his 'photograph mounted in a bracelet snap with coronet in raised gold', and others followed. Her grief over his loss is reflected in the character of her own portrait jewelry, such as a brooch with her photograph in her widow's weeds, surrounded by a crown of thorns [319], inscribed DE VOTRE MALHEUREUSE SOEUR ET AMIE / VR / 26 AVRIL 1863 (From your unhappy sister and friend / VR / 26 April 1863), given to the Duchesse d'Aumale on her birthday. In that same year, 1863, *Queen* magazine observed that

> the photographic portrait appears now to be one of the most fashionable ornaments: it is very small and is made as brooch, locket or bracelet. For brooches or lockets they are called secret photographs which are made to contain four portraits two of which are

314 *Dynastic Pride and Private Affection from Napoleon to World War I, 1800–1916*

> ostensible ones and be seen by any who open the lockets but the remaining two are only visible when a secret spring is touched. The prettiest mountings for these brooches and lockets are found with interlaced cords, one of them pearl, the other composed of gold of different colours.

Others were decorated with symbols of sentiment, such as the 'handsome locket with a turquoise and diamond forget-me-not containing their photographic portraits' which Baroness Bloomfield received from the King and Queen of Hanover.[80]

Another innovation, described in *Queen* magazine in 1865, was

> bracelets consisting of a band of gold ornamented by two locket medallions which opened and contained spaces for four portraits. These were ornamented, some with emeralds, and some with pearls and turquoises. One bracelet which we observed was merely a plain gold band with two clasps of purple enamel crossing it. The half of this opened and contained five photographs. Bracelets and brooches both are now constantly made to contain photographs; while lockets open in various ways and are capable of holding half a dozen portraits.

An example of the type was bequeathed in the will of the Duchesse de Talleyrand (1891) to her granddaughter, Vera de Kaunitz: 'a matt gold medallion, one side with chequerboard pattern of small pearls. She will find a portrait of her parents inside.' Distributed to close friends and relations as a souvenir, double portraits of the bride and bridegroom taken at the time of a marriage might be set in brooches surrounded

321, 322 *opposite* A gold locket seal designed as a weight measuring one *pud*, enclosing photographs of the Grand Duchess Olga (1851–1926) and her husband, King George of Greece (1845–1913), at the time of their marriage in 1867. A lapis lazuli seal at the base is engraved with the badge of the Royal Guelphic Order. Setting by August Holmström (1828–1903), workmaster for Carl Fabergé, 1867. H 22 mm.

320 A pair of gold locket cufflinks decorated with cabochon sapphire and diamond four-leaf clovers, enclosing tinted photographs of the Grand Dukes Kyrill, Boris and Andrei and their sister the Grand Duchess Elena, children of the Grand Duke Vladimir of Russia. Maker unknown, St Petersburg, *c.* 1883–84. D 17 mm.

316 *Dynastic Pride and Private Affection from Napoleon to World War I, 1800–1916*

by pearls and diamonds, tied together by a lover's knot, or enclosed within bracelet lockets, their ciphers on the covers. Mothers or grandmothers might wear photographs of children reproduced as miniatures mounted in gold as brooches or pendants, surrounded by the birthstones of the infant depicted. Other variants included cufflinks [320], miniature weights to hang from a bracelet [321, 322], and the watchcase, almost always at hand, which was now often similarly adopted for photographs.

To meet the demand for these personal mementoes, in 1900 the London jeweller Joseph Heming advertised in the *Illustrated London News* diamond cluster rings enclosing a minute photograph, covered by a white sapphire, imitating a portrait diamond. The firm offered to reduce any photograph supplied to the dimensions of the ring. It was so much easier to make duplicates of photographs than of hand-painted

323 Gold Russian Orthodox memorial cross enclosing a photograph of Alexander III, Emperor of Russia (1845–94), in a black border. Setting by Mikhail Perkhin, workmaster for Carl Fabergé, 1894–95. 46 × 21 mm.

miniatures that they were considered ideal for memorial jewelry, some openly displayed in rings or brooches, others hidden under a cover, enamelled black. For the Russian imperial family Fabergé inserted a small photograph of Alexander III in a black enamel frame into an Orthodox triple-armed gold cross, inscribed with the date of his death, '20 x 94', his cipher and the imperial crown [323].

So popular was photography, especially among amateurs after the invention of the hand-held camera in 1890, that Fabergé was required to produce frames for the many photographs of family and friends which were placed on tables, desks, cabinets and grand pianos. There are said to have been nearly a dozen frames, most of them by Fabergé, scattered on the desk of Nicholas II.[81] The stylistic source for many of the ornamental motifs was the Neoclassical art of the Louis XVI period: palmettes, acanthus, laurel, swags, garlands, Cupid's bow, quiver and flaming torch, ribbons and bowknots, applied to a coloured enamel or hardstone ground. Occasionally flowers – cornflowers or lilies – appear either above or flanking the image. The shapes vary, from architectural – like a pedimented doorcase – to miniature firescreens, to symbolic hearts, to geometric – circles, squares, rectangles and triangles [324]. Most flat surfaces were decorated with guilloché enamel patterns, sometimes with moiré effects, chosen from a range of 144 shades of colour, but Fabergé also used hardstone – aventurine, nephrite, rock crystal and bowenite – embellished with rose-cut diamonds and cabochon rubies. The backs were usually executed in ivory, though mother-of-pearl was used for the very smallest frames. From the simplest made of wood to the most luxurious, each frame is technically perfect, ideally suited to its purpose, and comparable to the best craftsmanship of the 18th-century masters.

324 A photograph of Princess Thyra of Denmark, Duchess of Cumberland (1853–1933), sister of Maria Feodorovna, Dowager Empress of Russia, set within a pearl border in a triangular silver-gilt frame outlined in arrowheads, with a guilloché radiate ground enamelled green – a gift to the Princess on her birthday, 29 September 1899, from her niece, the Grand Duchess Olga of Russia. Frame by Johan Viktor Aarne (1863–1904), workmaster for Carl Fabergé. H 55 mm.

5 The Portrait Diamond
1613–1906

Whereas the miniatures painted on ivory and vellum in watercolours surveyed in the preceding chapters are protected by crystal covers, a very small and rare group is covered by diamonds, flat on both sides, the top surface faceted at the edges. Known as lask or portrait diamonds, these come from the cleavage of irregularly shaped octahedrons. Reflections from the facets on the diamond light up the portrait; the highly polished limpid surface lets the portrait shine through with far more éclat than crystal and also draws the eye towards it. Only the very clearest stones could obtain this magical effect.

325 *opposite* John Churchill, 1st Duke of Marlborough (1650–1722), wearing the ribbon and star of the Order of the Garter. Detail of a portrait by Sir Godfrey Kneller, *c.* 1701. As a reward for his victory at the Battle of Blenheim, Queen Anne presented his wife with a miniature of the Duke covered by a portrait diamond.

An early enthusiast was Marie de Médicis, brought up amidst the splendour of the Palazzo Pitti in Florence, who as the wife of Henri IV of France owned a magnificent collection of pearl, diamond and coloured stone jewelry acquired from dealers all over Europe. Besides purchasing from the jeweller Paris Turquet 'a fine portrait jewel embellished with diamonds', in 1613 she paid the German Gilbert Hessing 1,050 *livres* for a gold ring enclosing the portraits of her son, Louis XIII, and his wife, Anne of Austria, beneath a large faceted diamond.[1] In her turn, Anne of Austria, according to a posthumous inventory of 1666, not only owned miniatures set in tortoiseshell and enamelled gold cases, and in a bracelet, surrounded by diamonds, but also 'a bracelet centrepiece set with a large flat diamond above a miniature within a border of closely set small diamonds' valued at 2,000 *livres*, which she bequeathed to her younger son, the Duc d'Orléans, and a ring 'set with a diamond above the miniature of the late King', that is Louis XIII.[2] In Britain, among the many rings with miniatures of Charles I only one is covered with a portrait diamond. Set in silver, with a crown above, the triangular table diamond covers a portrait of the King, whose initials, CR, are engraved on the back.[3]

A ruler with a name associated with great taste and luxury whose portrait, surmounted by his crown, was enhanced in this way is Grand Duke Cosimo III of Tuscany. It is listed in the posthumous inventory of the last Medici princess, his daughter, the Electress Palatine Anna Maria Ludovica: 'a small picture jewel with the miniature portrait of Grand Duke Cosimo in the centre covered with a large flat table diamond instead of a crystal, embellished with many brilliants, eight large, the others small, surmounted by the grand-ducal crown similarly embellished with brilliants'.[4]

There were others recorded during the 18th century. The military skills of John Churchill, 1st Duke of Marlborough [325], in the campaigns against Louis XIV were rewarded with valuable jewels by all the sovereigns of Europe, including Queen Anne at home. According to Mrs Delany,

> the Duchess of Marlboro' (ye famous) said she never had a present of a jewel from Queen Anne and 'tis notorious that when news came of the victory of Blenheim ye Queen gave her a portrait of ye Duke of Marlborough covered with a flat diamond with brilliant edges which cost £8000 – it is now in ye possession of ye Duke of Montagu's daughter ye present Duchess of Buccleuch.[5]

This must be 'the duke of Marlborough's picture cover'd with a large Diamond in a pearl braslett of 4 rows, with a Brilliant buckle and drop' listed in the Duchess's inventory[6] and later bequeathed to one of her daughters, the Duchess of Montagu; the diamond could be the one illustrated, though that is described as being in a ring [326]. The bracelet was the cause of a drama, as the Duchess of Marlborough explained in her letters, having first mentioned that the setting of miniatures in this way came from the Netherlands where 'it is the fashion to wear bracelets of diamonds and pictures about their rists buckl'd on in a manner that they cannot come off without undoing'. She then went on to say that when the bracelet, 'the most agreeable and pritty fine thing that I ever saw in my life', disappeared, the black footman, Ned, was accused of the theft and imprisoned. Her feelings when it was recovered were mixed:

> Tho I had fancied I would give twice the value of it again, yet when they brought it to me, instead

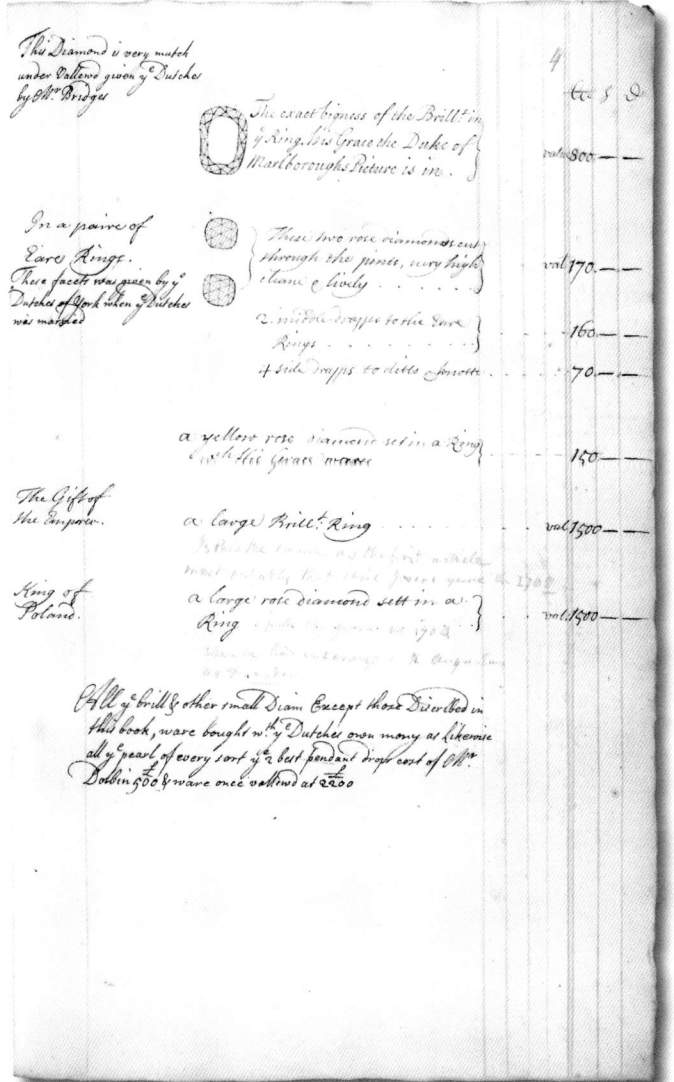

326 A page from the inventory of the Duchess of Marlborough's collection shows (at the top) a diamond that covered her husband's portrait in a ring.

The Portrait Diamond, 1613–1906 323

of being pleased I could not help bursting into a great passion of crying to think how much I had wronged a very inosent man and as soon as I had recovered myself I sent for the footman & gave him 50 pistoles to make amends for his ill lodging in prison assuring him at the same time that if hee would leave a great fault he has of drinking I would bee very kind to him.[7]

So rare is portrait diamond jewelry that it cannot be claimed that the Duchess of Marlborough started a fashion. One of the few survivals, without a provenance, dating from the 1770s, is a memorial brooch, round and enamelled royal blue, centred on a miniature of a young boy enclosed in an urn hung with trails of diamond leaves and covered by a portrait diamond [327].

A queen of England who wore her husband's miniature covered by a diamond in a ring given among his wedding presents in 1761 was the wife of George III, Charlotte of Mecklenburg-Strelitz [329].[8] Even more ambitious was their son, George, who as Prince of Wales ordered from Richard Cosway a pair of miniatures of himself, handsome in armour, and of Maria Fitzherbert, whom he married morganatically in 1785. Both were small pictures surrounded by diamonds, and covered with the two halves of a split diamond [328]. In his will of 1796 the Prince asked that 'my constant companion the picture of my beloved wife Mrs Fitzherbert may be interred with me suspended round my neck by a ribbon as I used to wear it while I lived, placed right upon my heart', and eventually his executor, the Duke of Wellington, having ascertained that the miniature was there, duly carried out these instructions. Mrs Fitzherbert's pair to it has descended in the family

327 Memorial brooch centred on an urn hung with festoons containing a miniature of a boy covered by a diamond, within a diamond border; the brooch is enamelled royal blue and edged with diamonds. English, 1770s. D 45 mm.

328 Locket with a miniature of George, Prince of Wales (the future George IV, 1762–1830), covered by a portrait diamond, within a diamond border, given to his wife, Mrs Fitzherbert. Miniature by Richard Cosway (1742–1821), 1785; setting contemporary. H 38 mm.

329 Ring with a miniature of George III, King of Great Britain and Ireland (1738–1820), under a diamond, surrounded by diamonds, given to his wife, Queen Charlotte, to wear on their wedding day. Miniature by Jeremiah Meyer (1735–89), 1761; setting contemporary. 12 × 10 mm.

The Portrait Diamond, 1613–1906 325

330 Brooch centred on a miniature of George IV after Sir Thomas Lawrence beneath a portrait diamond, in an enamelled frame embellished with two rows of diamonds. Miniature after c. 1820; setting by Carlo Giuliano (1731–95), c. 1880. D 34 mm.

331 *opposite, above* Ring with a miniature of William IV, King of Great Britain and Ireland (1765–1837), beneath a portrait diamond, within a brilliant-cut diamond border and shoulders. Probably 1831.

332 *opposite, below* Locket ring with a miniature of Edward VII, King of Great Britain and Ireland (1841–1910), beneath a portrait diamond, flanked by the royal cipher and crown at the shoulders. Miniature and setting 1901.

326 *The Portrait Diamond, 1613–1906*

of her adopted daughter, Mrs Dawson Damer, whose daughter married Earl Fortescue.⁹

According to his accounts with the jeweller Rundell, Bridge and Rundell, in 1800 as Prince Regent George acquired 'a yellow brilliant picture ring with secret spring and hair plait' and 'A brilliant locket with picture diamond in the centre with secret spring to hair plait and 16 brilliants for the loop and 8 rose diamonds'; in 1813 he added 'A ring with a curious picture diamond'.¹⁰ Whereas these have vanished, another miniature covered by a portrait diamond, after the portrait painted by Sir Thomas Lawrence when the Prince had become king, was reset later in the century in a shield-shaped enamelled brooch by the London jeweller Carlo Giuliano [330]. At least two other English monarchs commissioned portrait diamond rings, William IV [331] and Edward VII [332] – both probably to mark their coronations.

Very occasionally there are references to portrait diamonds owned by the French aristocracy. In 1780, for instance, the Maréchale de Richelieu bought from Ange-Joseph Aubert 'a medallion with a portrait surrounded by 16 good quality brilliants covered by a very fine brilliant, which opens'. Madame de Genlis told a story involving the miniature of the Prince de Conti, the kindest of men. When a woman friend asked for his miniature, on condition that it was set in the plainest of rings, he responded by having the picture encircled by the simplest gold rim, but covered by a flat diamond. Embarrassed, she kept the miniature but returned the diamond: whereupon he had it ground to a powder which he then, to dry the ink, scattered over the letter he wrote her in reply.¹¹

Possibly of French origin is an elegant brooch containing three miniatures, a lady in the centre, flanked by heads of

333 Ring with a miniature of a lady beneath a portrait diamond, surrounded by diamonds, within a later diamond outer border, c. 1780.

334 *opposite* Snuff box, the lid with miniatures of Prince Nikolaus Esterházy (1765–1833), his wife, two sons and daughter, each covered by a portrait diamond, within a chased gold border outlined in royal blue enamel and surrounded by diamonds. Miniatures Austrian School; box by Pierre-André Montauban (fl. 1804–20), c. 1805. w 80 mm.

gentlemen, one shown in profile, the other facing three quarters, each under a faceted diamond, within diamond borders, surmounted by bowknots [335–337]. The brooch can be divided so that the lady's picture can be worn as a medallion, and those of the two gentlemen, which have leafy branches below them, as earrings. In spite of the absence of a provenance, the quality of this jewel and the feat of matching three portrait diamonds could point towards a commission at the very highest level, perhaps from Russia.

Another such multiple commission came from the extravagant and autocratic Prince Nikolaus Esterházy. Famous for his diamond and pearl jewelry and said to be the richest subject in Europe, he turned down Napoleon's offer of the crown of Hungary. The lid of the snuff box that Prince Nikolaus ordered from Pierre-André Montauban in Paris is set with miniatures of himself, his wife, and their three children, each covered by a portrait diamond [334]. Of similar size to those of the Esterházy group, but displayed on its own, a miniature of a young woman is set in a ring beneath a diamond surrounded by a diamond border; much later its importance was emphasized by the addition of another line of larger stones [333].

After Napoleon's marriage to Marie-Louise in 1810 the Emperor's official jeweller, François-Regnault Nitot, revived the portrait diamond as part of the diamond parure that he created for the Empress, which was considered the most magnificent of the 19th century. She wears the tiara, comb, three-drop earrings, necklace and belt in the famous portrait of 1812 by Robert Lefèvre. The two bracelets in the parure – not shown in the portrait – consisted of diamond chains attached to centrepieces surrounded by diamonds enclosing miniatures, presumably of Napoleon and their son, the King

335–337 Silver and gold brooch – shown as its separate elements – with miniatures of a lady between two gentlemen, all beneath portrait diamonds, surmounted by diamond ribbons, the two gentlemen with sprays of leaves and collet-set diamonds below, the lady surrounded by a diamond border. The miniatures of the two gentlemen can be detached to wear as earrings, and that of the lady as a medallion. Miniatures and setting French or Russian, *c.* 1760. W 58 mm.

The Portrait Diamond, 1613–1906

338 Gold ring with a miniature of Peter the Great, Emperor of Russia (1682–1725), beneath a pink-coloured flat portrait diamond. Miniature by J. G. Danhauer, early 18th century; setting St Petersburg, contemporary. 16 × 20 mm.

339, 340 *opposite* A pair of pearl bracelets with centrepieces containing miniatures of King Maximilian I of Bavaria (1756–1825) and his second wife, Caroline of Baden (1776–1841), beneath portrait diamonds and surrounded by diamonds. Miniatures by Josef Heigel (1780–1837), *c.* 1800.

of Rome, covered with diamonds 'faceted so as to receive two portraits' weighing respectively 9.1 and 6.83 carats; the description noted that 'These two stones, unique both in shape and in limpidity and so perfectly matched, are beyond compare with any other brilliants'. In 1887 at the sale of the French crown jewels the smaller diamond was sold; the larger, without a miniature, was given to the Muséum d'Histoire Naturelle in Paris.

The Empress's bracelets may have influenced the Francophile King of Bavaria Maximilian I, who commissioned a similar pair with centrepieces enclosing miniatures of himself and his second wife, Caroline of Baden, beneath and surrounded by diamonds [339, 340]. Thereafter only a few French jewellers received commissions for such de luxe bracelets, an exception being the spectacular diamond centrepiece enamelled blue, 'with a large brilliant covering the portrait', supplied by Jules Fossin to the vastly rich Italian-born Duchesse de Galliera in 1852.[12]

Russia made this type of jewel her own. The earliest depicts Peter the Great, whose miniature – head only – by the German J. G. Danhauer covered by a pink flat diamond and secured by claws is set in a plain gold ring [338]. Some of the many miniatures given by Catherine the Great as badges of office and as marks of esteem and friendship must also have been embellished by diamond covers, though not all can have made so great an impression as that worn by Count Alexis Orlov-Chesmensky, brother of her favourite, Gregory Orlov, as seen by Catherine Wilmot: 'He is a monster in appearance and his strength is beyond belief – he made me shudder. He wears the empress's picture set in diamonds of enormous size and instead of a glass, 'tis a single diamond which covers the portrait.'[13]

341 Gothic-style enamelled bracelet, the centrepiece enclosing a miniature of Alexander I, Emperor of Russia (1777–1825), beneath the *Tafelstein*, a 25-carat portrait diamond. Miniature by Ivan Winberg (fl. 1825–46) after George Dawe. 40 × 29 mm.

Epitomizing Russian prodigality is the largest portrait diamond known, the historic 25-carat *Tafelstein* that covers the miniature of Alexander I, standing full-length in the military uniform which suited him so well, painted on ivory cut to the same irregular triangular shape as the wonderfully transparent stone [341]. It is set as the centrepiece of a gold bracelet within a pointed Gothic-style arch, embellished with trefoils, quatrefoils, flowers and foliage, surmounted by pinnacles, flanked by niches, bright with enamels in many colours. The Emperor's bust only, also in uniform, is covered by another pure and beautiful irregularly shaped diamond, weighing 22 carats, bordered with brilliants, in a medallion intended as the centrepiece of a pearl bracelet [342]. Another bust-length miniature of Alexander I, in profile, is set beneath an oblong scissor-cut diamond within a narrow row of small brilliants surrounded by another, larger, row; the whole is bordered by a ribbon frame and surmounted by a bowknot, to be worn as a medallion round the neck [343]. Similarly portrait diamond rings and a medallion depict Alexander's brother and successor, Nicholas I [344–346]: the 'Iron Tsar' always appears in military uniform, the model of autocracy. Although some may have been presented as official gifts, at least one such jewel belonged to his wife, the Empress Alexandra Feodorovna, who displayed a large stone over his portrait among the diamonds of all sizes in the showcases lining the walls of her private apartments.[14]

Each of the following generations of tsars is associated with this type of jewel, especially to mark their coronations. Alexander II, crowned in 1856, appears in brooches [347, 348]. A brooch designed as the Russian imperial crown with diamond-covered miniatures of both Alexander III, crowned in 1883, and Tsarina Maria Feodorovna, made by Bolin of

342 Centrepiece for a bracelet with a miniature of Alexander I beneath a 22-carat portrait diamond. Miniature by Domenico Bossi (1767–1858), *c.* 1800. 32 × 28 mm.

The Portrait Diamond, 1613–1906 335

344 Gold ring with a miniature of Nicholas I, Emperor of Russia (1796–1855), beneath a portrait diamond.

343 *below* Medallion with a miniature of Alexander I beneath a scissor-cut portrait diamond, within a double diamond border framed in ribbons surmounted by a bowknot. 36 × 28 mm.

345 *below right* Gold ring with a miniature of Nicholas I beneath a portrait diamond, within a diamond border. Miniature by R. Theer, Austrian; setting St Petersburg, 1830. D 18 mm.

346 Medallion centred on a miniature of Nicholas I beneath a portrait diamond, within laurel leaves and berries bordered by diamonds.

347 Pendant set with a miniature of Alexander II, Emperor of Russia (1818–81), emancipator of the serfs, beneath a portrait diamond, framed in diamonds, hanging from a spinel and diamond brooch, terminating in ribbons and a pearl.

348 Brooch containing a portrait miniature of Alexander II under a rectangular-cut diamond, with a border of pink diamonds; the lozenge-shaped outer border is mounted in gold and silver with a row of antique-cut diamonds.

The Portrait Diamond, 1613–1906 337

338 *The Portrait Diamond, 1613–1906*

349 *opposite* Brooch in the form of the Russian imperial crown enclosing miniatures of Alexander III, Emperor of Russia (1845–94), and his Empress, Maria Feodorovna (1847–1928), beneath portrait diamonds, bordered by diamonds and terminating in twin pearls. It was a gift to her mother, Queen Louise of Denmark, marking Alexander III's coronation in Moscow. Signed RS (Robert Schwan) for C. E. Bolin (fl. 1836–64), St Petersburg, 1883. w 53 mm.

St Petersburg, was presented to the Tsarina's mother, Queen Louise of Denmark [349]. To mark their miraculous escape from a railway accident in 1888, Alexander III gave the Tsarina a diamond cross centred on a head of Christ, beneath a portrait diamond, which was inherited by their grandson, Prince Dimitri Romanov.[15] Two other portrait jewels, a bracelet centrepiece and a pendant, are designed round miniatures of the Grand Dukes Nicholas [350] and Vladimir [351], brothers of Alexander III.

The next tsar, Nicholas II, wishing to give his bride Alexandra Feodorovna an Easter egg that expressed his feelings for her, in 1895 commissioned from Fabergé the 'Rosebud' egg [352, 353], decorated with flowers garlanding Cupid's arrows and surmounted by his miniature beneath a large portrait diamond; a rose, also symbolic of love, opened on a spring to reveal an imperial crown.[16] Photographed and painted many times, the imperial couple's four daughters, Olga, Tatiana, Maria and Anastasia, are also represented in a group of miniatures, each covered by a portrait diamond, surrounded by

350 A diamond bracelet, the centrepiece with a miniature of the Grand Duke Nicholas (1843–65), elder brother of Alexander III, beneath a 6-carat portrait diamond, within a border of small diamonds framed in twelve large brilliants.

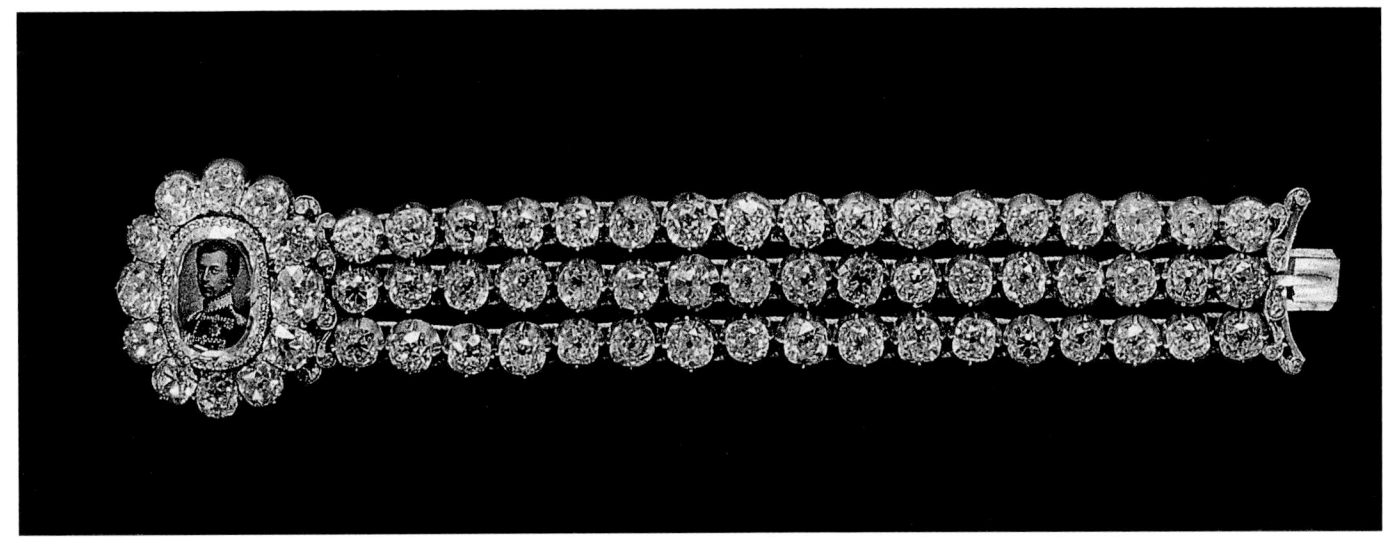

The Portrait Diamond, 1613–1906 339

351 *opposite* Pendant enclosing a miniature of the Grand Duke Vladimir (1847–1909) beneath a portrait diamond, within a diamond frame, below an imperial crown. 32 × 32 mm.

352, 353 Two views of the 'Rosebud' Easter egg, with a miniature of Nicholas II, Emperor of Russia (1868–1918), at the top beneath a portrait diamond. The egg was presented to the Empress at Easter 1895. By Mikhail Perkhin (1860–1903), workmaster for Carl Fabergé. H 68 mm.

The Portrait Diamond, 1613–1906 341

a frame of old-cut brilliants, mounted in reeded gold backs, with a collet-set diamond above the suspension loop [354]. The two eldest, Olga and Tatiana, depicted in heart-shaped pendants, were the 'Big Pair' and the two youngest, Maria and Anastasia, were the 'Little Pair'. These pendants, intended to be worn hanging from a chain at the neck or from a bracelet at the wrist, as a set or individually, belonged to a very close relation such as the Dowager Empress, or to a favourite aunt, the Grand Duchess Olga. It would be difficult to find a more personal and moving memento of these young women, so good-looking and happy, who were denied the chance of fulfilling their potential by the Bolsheviks who murdered them in 1918. Dating from around 1906, the group brings the long association of Russian royalty with the portrait diamond into the 20th century.

354 Pendants, each set with a miniature of one of the daughters of Nicholas II and Alexandra beneath a portrait diamond within a frame of old-cut brilliants, *c.* 1906. The heart-shaped frames hold images of the older daughters, Grand Duchesses Olga (1895–1918) and Tatiana (1897–1918); Maria (1899–1918) and Anastasia (1901–18) are in the oblong frames.

342 *The Portrait Diamond, 1613–1906*

The Engraved Diamond Portrait

Rarest of all are the portraits engraved on diamonds, a task so exacting and time-consuming that few gem engravers have ever been commissioned to produce them. According to some authors, Jacopo da Trezzo and Clement Birague succeeded in doing so around 1564, the latter portraying Don Carlos, heir to Philip II.[1] In the 18th century the connoisseur Philip von Stosch declared that the Roman engraver Giovanni Costanzi had completed a head of Nero, again on a diamond.[2] Another, of the young Habsburg Emperor Leopold II, in the collection of Henry Philip Hope, was described as 'a very good likeness of that monarch, in whose collection it was'.[3]

The challenge was taken up later in the 19th century by anonymous craftsmen who succeeded in engraving diamond intaglio portraits for rings and a locket.[4] Symbolic of opulence, this last [355, 356] was commissioned by the Amsterdam diamond company of Verschuur van der Voort for Willem III of the Netherlands to give his bride, Princess Emma of Waldeck Pyrmont, in 1879: recognizing its significance, she pinned it on her wedding dress. The portrait, which shows King Willelm facing left in profile engraved on a 13/15 carat stone, is surrounded by an openwork double border of rose-cut diamonds, surmounted by ribbons and a royal crown, the circlet set with rubies and emeralds. The locket, which has a container for hair at the back, is signed by the famous Parisian jeweller Oscar Massin.[5]

355, 356 *opposite* Front and back views of a locket set with an intaglio portrait of Willem III, King of the Netherlands (1817–90), engraved on a diamond, by Verschuur van der Voort, 1879; setting by Oscar Massin.

NOTES

Titles in the Bibliography are given here in shortened form.

Abbreviations:
AN = Archives Nationales, Paris
BL = British Library, London
PRO = Public Record Office, London
RAW = Royal Archives, Windsor

CHAPTER 1 (pp. 8–77)

[1] Muller, *Jewels in Spain*, p. 49.
[2] J. Babelon, *Jacopo da Trezzo*, p. 29.
[3] ibid., pp. 243–44.
[4] Nationalmuseum, Stockholm, Drawings Department.
[5] Sframeli, *I gioielli dei Medici*, p. 144, no. 73.
[6] E. Babelon, *Catalogue des Camées antiques et modernes de la Bibliothèque nationale*, no. 975.
[7] National Museums of Scotland.
[8] In addition to associating himself with Hercules, slayer of monsters, Henri IV adopted the motto 'Invia virtuti nulla est via' (There is no path closed to virtue).
[9] *Brilliant Europe*, exh. cat., p. 144.
[10] Bimbenet-Privat, *Les Orfèvres et l'orfèvrerie de Paris au XVIIe siècle*, II, no. 150, p. 429.
[11] Historical Manuscripts Commission, *The Manuscripts of His Grace the Duke of Rutland* (1905), p. 388.
[12] Strong, *Gloriana*, p. 168, note 71.
[13] BL, Royal ms. Appx. 68, no. 79.
[14] BL, Add. ms. 5751A, fols 218r–v.
[15] ibid., fols 229–235v.
[16] Strong, *Tudor and Jacobean Portraits*, I, p. 321, no. 1807, attributed to John Critz the Elder.
[17] *Princely Magnificence*, exh. cat., 1980–81, no. 44.
[18] *The Art of Gem Engraving from Alexander the Great to Napoleon III*, exh. cat., no. 56.
[19] Sframeli, *I gioielli dei Medici*, pp. 112–13, nos 53–55.
[20] Kunsthistorisches Museum, Vienna.
[21] Börner, *Deutsche Medaillenkleinode des 16. und 17. Jahrhunderts*, is a succinct account of the development of the Gnadenpfennig.
[22] ibid., p. 61, fig. I.
[23] Lebel, 'British–French Artistic Relations in the XVIth Century', pp. 274–76.
[24] Robertson, *Inventaires de la Royne Descosse Douairière de France*, pp. 16 and 11.
[25] ibid., p. 123.
[26] *The Queen's Image*, exh. cat., p. 37, no. 20.
[27] Viel-Castel, 'Commande de bijoux par la reine Catherine de Médicis, à Dujardin, orfèvre du roi Charles IX', pp. 41–45.
[28] Fréville, 'Notice historique sur les biens meublés de Gabrielle d'Estrées', p. 168; and Desclozeaux, *Gabrielle d'Estrées*, p. 292, for the aigrette with miniature of Henri IV.
[29] J. P. Babelon, *Lettres d'amour et écrits politiques*, no. 216.
[30] Bruel, 'Deux Inventaires de bagues, joyaux, pierreries et dorures de la Reine Marie de Médicis, 1609, 1610', p. 199, no. 45.
[31] For instance, the pair of rings enclosing miniatures of the Emperor Mathias and Empress Anna in the Kunsthistorisches Museum, Vienna.
[32] *Letters and Papers Foreign and Domestic of the Reign of Henry VIII* (London 1872), IV, Pt ii, no. 3169, 10 June 1527.
[33] Scarisbrick, *Jewellery in Britain 1066–1837*, p. 65.
[34] BL, Harl. ms. 611, fol. 2b.
[35] ibid., fol. 3b.
[36] Strong, *Gloriana*, p. 125.
[37] Scarisbrick, 'Anne of Denmark's Jewelry Inventory', p. 215, no. 230.
[38] Strong, *Gloriana*, p. 10, from Horace Walpole, *Anecdotes of Painting*.
[39] ibid., p. 30.
[40] Steene, *The Letters of Lady Arabella Stuart*, letter to the Earl of Shrewsbury, p. 183.
[41] Ungerer, 'Juan Pantoja de la Cruz and the Circulation of Gifts between the English and Spanish Courts, 1604–5', pp. 149 and 154.
[42] Tait, *The Waddesdon Bequest*, p. 178.
[43] Cammell, *The Great Duke of Buckingham*, p. 166.
[44] Gade, *Christian IV*, pp. 113–14, and *Smykket i dansk eje (Jewelry in Danish Collections)*, exh. cat., pp. 25–26.
[45] Heriot, *Memoir of George Heriot*, p. 197 (both cases were pawned in 1609), and p. 221 for the James I ring.
[46] Herbert, *Autobiography*, p. 79.
[47] PRO, Prob. 11/174, fol. 70.
[48] Delany, *Autobiography and Correspondence of Mary Granville, Mrs. Delany*, III, 2nd ser., p. 173.

CHAPTER 2 (pp. 78–153)

[1] E. Babelon, *Histoire de la gravure sur gemmes en France*, pl. XII, no. 6.
[2] Clément, *Lettres, Instructions et mémoires de Colbert*, Posthumous Inventory, p. 388, no. 380, 'une agate-onyx représentant le portrait du Roy'; no. 381, also agate onyx, is of Cardinal Mazarin, whom Colbert had served and who in his will recommended him to the King 'étant fidèle'.
[3] Dalton, *Catalogue of the Finger Rings . . . in the British Museum*, no. 1368. The back of the bezel is enamelled with a motif similar to a design by Pierre Marchand.
[4] Scarisbrick, *Rings: Jewelry of Power, Love and Loyalty*, ills 253 and 254. The date of the King's execution is at the back of the bezel.
[5] Green, *Calendar of State Papers, Domestic*. Thomas Simon was paid £850 for a jewel to be presented to the ambassador of Sweden in 1656 (p. 115).
[6] Weber, *Geschnittene Steine aus altbayerischen Besitz*, nos 234–42.
[7] Eichler and Kris, *Die Kameen in Kunsthistorischen Museum*, nos 438–43 (pendants) and 444 and 445 (rings) on the same theme.
[8] ibid., no. 442, p. 185, fig. 81.
[9] Shaw, 'Pieter van Roestraeten and the English *Vanitas*', p. 405, fig. 23.
[10] Muller, *Jewels in Spain*, p. 109.
[11] Maze-Sencier, *Le Livre des collectionneurs*. In 1705 the Marchese Ranuccini received 'un médaillier de l'Histoire du Roi de 280 médailles, dont 7 d'or et les autres argent' (2,374 livres); similarly the Papal Nuncio Lorenzo Fieschi the same but 86 gold, and 195 silver (12,065 livres). Maze-Sencier quotes extensively from the *Registre des Présents du Roi*, and his citations have been used throughout this text.
[12] ibid.
[13] Whitelocke, *Journal of the Swedish Embassy in the Years 1653–1654*, II, pp. 199–209.
[14] Masson, *Queen Christina*, p. 196.
[15] Josten, 'Elias Ashmole'.
[16] Börner, *Deutsche Medaillenkleinode des 16. und 17. Jahrhunderts*, pl. 69, cat. no. 145.
[17] ibid., pls 16, 17, cat. nos 25, 28.
[18] Reynolds, *The Sixteenth and Seventeenth-Century Miniatures in the Collection of Her Majesty the Queen*, no. 426, p. 287.
[19] Scarisbrick, *Ancestral Jewels*, pl. 91, in the collection of the Duke of Hamilton.
[20] Noble, *Memoirs of the Protectoral House of Cromwell*, I, p. 308.
[21] Victoria and Albert Museum, London.
[22] Scarisbrick, *Ancestral Jewels*, p. 43, pls 49, 50.
[23] Haile, *Queen Mary of Modena*, pp. 518–21.
[24] Dorothy Osborne, before engaging the artist, 'consulted my glass every morning . . . but could never find my face in a condition to admit on't and when I was not satisfied with it myself, I had no reason to hope that anyone else should'. *Letters of Dorothy Osborne to Sir William Temple*, p. 59 and p. 109, 13 June 1654.
[25] Scarisbrick, *Jewellery in Britain 1066–1837*, p. 215.
[26] Olausson, 'Bejewelled Monarchs', in *Precious Gems*, exh. cat., p. 14.
[27] Bimbenet-Privat, *Les Orfèvres et l'orfèvrerie de Paris au XVIIe siècle*, II, discusses French miniatures and their settings in depth.
[28] AN, T 1520.
[29] Gauthier, 'Le Portrait de Béatrix de Cusance au Musée du Louvre et l'inventaire de ses bijoux en 1663', p. 136, nos 48–51.
[30] AN, T* 479/2.
[31] AN, T 532/3 (Vente après décès des meubles de Marie Charron, veuve de Jean-Baptiste Colbert).
[32] Cordey, 'Inventaire après décès d'Anne d'Autriche', pp. 265, 272.
[33] For the miniature of the Comtesse d'Olonne, see Grace, 'A Celebrated Miniature of the Comtesse d'Olonne', pp. 3–21.
[34] Bimbenet-Privat, *Les Orfèvres et l'orfèvrerie de Paris au XVIIe siècle*, II, p. 400.
[35] Orléans, Inventory. Muller, *Jewels in Spain*, quotes from this document.

Notes 345

36 Saint-Simon, *Mémoires*, I, pp. 565–66.
37 Bimbenet-Privat, *Les Orfèvres et l'orfèvrerie de Paris au XVIIe siècle*, II, p. 513.
38 Maze-Sencier, *Le Livre des collectionneurs*, is the source of this information from the *Registres des Présents*.
39 Perini, 'Malvasia's Connexions with France and Rome', pp. 410–12.
40 Scholten, 'Concerning the *conterfeyt-boot* Miniature Case of Louis XIV', in *A Sparkling Age*, exh. cat., pp. 55–62, cat. no. 95.
41 Tillander-Godenhielm, 'The Russian Imperial Award System under Nicholas II', pp. 149–79.

CHAPTER 3 (pp. 154–223)

1 Quoted by Mansel, *The Prince of Europe: The Life of Charles-Joseph de Ligne*, p. 87.
2 Hackenbroch and Sframeli, *I gioielli dell'Elettrice Palatina al Museo degli Argenti*, pp. 158–76, nos 68, 786 and 785.
3 Maze-Sencier, *Le Livre des collectionneurs*.
4 E. Babelon, *Histoire de la gravure sur gemmes en France*, pl. XIII, no. 2.
5 Bapst, *Inventaire de Marie-Josèphe de Saxe*, p. 149.
6 Maze-Sencier, *Le Livre des collectionneurs*, lists many examples of snuff boxes and jewelry with miniatures but not 'en relief'.
7 AN, T* 299/5, 6, 7, 'Journal du Joaillier Aubert' 1767–70/ 1773–75/ 1775–81. Marcel, 'Aubert d'Avignon, ioaillier du roi et garde de diamants de la couronne', pp. 89–111.
8 Heuzé, 'Les Simon, une dynastie de graveurs sur médailles', fig. 12a and b, but missing from Musée Carnavalet, Paris.
9 Hertz, *Catalogue of the Collection of Pearls and Precious Stones formed by Henry Philip Hope*, pl. VII, no. 47.
10 The accounts of George IV as Prince of Wales, Regent and King are in the Royal Archives at Windsor: Charles James Fox cameo ring RAW 25648, King of Prussia RAW 25650/3.
11 Minto, *The Life and Letters of Sir Gilbert Elliot, 1st Earl of Minto* (London 1874), I, p. 326.
12 Christie's sale, 17 May 1819, nos 33 and 59.
13 *The Art of Gem Engraving from Alexander the Great to Napoleon III*, exh. cat., no. 74.
14 Maze-Sencier, *Le Livre des collectionneurs*.
15 Allemagne, *Les Accessoires du costume et du mobilier*, I, pp. 9 and 10.
16 Genlis, *Mémoires*, I, p. 42.
17 AN, Minutier central, étude XXI, 141, 27 Sept. 1749.
18 'Registres comptables du marchand bijoutier joaillier successeur de la Veuve Demay et Masson, à l'enseigne "A La Descente du Pont Neuf."' Institut National de l'histoire de l'art, Paris, ms 129/1.
19 Maze-Sencier, *Le Livre des collectionneurs*, p. 498.
20 Diderot, *Letters to Sophie Voland*, pp. 19–20.
21 AN, T 434.
22 AN, T 197.
23 Garnier-Pelle et al., *Portraits des maisons royales et impériales de France et d'Europe: les miniatures du Musée Condé à Chantilly*, no. 143.
24 Quoted by Guillebon, 'Un Suédois peintre du roi et des enfants de France: le miniaturiste Hall', pp. 78–79.
25 AN, Minutier central, étude CXV, 610.
26 AN, T* 584–52.
27 Bapst, *Inventaire de Marie-Josèphe de Saxe*, p. 148. According to Bapst, p. 22, the Dauphin was so attached to the bracelet miniatures of his first wife that he asked Marie-Josèphe to show her love for him by wearing them in her memory. Marie-Josèphe agreed to do so.
28 Spencer-Stanhope, *The Letter-Bag of Lady Elizabeth Spencer-Stanhope*, I, p. 41.
29 Mitford, *Voltaire in Love*, p. 271.
30 Montet, *Souvenirs*, pp. 307–8.
31 Yonan, 'Portable dynasties', p. 186 and note 25, discusses the significance of this gift, which is the object of a forthcoming study by Alden Gordon on the exchange of miniatures between Madame de Pompadour, the Empress Maria Theresa and Count Kaunitz. I am also indebted to Michael Yonan for his account, in the same article, of the box with thirteen Habsburg family miniatures.
32 Grootenboer, 'Treasuring the Gaze: Eye Miniature Portraits and the Intimacy of Vision', pp. 496–507.
33 *Country Life*, 19 April 1956, p. 811.
34 Boscawen, *Admiral's Wife: The Life and Letters of the Hon. Mrs Edward Boscawen*, p. 163.
35 Christie's sale, 17 May 1819, no. 64. Pointon, '"Surrounded with Brilliants": Miniature Portraits in Eighteenth Century England', pp. 48–71, discusses and illustrates Queen Charlotte's adoption of jewelled miniatures.
36 Walker, *Eighteenth and Early Nineteenth Century Miniatures in the Collection of Her Majesty the Queen*, pp. 156–57.
37 Coke, *The Letters and Journals of Lady Mary Coke*, II, p. 56.
38 Delany, *Autobiography and Correspondence of Mary Granville, Mrs. Delany*, III, 2nd ser., p. 216.
39 Walker, *Eighteenth and Early Nineteenth Century Miniatures in the Collection of Her Majesty the Queen*, p. 84.
40 ibid., no. 169.
41 BL, Althorp Papers F126.
42 *The Intimate Portrait*, exh. cat., p. 17 and fig. 4 – Mrs Fitzherbert's eye in a locket.
43 Scarisbrick, *Rings, Symbols of Power, Wealth and Affection*, pp. 127–28.
44 Scarisbrick, *Jewellery in Britain 1066–1837*, pp. 268–69, also 'The Jewelry of Treason', *Country Life*, 182 (1988), pp. 128–29.
45 Oman, *British Rings*, p. 122, 82b.
46 Maugras, *La Marquise de Boufflers*, pp. 216–17.
47 Barbara Kerrich on 3 February 1748 describes the much-talked-about marriage of Mr Folkes with the daughter of Dr Browne, and notes that the bride's dress and jewels included 'a fine repeating watch with his picture set round with diamonds'. Surry, *Your Affectionate and Loving Sister: the Correspondence of Barbara Kerrich and Elizabeth Postlethwaite*.
48 Christie's sale, 27 March 1984, lot 200.
49 La Roche, *Sophie in London*, p. 246.
50 Scarisbrick, *Jewellery in Britain 1066–1837*, p. 338.
51 Hackenbroch and Sframeli, *I gioielli dell'Elettrice Palatina al Museo degli Argenti*, no. 22.
52 Garnier-Pelle et al., *Portraits des maisons royales et impériales de France et d'Europe: les miniatures du Musée Condé à Chantilly*, no. 192.
53 Christie's sale, Geneva, 17/18 May 1994, lot 345.
54 Holland, *Spanish Journal of Lady Holland*, p. 28.
55 Casanova, *Memoirs of Jacques Casanova de Seingalt*, p. 159, and p. 184 for the medallion and a snuff box *à secret*.
56 Olausson, 'Bejewelled Monarchs', in *Precious Gems*, exh. cat., p. 18, illustrates a portrait by Franz Gerhard von Kügelgen of Princess Charlotta von Liewen, governess to the future Emperor Alexander I, wearing diamond pendants set with miniatures of his grandmother and mother, Catherine the Great and the Empress Maria Feodorovna, and two more framed in pearls in the clasps of her bracelets.
57 *Memoirs of the Princess Dashkov*, I, p. 333.
58 *Illustrated London News*, vol. 64, p. 22.

CHAPTER 4 (pp. 224–319)

1 National Gallery of Scotland, Edinburgh.
2 Museo Napoleonico, Rome.
3 Garside, *Jewelry Ancient to Modern*, no. 652.
4 Christie's sale 1962.
5 Tassinari, 'Glyptic Portraits of Eugène de Beauharnais: the Intaglios by Giovanni Beltrami and the Cameo by Antonio Berini', pp. 43–64.
6 *The Art of Gem Engraving from Alexander the Great to Napoleon III*, exh. cat., no. 82.
7 *The Connoisseur*, 1908, p. 230.
8 *Smykket i dansk eje* (*Jewelry in Danish Collections*), exh. cat., no. 214.
9 Heuzé, 'Les Simon, une dynastie de graveurs sur médailles', pp. 201–28.
10 Formerly Esmerian Collection, sold by S. J. Phillips, now private collection USA.
11 Hartop, *Royal Goldsmiths: the Art of Rundell & Bridge*, no. 67: snuff box set with cornelian intaglio of George IV within gold border chased with badge and motto of the Royal Guelphic Order. The intaglio is by Benedetto Pistrucci. For a comprehensive account of the medallist and gem-engraver Pistrucci see Pirzio Biroli, *I modelli in cera di Benedetto Pistrucci*.
12 Aschengreen Piacenti and Boardman, *Ancient and Modern Gems and Jewels in the Collection of Her Majesty the Queen*, no. 273.
13 RAW 26161.
14 Aschengreen Piacenti and Boardman, *Ancient and

Modern Gems and Jewels in the Collection of Her Majesty the Queen, no. 227.
15 *Victoria and Albert, Art and Love*, exh. cat., no. 9.
16 ibid., no. 244, for a full account of this Order.
17 Dickmann de Petra and Barberini, *Tommaso e Luigi Saulini*, illustrate drawings of sitters identified as American: George Washington Green (B 140), Mr F. Wright (B 189), Samuel M. Dossey (B 200), Dr Gordon Estess (B 220), and Mr S. H. Benoizt (C 29).
18 Fossin ledgers, Chaumet Archives, Paris.
19 Tolles, 'Augustus Saint-Gaudens in the Metropolitan Museum of Art', p. 61.
20 *The Art of Gem Engraving from Alexander the Great to Napoleon III*, exh. cat., no. 221.
21 Montet, *Souvenirs*.
22 Ligne, *Souvenirs*, p. 178.
23 Sothebys sale, London, 16 May 1991, no. 426.
24 Tassinari, 'I ritratti dello zar Nicola I incise su intaglie e cammei'.
25 Dickmann de Petra and Barberini, *Tommaso e Luigi Saulini*, illustrate drawings and cameos of Russian sitters.
26 Sotheby's sale, Monte Carlo, 25 June 1976, lot 555. Given to his daughter Elena, Princess Nicholas of Greece.
27 Dickmann de Petra and Barberini, *Tommaso e Luigi Saulini*, p. 72.
28 In 1819 Pistrucci was commissioned to create the Waterloo victory medal and thereafter others of celebrated events and individuals. See Pirzio Biroli, *I modelli in cera di Benedetto Pistrucci*.
29 RAW 25995.
30 RAW 25996.
31 RAW 26004.
32 Tait, *The Art of the Jeweller: A Catalogue of the Hull Grundy Gift to the British Museum*, no. 361 (pendant setting later, by John Brogden, fl. 1842–85): one of 650 gold and 800 silver medals struck of Benedetto Pistrucci's coronation medal.
33 Scarisbrick, *Jewelry in Britain 1066–1837*, p. 326, nos 117, 118.
34 Tait, *The Art of the Jeweller: A Catalogue of the Hull Grundy Gift to the British Museum*, no. 365.
35 ibid., no. 362: double, the two pins linked by a gold chain, each pin surmounted by a blue enamel snake with diamond eyes framing a swivel medal set in gold: a double portrait of Queen Victoria and Prince Albert, and the head of the infant Prince of Wales with his emblem of ostrich plumes, inscribed with his name, dates of birth and christening at Windsor.
36 ibid., no. 363.
37 Bury, *Jewellery 1789–1910*, II, pl. 332/D: pin with medallic portrait of Queen Victoria by Alfred Gilbert set round with diamonds by the jeweller Joseph Heming.
38 Tait, *The Art of the Jeweller: A Catalogue of the Hull Grundy Gift to the British Museum*, no. 359: medal of Princess Pauline Borghese by Bertrand Andrieu mounted as a brooch surrounded by a wreath of flowers executed in gold of various colours.
39 Hartop, *Royal Goldsmiths: the Art of Rundell & Bridge*, fig. 24, p. 35, presented to the 6th Duke of Devonshire.
40 Bloomfield, *Reminiscences of Court and Diplomatic Life*.
41 Marquardt, *Schmuck*, p. 297, no. 484.
42 ibid., p. 346, no. 696, and Sotheby's sale, Geneva, 17 November 1992.
43 Marquardt, *Schmuck*, p. 278, no. 386.
44 Clary, *Trois Mois à Paris*, p. 245.
45 Chavanne et al., *Jean-Baptiste Isabey*, p. 129, no. 63bis.
46 Dernelle, *Mémoires de Mademoiselle Avrillion*, p. 282.
47 Scarisbrick, *Chaumet*, pp. 35–36.
48 Chavanne et al., *Jean-Baptiste Isabey*, no. 100.
49 Biagi, *Le lettere di Joachim Murat alla figlia Laetizia*, Letter XX.
50 *The Memoirs of Chateaubriand*, tr. R. Baldick (London 1961), p. 372.
51 Breguet bill, 19 September 1807, no. 2080.
52 Chavanne et al., *Jean-Baptiste Isabey*, no. 70.
53 Fossin ledgers, Chaumet Archives, Paris.
54 Karr, *Les Guêpes*, p. 159.
55 Baronne de Montet, *Souvenirs*, p. 341.
56 *Entre Cour et Jardin, Marie-Caroline, duchesse de Berry*, exh. cat.
57 Garnier-Pelle et al., *Portraits des maisons royales et impériales de France et d'Europe: les miniatures du Musée Condé à Chantilly*, no. 148. The box was given by Madame Adélaïde to mark the christening of their godson, the Duc d'Aumale, in 1825.
58 Christie's sale, Paris, 28 October 2008.
59 *Souvenirs de la Princesse de Ligne* (Brussels and Paris 1923), p. 76.
60 Garnier-Pelle et al., *Portraits des maisons royales et impériales de France et d'Europe: les miniatures du Musée Condé à Chantilly*, p. 13, fig. 3.
61 Fossin ledgers, Chaumet Archives, Paris.
62 Aspinall, *Letters of George IV 1812–30*, I, no. 340.
63 Frampton, *Journal of M. Frampton*, p. 279.
64 RAW 25920.
65 Walker, *Eighteenth and Early Nineteenth Century Miniatures in the Collection of Her Majesty the Queen*, no. 923.
66 ibid.
67 *Victoria and Albert, Art and Love*, exh. cat., nos 2 and 20.
68 ibid., no. 7.
69 ibid., no. 16.
70 Garnier-Pelle et al., *Portraits des maisons royales et impériales de France et d'Europe: les miniatures du Musée Condé à Chantilly*, no. 245.
71 *Victoria and Albert, Art and Love*, exh. cat., nos 257 and 258: bracelets commissioned by Prince Albert for Queen Victoria. There are six miniatures of their children in no. 257, the other three in no. 258. Each miniature is enclosed in a pearl locket enamelled with blue foliate scrolls, containing a lock of hair, inscribed with the name and date of the sitter.
72 *Exhibition of Royal and Historic Treasures in Aid of 'The Heritage'*, exh. cat., p. 73, no. 17.
73 Scarisbrick, *Jewellery in Britain 1066–1837*, p. 337.
74 Broughton, *Recollections*, I, p. 231.
75 Wassenaer, *A Visit to St. Petersburg 1824–1825*, p. 43.
76 Scarisbrick, *Ancestral Jewels*, p. 75.
77 Tillander-Godenhielm, 'The Russian Imperial Award System under Nicholas II', pp. 149–79.
78 *Victoria and Albert, Art and Love*, exh. cat., no. 259.
79 ibid., no. 260. Another example, a brooch enclosing this photograph, is illustrated in Garnier-Pelle et al., *Portraits des maisons royales et impériales de France et d'Europe: les miniatures du Musée Condé à Chantilly*, no. 244.
80 Bloomfield, *Reminiscences of Court and Diplomatic Life*, p. 345.
81 Solodkoff, *Fabergé*.

CHAPTER 5 (pp. 320–43)

1 Batiffol, *La Vie intime d'une reine de France au XVIIe siècle*, II, p. 90.
2 Cordey, 'Inventaire apres décès d'Anne d'Autriche', pp. 265, 272, 274.
3 Sharp, 'Notes on Stuart Jewelry', p. 230. Collection Colonel le Rossignol.
4 Hackenbroch and Sframeli, *I gioielli dell'Elettrice Palatina al Museo degli Argenti*, p. 161, no. 67.
5 Delany, *Autobiography and Correspondence of Mary Granville, Mrs. Delany*, III, 2nd ser., p. 178.
6 BL, Add. ms. 61472, fols 206–207b.
7 Green, *Sarah, Duchess of Marlborough*, pp. 190–92, also Garrard accounts 1829, 'A bracelet with a very fine table diamond covering a portrait of the great Duke of Marlborough'.
8 Walker, *Eighteenth and Early Nineteenth Century Miniatures in the Collection of Her Majesty the Queen*, p. 127, no. 250.
9 ibid., p. 98.
10 For 1800, RAW 25687; for 1813, RAW 25848.
11 Genlis, *Mémoires*, p. 303.
12 Scarisbrick, *Chaumet*, p. 138.
13 Wilmot, *The Russian Journals of Martha and Catherine Wilmot 1803–1808*, pp. 67–68.
14 Grunwald, *Nicholas I*.
15 Christie's sale, London, 22 March 1961, lot 10.
16 *Fabergé, Joaillier des Romanov*, exh. cat., pp. 43–45.

THE ENGRAVED DIAMOND PORTRAIT (pp. 344–45)

1 J. Babelon, *Jacopo da Trezzo*, p. 37.
2 Mariette, *Traité des pierres gravées*, I, p. 141.
3 Hertz, *Catalogue of the Collection of Pearls and Precious Stones formed by Henry Philip Hope*, p. 29, no. 41.
4 Story-Maskelyne, *Report on Jewellery and Precious Stones*, p. 601.
5 *Diamant van ruwe steen tot sieraad*, exh. cat.

BIBLIOGRAPHY

Allemagne, H. d' *Les Accessoires du costume et du mobilier* (Paris 1928)

Aschengreen Piacenti, K., and John Boardman *Ancient and Modern Gems and Jewels in the Collection of Her Majesty the Queen* (London 2008)

Aspinall, A. *The Letters of George IV 1812–30* (London 1938)

Babelon, E. *Catalogue des camées antiques et modernes de la Bibliothèque nationale* (Paris 1897)

— *Histoire de la Gravure sur gemmes en France* (Paris 1902)

Babelon, J. *Jacopo da Trezzo et la construction de l'Escurial* (Paris 1922)

Babelon, J. P. *Lettres d'amour et écrits politiques* (Paris 1988)

Bapst, G. *Inventaire de Marie-Josèphe de Saxe, Dauphine de France* (Paris 1883)

Batiffol, L. *La Vie intime d'une reine de France au XVIIe siècle* (Paris 1931)

Biagi, G. *Le lettere di Joachim Murat alla figlia Laetizia* (Rome 1893)

Bimbenet-Privat, M. *Les Orfèvres et l'orfèvrerie de Paris au XVIIe siècle* (Paris 2002)

Bloomfield, Baroness *Reminiscences of Court and Diplomatic Life* (London 1883)

Börner, L. *Deutsche Medaillenkleinode des 16. und 17. Jahrhunderts* (Leipzig 1981)

Boscawen, E. *Admiral's Wife: The Life and Letters of the Hon. Mrs Edward Boscawen*, ed. C. Aspinall Oglander (London 1940)

Brewer, J. C., ed. *Letters and Papers, foreign and domestic of the reign of Henry VIII, preserved at the Public Record Office* (London 1872)

Broughton, Lord *Recollections*, ed. Lady Dorchester (London 1909)

Bruel, F. L. 'Deux Inventaires de bagues, joyaux, pierreries et dorures de la Reine Marie de Médicis, 1609, 1610', *Archives de l'Art français*, II (Paris 1908)

Bury, S. *Jewellery 1789–1910* (Woodbridge 1991)

Cammell, C. R. *The Great Duke of Buckingham* (London 1939)

Casanova, G. *Memoirs of Jacques Casanova de Seingalt* (London and Amsterdam 1922)

Chavanne, B., et al. *Jean-Baptiste Isabey 1767–1855, Portraitiste de l'Europe* (Paris 2006)

Clary, C. *Trois Mois à Paris* (Paris 1914)

Clément, P., ed. *Lettres, Instructions et mémoires de Colbert*, VII (Paris 1873)

Coke, M. *Letters and Journals of Lady Mary Coke*, ed. A. J. Home, II (Bath 1970)

Cordey, J. 'Inventaire après décès d'Anne d'Autriche', *Bulletin de la Société de l'histoire de l'art français* (Paris 1930)

Dalton, K. 'Art For the Sake of Dynasty', in Peter Erickson and Clark Hulse, eds., *Early Modern Visual Culture: Representation, Race and Empire in Renaissance England* (Philadelphia, Pa., 2000)

Dalton, O. M. *Catalogue of the Finger Rings, Early Christian, Byzantine, Teutonic, Medieval and Later in the British Museum* (London 1912)

Dashkov, Princess *Memoirs of the Princess Dashkov written by herself*, ed. Mrs W. Bradford (London 1840)

Delany, M. *The Autobiography and Correspondence of Mary Granville, Mrs. Delany*, ed. Lady Llanover (London 1862)

Dernelle, M., ed. *Mémoires de Mademoiselle Avrillion* (Paris 1969)

Desclozeaux, L. *Gabrielle d'Estrées* (Paris 1889)

Dickmann de Petra, M., and F. Barberini *Tommaso e Luigi Saulini* (Rome 2006)

Diderot, Denis *Letters to Sophie Voland*, ed. P. France (Oxford 1972)

Duffy, S., and C. Vogtherr *Miniatures in the Wallace Collection* (London 2010)

Eichler, F., and E. Kris *Die Kameen in Kunsthistorischen Museum* (Vienna 1927)

Frampton, M. *The Journal of M. Frampton, 1779–1846*, ed. H. G. Mundy (London 1885)

Fréville, E. de 'Notice historique sur les biens meublés de Gabrielle d'Estrées', *Bibliothèque de l'Ecole des Chartes*, III (Paris 1841–42)

Gade, J. *Christian IV* (London 1928)

Garnier-Pelle, N., et al. *Portraits des maisons royales et impériales de France et d'Europe: les miniatures du Musée Condé à Chantilly* (Paris 2007)

Garside, A., ed. *Jewelry Ancient to Modern* (Baltimore, Md, 1979)

Gauthier, J. 'Le Portrait de Béatrice de Cusance au Musée du Louvre et l'inventaire de ses bijoux en 1663', *Académie des Sciences, Belles Lettres et Arts de Besançon, Procès verbaux et mémoires* (Besançon 1897)

Genlis, Madame de *Mémoires* (Paris 1928)

Grace, P. 'A Celebrated Miniature of the Comtesse d'Olonne', *Philadelphia Museum of Art Bulletin*, vol. 83, no. 353, Autumn 1986

Green, D. *Sarah, Duchess of Marlborough* (London 1967)

Green, M. A. E., ed. *Calendar of State Papers, Domestic, 1656–67* (London 1884)

Grootenboer, H. 'Treasuring the Gaze: Eye Miniature Portraits and the Intimacy of Vision', *Art Bulletin*, vol. 88, 2006

Grunwald, C. de *Nicholas I* (London 1954)

Guillebon, R. de Plinval de 'Un Suédois, Peintre du Roi et des Enfants de France: le miniaturiste Hall', *L'Estampille, L'Objet d'Art*, no. 354, January 2001

Hackenbroch, Y., and M. Sframeli *I gioielli dell'Elettrice Palatina al Museo degli Argenti* (Florence 1988)

Haile, M. *Queen Mary of Modena, Her Life and Letters* (London 1905)

Hartop, C. *Royal Goldsmiths: the Art of Rundell & Bridge, 1797–1843* (Cambridge 2005)

Herbert, Lord *Autobiography: A Collection of the Most Instructive and Amusing Lives Ever Published*, VIII (London 1830)

Heriot, G. *Memoir of George Heriot, Jeweller to King James VI* (Edinburgh 1822)

Hertz, B. *Catalogue of the Collection of Pearls and Precious Stones formed by Henry Philip Hope* (London 1839)

Heuzé, M. 'Les Simon, une dynastie de graveurs sur médailles', *Bulletin de la Société de l'histoire de l'art français*, 2002

Holland, E. *Spanish Journal of Lady Holland* (London 1910)

Josten, C. H. 'Elias Ashmole F.R.S. 1617–1692', *Notes and Records of the Royal Society of London*, vol. 15, July 1960

Karr, A. *Les Guêpes* (Paris 1858)

La Roche, S. von *Sophie in London*, transl. C. Williams (London 1933)

Lebel, G. 'British–French Artistic Relations in the XVIth Century', *Gazette des Beaux-Arts*, ser. 6, vol. XXXIII, 1948, pp. 273–77

Ligne, Princesse de *Souvenirs de la Princesse de Ligne (1815–1850)* (Brussels and Paris 1923)

Mansel, P. *Prince of Europe: The Life of Charles-Joseph de Ligne* (London 2005)

Marcel, N. 'Aubert d'Avignon, joaillier du roi et garde de diamants de la couronne', *Mémoires de l'Académie de Vaucluse*, ser. 2, vol XIX, 1919

Mariette, P. *Traité des Pierres gravées* (Paris 1750)

Marquardt, B. *Schmuck: Realismus und Historismus 1850–1895* (Munich 1998)

Masson, G. *Queen Christina* (London 1974)

Maugras, G., ed. *La Marquise de Boufflers* (Paris 1907)

Maze-Sencier, A. *Le Livre des collectionneurs* (Paris 1885)

Minto, 1st Earl of *The Life and Letters of Sir Gilbert Elliot, First Earl of Minto*, ed. Countess of Minto (London 1874)

Mitford, N. *Voltaire in Love* (London 1957)

Montet, Baronne du *Souvenirs* (Paris 1904)

Muller, P. *Jewels in Spain* (New York 1972)

Noble, M. *Memoirs of the Protectoral House of Cromwell* (London 1787)

Olausson, M. 'Bejewelled Monarchs: From Mark of Favour to Royal Emblem', in *Precious Gems*, exh. cat., Stockholm, 2000

Oman, C. *British Rings* (London 1973)

Orléans, M.-L. d' Inventory, 1689; vol. 5269, Registro de Escrituras de Don Francisco Arévalo, Real Bureo, Archivo General de Palacio, Madrid

Osborne, D. *Letters of Dorothy Osborne to Sir William Temple*, ed. G. M. Smith (Oxford 1928)

Perini, G. 'Malvasia's Connexions with France and Rome', *Burlington Magazine*, CXXXII, no. 1047, June 1990

Pirzio Biroli, L. *I modelli in cera di Benedetto Pistrucci* (Rome 1989)

Pointon, M. '"Surrounded with Brilliants": Miniature Portraits in 18th Century England', *Art Bulletin*, vol. 83, 2001

Remington, V. *Victorian Miniatures in the Collection of Her Majesty the Queen* (London 2010)

Reynolds, G. *The Sixteenth- and Seventeenth-Century Miniatures in the Collection of Her Majesty the Queen* (London 1999)

Robertson, J., ed. *Inventaires de la Royne Descosse Douairiere de France 1556–1569* (Edinburgh 1863)

Saint-Simon, Louis de Rouvroy, Duc de *Mémoires*, I (Paris 1983)

Scarisbrick, D. *Ancestral Jewels* (London 1984)

— 'Anne of Denmark's Jewellery Inventory', *Archaeologia*, vol. 109, 1991

— *Jewellery in Britain 1066–1837* (Norwich 1994)

— *Chaumet, Master Jewellers since 1780* (Paris 1995)

— *Rings: Symbols of Power, Wealth and Affection* (London 1993)

— *Rings: Jewelry of Power, Love and Loyalty* (London 2007)

Sframeli, M. *I gioielli dei Medici* (Florence 2003)

Sharp, A. 'Notes on Stuart Jewellery', *Proceedings of the Society of Antiquaries of Scotland*, 1923

Shaw, L. B. 'Pieter van Roestraten and the English *Vanitas*', *Burlington Magazine*, CXXXII, June 1990

Solodkoff, A. von *Fabergé* (London 1988)

Spencer-Stanhope, E. *The Letter-Bag of Lady Elizabeth Spencer-Stanhope*, ed. A. M. W. Stirling (London 1913)

Steene, S. J. *The Letters of Lady Arabella Stuart* (Oxford 1994)

Story-Maskelyne, M. H. N. *Report on Jewellery and Precious Stones; Report on the Paris Universal Exhibition, 1867*, II, Class 36 (London 1868)

Strong, R. *Tudor and Jacobean Portraits* (National Portrait Gallery, London 1969)

— *Gloriana: The Portraits of Queen Elizabeth I* (London 1987)

Surry, N., ed. *Your Affectionate and Loving Sister: The Correspondence of Barbara Kerrich and Elizabeth Postlethwaite 1733–1751* (Dereham 2000)

Tait, H., ed. *The Art of the Jeweller: A Catalogue of the Hull Grundy Gift to the British Museum* (London 1984)

— *The Waddesdon Bequest*, I, *The Jewels* (London 1986)

Tassinari, G. 'Glyptic Portraits of Eugène de Beauharnais: the Intaglios by Giovanni Beltrami and the Cameo by Antonio Berini', *Journal of the Walters Art Museum*, vol. 60/61, 2003

— 'I ritratti dello zar Nicola I incise su intaglie e cammei', *Zeitschrift für Kunstgeschichte*, 68, 2005, Heft 3

Tillander-Godenhielm, U. 'The Russian Imperial Award System under Nicholas II 1894–1917', *Journal of the Finnish Antiquarian Society*, 2005

Tolles, T. 'Augustus Saint-Gaudens in the Metropolitan Museum of Art', *Metropolitan Museum of Art Bulletin*, Spring 2009

Ungerer, G. 'Juan Pantoja de la Cruz and the Circulation of Gifts between the English and Spanish Courts, 1604–5', *Shakespearean Studies*, 26, 1993

Vachaudez, C. *Bijoux des reines et princesses de Belgique* (Brussels 2004)

Viel-Castel, H. de 'Une Commande de bijoux par la Reine Catherine de Médicis, à Dujardin, orfèvre du roi Charles IX', *Archives de l'Art français*, III, 1853–55

Walker, R. *The Eighteenth and Early Nineteenth Century Miniatures in the Collection of Her Majesty the Queen* (Cambridge 1992)

Wassenaer, C. van *A Visit to St. Petersburg 1825–1825*, transl. and ed. I. Vinogradoff (Norwich 1994)

Weber, I. *Geschnittene Steine aus altbayerischen Besitz* (Munich 2001)

Whitelocke, B. *A Journal of the Swedish Embassy in the Years 1653–1654, impartially written by the ambassador, Bulstrode Whitelocke*, ed. H. Reeve (London 1855)

Wilmot, M. and C. *The Russian Journals of Martha and Catherine Wilmot 1803–1808*, ed. H. M. Hyde (London 1934)

Yonan, M. 'Portable Dynasties: Imperial Gift-Giving at the Court of Vienna in the Eighteenth Century', in *Gift-Giving in 18th Century Courts*, special issue of *The Court Historian*, vol. 14, 2, December 2009

EXHIBITION CATALOGUES

The Art of Gem Engraving from Alexander the Great to Napoleon III, Hakone and Fukuoka, Japan, 2008 (D. Scarisbrick)

Brilliant Europe, ING Cultural Centre, Brussels, 2008 (D. Scarisbrick et al.)

Diamant van ruwe steen tot sieraad, Museon, The Hague, 2002–3 (René Brus)

Entre Cour et Jardin, Marie-Caroline, duchesse de Berry, Musée de l'Ile de France, Sceaux, 2007

Exhibition of Royal and Historic Treasures in Aid of 'The Heritage' (The Heritage Craft Schools, Chailey, Sussex), held at 145 Piccadilly, London, 29 June–29 September 1939

Fabergé, Joaillier des Romanov, ING Cultural Centre, Brussels, 2005

Gioielli regali, ori, smalti, coralli e pietre preziose, Royal Palace, Caserta, 2005

The Intimate Portrait, British Museum, 2008 (S. Lloyd and K. Sloan)

Precious Gems, Nationalmuseum, Stockholm, 2000 (E. Welander-Berggren)

Princely Magnificence, Victoria & Albert Museum, London, 1980–81 (A. Somers Cocks)

The Queen's Image, Scottish National Portrait Gallery, Edinburgh, 1987 (H. Smales and D. Thomson)

Smykket I dansk eje (Jewelry in Danish Collections), Danske Kunstindustrimuseet, Copenhagen 1960

A Sparkling Age, Diamond Museum, Antwerp, 1993 (J. Walgrave)

Victoria and Albert, Art and Love, Queen's Gallery, London, 2010 (J. Marsden)

PRIMARY SOURCES

Archives Nationales, Paris
Archivo General de Palacio, Madrid
British Library, London
Chaumet Archives, Paris
Institut National de l'Histoire de l'Art, Paris
Royal Archives, Windsor

ACKNOWLEDGMENTS FOR ILLUSTRATIONS

1 Private Collection; 2 Szépművészeti Múzeum, Budapest; 3 Courtesy A La Vieille Russie, New York; 4 Kunsthistorisches Museum, Vienna; 5 Galleria degli Uffizi, Florence © 2010. Photo Scala, Florence – courtesy of the Ministero Beni e Attività Culturali; 6, 7 Kunsthistorisches Museum, Vienna; 8, 9 Private Collection. Courtesy Albion Art Jewellery Institute, Japan; 10, 11 Museo degli Argenti, Florence © 2010. Photo Scala, Florence – courtesy of the Ministero Beni e Attività Culturali; 12 Private Collection; 13, 14 Museo degli Argenti, Florence © 2010. Photo Scala, Florence – courtesy of the Ministero Beni e Attività Culturali; 15 Prado, Madrid, Spain/Giraudon/The Bridgeman Art Library; 16 Museo degli Argenti, Florence © 2010. Photo Scala, Florence – courtesy of the Ministero Beni e Attività Culturali; 17 By permission of the Governing Body of Christ Church, Oxford; 18, 19 Albion Art Collection, Japan; 20 Museo degli Argenti, Florence © 2010. Photo Scala, Florence – courtesy of the Ministero Beni e Attività Culturali; 21, 22 Private Collection; 23 Bibliothèque Nationale de France, Paris; 24 © Ashmolean Museum, University of Oxford/The Bridgeman Art Library; 25 Bibliothèque Nationale de France, Paris; 26 Private Collection; 27 © Society of Antiquaries of London; 28 © V&A Images/Victoria & Albert Museum, London; 29 © National Portrait Gallery, London; 30 Kunsthistorisches Museum, Vienna; 31, 32 © V&A Images/Victoria & Albert Museum, London; 33 Museo degli Argenti, Florence © 2010. Photo Scala, Florence – courtesy of the Ministero Beni e Attività Culturali; 34 Kunsthistorisches Museum, Vienna; 35 Galleria degli Uffizi, Florence © 2010. Photo Scala, Florence - courtesy of the Ministero Beni e Attività Culturali; 36 © V&A Images/Victoria & Albert Museum, London; 37 Münzkabinett, Staatliche Kunstsammlungen Dresden; 38 Grünes Gewölbe, Staatliche Kunstsammlungen Dresden; 39 Staatliche Münzsammlung, Munich; 40 Private Collection; 41 Bayerisches Nationalmuseum, Munich; 42 Staatliche Münzsammlung, Munich; 43, 44 © The Trustees of the British Museum, London; 45–48 © V&A Images/Victoria & Albert Museum, London; 49 The Danish Royal Collection, Rosenborg Castle, Copenhagen; 50 Rubenshuis, Antwerp © Collectiebeleid; 51, 52 © The Trustees of the National Museums of Scotland, Edinburgh; 53–56 Kunsthistorisches Museum, Vienna; 57 Courtesy the Weiss Gallery, London; 58 © Ashmolean Museum, University of Oxford/The Bridgeman Art Library; 59 Landesmuseum Württemberg, Stuttgart, photo Dr Ulrich Klein; 60 Grünes Gewölbe, Staatliche Kunstsammlungen Dresden; 61 © V&A Images/Victoria & Albert Museum, London; 62 Victoria & Albert Museum, London; 63 Plymouth City Museum & Art Gallery; 64–66 © V&A Images/Victoria & Albert Museum, London; 67–69 Kunsthistorisches Museum, Vienna; 70–72 © The Trustees of the British Museum, London; 73, 74 Fitzwilliam Museum, University of Cambridge/The Bridgeman Art Library; 75 Private Collection; 76, 77 Museo Nacional de Arte Decorativo, Buenos Aires, Argentina; 78–80 Private Collection; 81 © York Museums Trust (York Art Gallery)/The Bridgeman Art Library; 82–84 Bibliothèque Nationale de France, Paris; 85, 86 Courtesy S. J. Phillips Ltd, London; 87 © National Portrait Gallery, London; 88 Cromwell Museum, Huntingdon; 89–91 Kunsthistorisches Museum, Vienna; 92 Kunsthistorisches Museum, Vienna/akg images/Erich Lessing; 93 Kunsthistorisches Museum, Vienna; 94, Musée de la Monnaie

de Paris, photo Jean-Jacques Castaing; 95 Bibliothèque Nationale de France, Paris; 96 York Museums Trust (York Art Gallery)/The Bridgeman Art Library; 97 Rijksmuseum, Amsterdam; 98 Courtesy S. J. Phillips Ltd, London; 99 akg images; 100 The Royal Coin Cabinet, Stockholm; 101 © Ashmolean Museum, University of Oxford/ The Bridgeman Art Library; 102, 103 Courtesy S. J. Phillips Ltd, London; 104 Staatliche Münzsammlung, Munich; 105 Private Collection; 106 Walters Art Museum, Baltimore; 107–109 Private Collection; 110 Rijksmuseum, Amsterdam; 111, 112 © The Trustees of the National Museums of Scotland, Edinburgh; 113, 114 The Danish Royal Collection, Rosenborg Castle, Copenhagen; 115, 116 Private Collection. Courtesy David Lavender Antiques; 117 Courtesy S. J. Phillips Ltd, London; 118, 119 Trustees of the Grimsthorpe and Drummond Castle Estates; 120, 121 The Royal Collection © 2010 Her Majesty Queen Elizabeth II; 122–124 © The Trustees of the British Museum, London; 125, 126 Private collection; 127 Rigsarkivet, Copenhagen; 128 Courtesy the Weiss Gallery, London; 129–141 The Danish Royal Collection, Rosenborg Castle, Copenhagen; 142 The Royal Armoury, Stockholm, photo Göran Schmidt; 143, 144 Nationalmuseum, Stockholm; 145 © Museen für Kunst und Kulturgeschichte der Hansestadt Lübeck; 146 The Royal Armoury, Stockholm, photo Göran Schmidt; 147 © Musée international d'horlogerie, La Chaux-de-Fonds, Switzerland; 148 The Earl of Sandwich; 149–151 Kunsthistorisches Museum, Vienna; 152 Private Collection; 153 Musées d'art et d'histoire, Geneva; 154, 155 Musée du Louvre, Paris, D.A.G. © RMN/Gérard Blot; 156, 157 Philadelphia Museum of Art: Gift of Mrs Lessing J. Rosenwald, 1961; 158 Private Collection; 159 The Royal Collection © 2009 Her Majesty Queen Elizabeth II; 160 Private Collection; 161, 162 Musée du Louvre, Paris, © RMN/Jean-Gilles Berizzi; 163, 164 © Christie's Images Ltd (2001); 165 Courtesy Sotheby's; 166–170 Victoria & Albert Museum, London; 171, 172 Bibliothèque Nationale de France, Paris; 173 Harvard Art Museum, Fogg Art Museum, Cambridge, Mass. Bequest of Charles E. Dunlap, 1966.47. Photo: Imaging Department © President and Fellows of Harvard College; 174 Albion Art Collection, Japan; 175 Private Collection. Courtesy S. J. Phillips Ltd, London; 176 © Christie's Images Ltd (2008); 177 Bibliothèque Nationale de France, Paris; 178 The Danish Royal Collection, Rosenborg Castle, Copenhagen; 179 The Royal Collection © 2010 Her Majesty Queen Elizabeth II; 180 Tweed Investments Ltd; 181 Private Collection; 182 Courtesy Sotheby's; 183 Fiorentina S.A., deposited in the Ciechanowiecki Foundation at the Royal Castle, Warsaw; 184 Kremlin Armoury, Moscow; 185 The State Hermitage Museum, St Petersburg. Photograph © The State Hermitage Museum/Photo by Vladimir Terebenin, Leonard Kheifets, Yuri Molodkovets; 186 Zucker Family Collection; 187 The State Hermitage Museum, St Petersburg. Photograph © The State Hermitage Museum/Photo by Vladimir Terebenin, Leonard Kheifets, Yuri Molodkovets; 188 © Society of Antiquaries of London; 189 Szépművészeti Múzeum, Budapest; 190 Private Collection; 191 Courtesy S. J. Phillips Ltd, London; 192 © The Rosalinde and Arthur Gilbert Collection on loan to the Victoria & Albert Museum, London; 193 The State Hermitage Museum, St Petersburg. Photograph © The State Hermitage Museum/Photo by Vladimir Terebenin, Leonard Kheifets, Yuri Molodkovets; 194 The Trustees of the Bowood Collection; 195 Bibliothèque Nationale de France, Paris; 196 Musée Carnavalet, Paris/Roger-Viollet/Topfoto; 197 Private Collection; 198 Kunsthistorisches Museum, Vienna; 199, 200 Christie's Images Ltd; 201 Musée Condé, Chantilly © RMN (Domaine de Chantilly)/René-Gabriel Ojéda; 202 Christie's Images Ltd; 203–205 Wallace Collection, London/The Bridgeman Art Library; 206, 207 Kunsthistorisches Museum, Vienna; 208 Victoria & Albert Museum, London; 209 Musée Carnavalet, Paris/Roger-Viollet/Topfoto; 210, 211 Private Collection. Courtesy S. J. Phillips Ltd, London; 212 © The Holburne Museum, Bath/Bridgeman Art Library; 213 Trustees of the Grimsthorpe and Drummond Castle Estates; 214, 215 The Royal Collection © 2010 Her Majesty Queen Elizabeth II; 216, 217 Tweed Investments Ltd; 218 Trustees of the Grimsthorpe and Drummond Castle Estates; 219–221 © Wallace Collection, London/The Bridgeman Art Library; 222, 223 Courtesy Bonhams; 224, 225 The Collection at Blair Castle, Perthshire; 226 Caserta, Courtesy of the Ministero per i Beni e le Attività Culturali; 227 Grünes Gewölbe, Staatliche Kunstsammlungen Dresden; 228 The State Hermitage Museum, St Petersburg. Photograph © The State Hermitage Museum/Photo by Vladimir Terebenin, Leonard Kheifets, Yuri Molodkovets; 229 Courtesy Sotheby's; 230, 231 Malmaison, châteaux de Malmaison et Bois-Préau © RMN/Gérard Blot; 232 Private Collection; 233, 234 Albion Art Collection, Japan; 235 Nationalmuseum, Stockholm; 236 Private Collection; 237 Albion Art Collection, Japan; 238 Courtesy Mr and Mrs Alain Moatti; 239, 240 Kunsthistorisches Museum, Vienna; 241 Zucker Family Collection; 242, 243 Private Collection; 244, 245 The Royal Collection © 2010 Her Majesty Queen Elizabeth II; 246 © V&A Images/Victoria & Albert Museum, London; 247 Courtesy S. J. Phillips Ltd, London; 248 Albion Art Collection, Japan; 249 © 2010 Image copyright The Metropolitan Museum of Art, New York/Art Resource/Scala, Florence; 250 © The Trustees of the British Museum, London; 251, 252 Albion Art Collection, Japan; 253 Courtesy Bonhams; 254 Private Collection. Courtesy Albion Art Jewellery Institute, Japan; 255 Fitzwilliam Museum, Cambridge; 256 Walters Art Museum, Baltimore; 257 Courtesy Christopher Hartop; 258 Royal Institute of Painters in Water Colours, London; 259 © Museum of London; 260 The State Hermitage Museum, St Petersburg. Photograph © The State Hermitage Museum/Photo by Vladimir Terebenin, Leonard Kheifets, Yuri Molodkovets; 261, 262 Walters Art Museum, Baltimore; 263 Musée Condé, Chantilly © RMN (Domaine de Chantilly)/René-Gabriel Ojéda; 264 The Danish Royal Collection, Rosenborg Castle, Copenhagen; 265 Malmaison, châteaux de Malmaison et Bois-Préau © RMN/Gérard Blot; 266 The Royal Court, Sweden, photo Alexis Daflos; 267 Collection Fondation Napoléon, Paris/Photo12.com, photo Patrice Maurin-Berthier; 268 Christie's Images Ltd; 269 Collection Fondation Napoléon, Paris/Photo12.com, photo Patrice Maurin-Berthier; 270 Museo Napoleonico, Comune di Roma – Sovraintendenza ai Beni Culturali; 271–273 Private Collection; 274, 275 Musée des Arts décoratifs, Bordeaux; 276 Christie's Images Ltd; 277 Musée Condé, Chantilly © RMN (Domaine de Chantilly)/René-Gabriel Ojéda; 278 Private Collection; 279, 280 Christie's Images Ltd; 281 Private Collection; 282, 283 Courtesy Sotheby's; 284 Fondation Napoléon, Paris, photo Vincent Mercier; 285 Château de Compiègne © RMN/Gérard Blot; 286 Chaumet Archives, Paris; 287 Musée Condé, Chantilly © RMN (Domaine de Chantilly)/René-Gabriel Ojéda; 288 Galerie du Château d'Eau de Toulouse. Print by Jean Dieuzaide from an original negative in the possession of Dr François Emile-Zola, the writer's grandson. © ADAGP, Paris and DACS, London 2010; 289, 290 Courtesy S. J. Phillips Ltd, London; 291 The House of Orange-Nassau Historic Collections Trust, The Netherlands; 292 The State Hermitage Museum, St Petersburg. Photograph © The State Hermitage Museum/Photo by Vladimir Terebenin, Leonard Kheifets, Yuri Molodkovets; 293 Private Collection. Courtesy David Lavender Antiques; 294 The Royal Collection © 2010 Her Majesty Queen Elizabeth II; 295 Kunsthistorisches Museum, Vienna; 296 Albion Art Collection, Japan; 297, 298 Christie's Images Ltd; 299 Royal Husgerådskammaren, Stockholm; 300 Private Collection; 301, 302 Courtesy Bonhams; 303 Brodick Castle, Isle of Arran, ScotlandsImages.com/ National Trust for Scotland; 304 Musée Carnavalet, Paris/ Roger-Viollet/Topfoto; 305, 306 The State Hermitage Museum, St Petersburg. Photograph © The State Hermitage Museum/Photo by Vladimir Terebenin, Leonard Kheifets, Yuri Molodkovets; 307 © The Rosalinde and Arthur Gilbert Collection on loan to the Victoria & Albert Museum, London; 308 The State Hermitage Museum, St Petersburg. Photograph © The State Hermitage Museum/Photo by Vladimir Terebenin, Leonard Kheifets, Yuri Molodkovets; 309 National Museum of Finland, Helsinki; 310 Courtesy Sotheby's; 311 Hillwood Estate, Museum & Gardens; Bequest of Marjorie Merriweather Post, 1973 (Acc. no. 11.241). Photo by E. Owen; 312 Courtesy Sotheby's; 313 Courtesy A La Vieille Russie, New York; 314, 315 Link of Times Foundation, Moscow; 316, 317 Collection Comte Charles-André Walewski. Photographer Xavier Reboud; 318 The Royal Collection © 2010 Her Majesty Queen Elizabeth II; 319, Musée Condé, Chantilly © RMN (Domaine de Chantilly)/René-Gabriel Ojéda; 320–322 Courtesy Sotheby's; 323 The State Hermitage Museum, St Petersburg. Photograph © The State Hermitage Museum/Photo by Vladimir Terebenin, Leonard Kheifets, Yuri Molodkovets; 324 Courtesy Sotheby's; 325 © National Portrait Gallery, London; 326 British Library, London; 327 Christie's Images Ltd; 328 Courtesy Earl Fortescue; 329 The Royal Collection © 2010 Her Majesty Queen Elizabeth II; 330 Albion Art Collection, Japan; 331 Private Collection; 332 Albion Art Collection, Japan; 333 De Beers Collection, London; 334 Courtesy Sotheby's; 335–337 Zucker Family Collection; 338 The State Hermitage Museum, St Petersburg. Photograph © The State Hermitage Museum/Photo by Vladimir Terebenin, Leonard Kheifets, Yuri Molodkovets; 339, 340 Courtesy Sotheby's; 341 Private Collection; 342, 343 Courtesy S. J. Phillips Ltd, London; 344 Zucker Family Collection; 345 The State Hermitage Museum, St Petersburg. Photograph © The State Hermitage Museum/Photo by Vladimir Terebenin, Leonard Kheifets, Yuri Molodkovets; 346, 347 From *Russia's Treasure of Diamonds and Precious Stones* (catalogue prepared after the Revolution under the supervision of A. E. Fersman, Moscow 1925–26), courtesy Stefano Papi; 348 Private Collection; 349 Courtesy Amalienborgmuseet, Copenhagen; 350 From *Russia's Treasure of Diamonds and Precious Stones* (catalogue prepared after the Revolution under the supervision of A. E. Fersman, Moscow 1925–26), courtesy Stefano Papi; 351 Zucker Family Collection; 352, 353 Link of Times Foundation, Moscow; 354 Zucker Family Collection; 355, 356 Historical Collections of the House of Orange-Nassau, photo René Brus.

INDEX

Page numbers in *italic* refer to illustrations and their captions

Aarne, Johan Viktor *319*
Abondio, Alessandro *38*
Accarisi *248, 249*
Adelaide, Queen of Great Britain and Ireland *277, 285*
Ador, Jean-Pierre *184*
Ahlstedt, Fredrik *304*
Albert, Prince Consort *241, 250, 253, 288–89, 293, 309, 313, 314*
Albrecht V of Bavaria *33, 35*
Alençon, Duchesse d' *58*
Alexander, John *170, 171*
Alexander I, Emperor of Russia *244, 246, 253, 257, 302–3, 334, 335, 336*
Alexander II, Emperor of Russia *300, 304, 305, 335, 337*
Alexander III, Emperor of Russia *304, 318, 318, 335, 338, 339*
Alexandra Feodorovna, *307, 310, 335, 339*
Alexeyev, Basil Vladimirovich *254*
Anastasia, Grand Duchess *342, 343*
Andrieu, Bertrand *253, 255*
Angoulême, Duc d' *269, 271*
Anna, Queen of the Netherlands *283, 283, 300*
Anne, Princess Royal *168, 169*
Anne, Queen of England and Ireland *64, 70, 71, 72, 73, 83*
Anne of Austria, Queen of France *136–37, 146, 322*
Appiani, Andrea *225, 226, 227*
Arakcheev, Count Alexei *302*
'Armada' Jewel *40, 48, 49*
Artois, Comte d' *162*
Ashmole, Elias *102, 103*
Atholl, 4th Duke of *218, 218*
Aubert, Ange-Joseph *162, 186–87, 191, 194*
Augustin, Jean-Baptiste-Jacques *260, 261, 264*
Augustus, Emperor *226*
Aumale, Duc d' *280, 281*
Aumale, Duchesse d' *280, 281, 292, 314, 314*

Barbour, William *33, 34*
Barbour Jewel *33, 34*
Barrier, François-Julien *158*
Beaufort, 7th Duke of *243, 243*
Beauharnais, Hortense de *231*
Beck, David *100*
Beltrami, Giovanni *233–34, 235*
Bencini, Antonio *202, 203*
Benoist, Antoine *94*
Berry, Duc de *269, 270*
Berry, Duchesse de *270, 271*
Bezborodko, Alexander *173, 174*
Blanc, Marie-Félix *258*

Bolin, C. E. *335, 338*
Bonaparte, Jérome *279, 280*
Bonaparte, Joseph *232, 233*
Bonaparte, Julie *229, 232, 233*
Bonaparte, Roland *258*
Bone, Henry *284, 286, 287*
Bossi, Domenico *303, 335*
Boucher, François *160, 161*
Bourbon, Louis-Henri-Antoine de *194, 197*
Bourbon, Luisa Carlotta Maria Isabella de *269, 271*
Bourbon, Maria Giuseppa de *218, 219*
Bourbon-Condé, Anne-Geneviève de *141*
Bourdon, Sébastien *129*
Branicka, Alexandra, Countess *155, 223*
Briot, Nicholas *98, 99*
Brompton, Richard *223*
Bronzino, Agnolo *8, 9, 36, 37*
Byron, Lord *295, 299*

Carlos, Don *16, 18*
Carolina Augusta, Empress of Austria *234, 235*
Caroline of Baden *332, 333*
Caroline Amalia, Queen of Denmark *256, 257, 257*
Carwardine, Penelope *215*
Castellani, Augusto *249, 249*
Catherine II (the Great), Empress of Russia *155, 175, 177, 183, 184, 221, 222, 223, 332*
Catherine de Médicis, Queen of France *21, 23, 54, 54, 55, 57*
Charles I, King of England *83, 98, 99, 108–11, 180, 183, 214, 322*
Charles II, King of England *108, 112, 113, 130, 135, 138, 147*
Charles III, King of Spain *218, 219*
Charles V, Emperor *11, 13, 86, 90, 91*
Charles IX, King of France *54, 54, 55, 57*
Charles Alexander, Archduke *202, 203*
Charlotte, Princess *237, 239*
Charlotte, Queen of Great Britain and Ireland *208, 209, 284, 324, 325*
Châtelet, Madame du *194, 200–201*
Chinard, Joseph *229, 232*
Christensen, C. *257*
Christian IV, King of Denmark *48, 50, 51, 70, 73, 123, 124*
Christian VI, King of Denmark *180, 182*
Christian VII, King of Denmark *165, 167*
Christian VIII, King of Denmark *256, 257, 257*
Christina, Queen of Sweden *99, 100, 101, 112, 123, 129*
Claypole, Betty *83, 84*
Clement XII, Pope *166*

Clouet, François, the Younger *6, 55, 57*
Clouet, Jean *52*
Condé, Prince de *194, 197*
Constantin, Abraham *263*
Cooper, Alexander *106, 123, 126–27, 130*
Cooper, Samuel *106, 112*
Costa, Brigadier Bartolomeu da *165*
Cosway, Richard *213, 324, 325*
Counis, Salomon-Guillaume *269, 270*
Coventry, Countess of *215*
Crofton, Hon. William George *296–97*
Cromwell, Oliver *83, 84, 85, 99, 101, 112*

Dadler, Sebastian *95, 97*
Dafrique, Félix *238, 240*
Dahl, Emil Ferdinand *257*
Damhart, Joseph *235*
Danhauer, J. G. *332, 332*
Daniel, Abraham *217*
Dashkov, Princess Catherine *222*
Dawe, George *302, 334*
De Felici *248, 249*
Delaune, Etienne *6, 24, 27, 57, 57*
Dennel, Antoine-François *193*
Des Granges, David *106, 117, 120–21*
Devonshire Parure *274, 276, 277*
Digby, Venetia, Lady *106, 107*
Dinglinger, Georg Friedrich *220, 221*
Dix, Arnould *152, 152, 153*
Dorothea of Baden *58*
Drake, Sir Francis *60, 61, 63*
Drake Jewel *60, 61, 62, 63*
Drausch, Valentin *34*
Drouais, Hubert *200–201*
Drummond, James *214*
Drummond, John *170*
Duchesne, Jean-Baptiste-Joseph *283*
Duflos, Augustin *156–57*
Dujardin, François *6, 54, 55, 57*

Edward VII, King of England *327, 327*
Elena, Grand Duchess *307*
Elizabeth I, Queen of England *30, 30, 31, 33, 34, 40, 46–47, 48, 49, 60, 61, 63, 64–65, 70*
Ernst, Duke of Bavaria *42, 45, 102, 104*
Essex, William *277, 288–89, 289*
Este, Isabella d' *36, 36*
Esterházy, Prince Nikolaus *328, 329*
Estrées, Gabrielle d' *57*
Eugénie, Empress *229, 231, 233, 274, 279*

Fabergé, Carl *5, 6, 300, 306–11, 317–19, 339, 341*
Faija, Guglielmo *293*
Farnese, Elizabeth *147, 149*
Ferdinand I, Grand Duke *36*
Ferdinand III, Emperor *86, 87, 89*
Fitzclarence, Lady Augusta *285*

Fitzherbert, Mrs Maria *211, 213, 324, 325, 327*
Flahaut, Comtesse de *188*
Fleurimont, G.-R. *178, 179*
Fossin, Jules *274, 280, 280, 309, 332*
François I, King of France *21, 52, 58, 61*
Franz I, Emperor *2, 178, 181, 202, 203*
Franz II, Emperor *235*
Fraser, William *229, 229*
Frederick, Duke of York *208, 210, 211, 237, 237*
Frederick II, King of Denmark *50*
Frederick II, King of Prussia *183, 185*
Frederick III, King of Denmark *102, 103, 123, 126–27*
Friedrich, Grand Duke *258, 259*
Friedrich III, Duke of Holstein-Gottorp *40*
Friedrich August II of Saxony *220, 221*
Friedrich Wilhelm, Elector of Brandenburg *102, 103*
Froment-Meurice, Emile *280, 281*

Gaillard, Jean *162, 191*
Gainsborough, Thomas *212*
Galle, André *255*
Garrards *238, 288–89, 289*
George, King of Greece *317*
George, 3rd Earl of Cumberland *73, 74–75*
George II, King of Great Britain and Ireland *206, 208*
George III, King of Great Britain and Ireland *183, 208, 209, 211, 212, 324, 325*
George IV, King of Great Britain and Ireland (as Prince of Wales) *169, 169–71, 208, 210, 211, 213, 234, 250, 286, 324, 325, 327,* (as King) *234, 236, 237, 250, 251, 284, 287, 326, 327*
Gérard, François *263*
Gerhard, Hubert *44*
Gibson, Richard *114*
Gilbert, Alfred *252, 253*
Gipfel, Gabriel *6, 39–40, 41*
Giroux, Alphonse *271*
Giuliano, Carlo *326, 327*
Gnadenpfennige *38, 39, 39–40, 42–45, 99, 102, 104–5*
Godolphin, William *135*
Goodricke, Daniel *79, 95, 96*
Gori, A. F. *180*
Gouillon, Louis *128*
Grant, Sir Francis *298*
Grenville, Sir Bevil *117, 120–21*
Grenville Jewel *117, 120–21*
Gresley, Sir Thomas *73, 76–77*
Gresley Jewel *73, 76–77*
Guay, Jacques *158, 159, 161, 162, 163*
Gustavus Adolphus, King of Sweden *79, 95, 96, 97, 99, 128*

Habsburg snuff box *202, 203*
Hamilton, Duchess of *298*
Hancock, C. F. *274, 276, 277, 290*
Harington, Sarah *123, 125*
Harley, Lady Brillana *122, 123*
Hatton, Sir Christopher *30, 32*
Haüer, Johann Paulus *106, 106*
Heckhel, A. *210*
Hedvig Eleonora, Queen *123, 130, 131*
Heigel, Josef *333*
Heming, Joseph *317*
Henri II, King of France *21, 54*
Henri IV, King of France *24, 26, 57, 159, 161, 162, 187*
Henrietta Maria, Queen of England *108, 109, 214*
Henry VIII, King of England *52, 58, 61*
Herbert, Lord *73*
Heriot, George *6, 70, 71, 73*
Heyden, Count Fedor Logginovich *304*
Hilliard, Nicholas *6, 46, 48, 49, 60, 61, 63–64, 64–65, 68–69, 70, 73, 74–77*
Holbein, Hans *61*
Hollaender, Hans *123, 124*
Holmström, August *317*
Hone, Horace *296–97*
Horenbout, Lucas *61*
Huntington, Daniel *242, 243*
Hyde, Anne *112, 114*

Isabel Clara Eugenia, Infanta of Spain *17, 18*
Isabey, Jean-Baptiste *231, 260, 262, 265–66, 267*

Jacquemin, Pierre-André *159, 161*
Jaeger, Johann Caspar *174, 175, 177*
Jagger, Charles *277*
James I of England and VI of Scotland *7, 64, 66–67, 68–69, 70, 83*
James II of England and VII of Scotland *115, 147*
James III, the Old Pretender *170, 171, 180*
James V, King of Scotland *53, 54*
Jeuffroy, Romain-Vincent *253*
Johann Georg I, Elector of Saxony *39, 39*
Johnson, Cornelius *123, 125*
Joinville, Prince de *312*
Josephine, Empress *225, 226, 227, 229, 230, 260, 262*

Karl X Gustav, King of Sweden *123, 130, 130, 131*
Karl XI, King of Sweden *130, 132*
Karl Ludwig of Bavaria *103*
Keibel, Johann Wilhelm *254*
Keibel, Samuel Otto *303*

Kellerthaler, Daniel 39
Kent, Duchess of 292, 293, 309, 313
Klepikou, Alexis 247
Kneller, Sir Godfrey 118–19, 321
Knieper, Hans 50
Kügelgen, Franz Gerhard von 246
Kurtz, Paul 123, 126–27

Labille-Guiard, A. 188
Lalique, René 280, 281
Lang, Edwin 62
Lawrence, Sir Thomas 326, 327
Le Moine, François 179
Le Tessier de Montarsy, Laurent 144, 150–51
Le Tessier de Montarsy, Pierre 146, 150–51, 152
Lebas, Paul 238, 240
Lefebvre, François 106, 134, 136–37, 149
Lefevre, Robert 328
Légaré, Gedeon 138
Légaré, Gilles 106, 107, 129, 133, 138, 139, 140–43
Legrand, Alexandre 273
Lely, Sir Peter 109
Lemersier, Balthazar 29, 30
Lempereur 138
Leopold I, Emperor 91, 91
Leopold Wilhelm, Archduke 86, 88–89
Leschaudel, Antoine 196
Livingston, Lady Anne 70, 71, 72
Londonderry, 7th Marquis of 295, 295
Longueville, Duchesse de 138, 141
Lorme, Emilie de 271
Louis XIII, King of France 24, 28, 30, 80, 81, 322
Louis XIV, King of France 6, 80, 82, 92, 93, 94, 136–37, 138, 144, 145, 146–47, 148, 149, 150–51
Louis XV, King of France 159, 160, 161, 165, 178, 187, 191, 192
Louis XVI, King of France 162, 162, 165, 191, 193
Louis-Philippe, King of France 233, 269, 272, 275
Louise, Grand Duchess 258, 259
Louise, Queen of the Belgians 274, 289, 290
Louise, Queen of Denmark 338, 339
Ludwig, Duke of Württemberg 58
Ludwig I, King of Bavaria 282, 283
Ludwig, Karl 43
Lyte, Thomas 64, 68–69
Lyte Jewel 64, 68–69, 70

Mack, Franz von 202, 203
Magdalena Sibylla of Saxony 39, 39
Maler, Valentin 43
Margaret, Queen of Spain 64
Maria, Grand Duchess 342, 343

Maria I, Queen of Portugal 164, 165
Maria Amalia, Queen of Spain 218, 219
Maria Feodorovna, Empress 244, 246, 306, 311, 335, 338
Maria Giuseppa, Infanta 218, 219
Maria Josepha, Archduchess 221
Maria Luisa, Queen of Spain (Marie-Louise d'Orléans) 135, 138, 144
Maria Theresa, Empress 2, 178, 181, 202, 203, 204
Marie de Médicis, Queen of France 24, 57–58, 322
Marie-Amélie, Queen of France 269, 272, 274
Marie-Antoinette, Queen of France 162, 162–63, 192, 195, 202, 268–69
Marie-Josèphe de Saxe 161, 193, 196
Marie-Joséphine of Savoy 192
Marie-Louise, Empress 26, 255, 262, 263, 328, 332
Marie-Thérèse of Savoy 191
Marlborough, Duchess of 323–24, 323
Marlborough, Duke of 321, 323
Martin, Jean 173, 174
Mary I, Queen of England 33, 34, 61
Mary of Modena, Queen of England 112, 116, 117
Mary Stuart, Queen of Scots 21, 22, 24, 25, 53, 54
Massin, Oscar 344
Maximilian I, King of Bavaria 332, 333
Maximilian II Emanuel, Elector 102, 105
Maximilian III, Archduke of Austria 38, 39
Mayer, R. 259
Mazarin, Cardinal 138, 139
Mazzini, Giuseppe 248, 249
Medici, Anna Maria Ludovica de' 158
Medici, Bia de' 9, 36, 37
Medici, Cosimo I de' 9, 18–21, 19, 20, 21, 36, 37
Medici, Gian Gastone de' 158
Médicis: see Catherine de and Marie de
Mellerio 279
Mengs, Anton Raphael 218, 219
Meyer, Jeremiah 325
Meyer, Maurice 278
Meytens, Martin van 2, 178, 181
Miers, John 218, 218
Mignard, Pierre 150–51
Mitoir, Charles-Benoît 301
Moncornet, Balthazar 29
Montauban, Pierre-André 228, 328, 329
Montgolfier, Joseph and Etienne de 190
Moreau, Jean-Michel 189
Morelli, Nicola 229, 233
Morikofer, Jean-Melchior 180, 183, 185
Morlière, Christophe 78

Moser, G. M. 210
Müller, Philipp Heinrich 105
Murat, Caroline 264, 265

Napoleon I, Emperor 225, 226, 227, 228, 229, 233, 253, 255, 260–62, 328
Napoleon III, Emperor 229, 231, 233, 274, 278, 279, 280
Natter, Lorenz 165
Neuber, J. C. 200–201
Nicholas, Grand Duke 339, 339
Nicholas, Prince of Greece 307
Nicholas I, Emperor of Russia 244, 247, 253, 254, 257, 335, 336, 337
Nicholas II, Emperor of Russia 300, 307, 308, 309, 310–11, 339, 341, 342, 343
Nitot, François-Regnault 226, 228, 262, 263, 328
Nocret, Jean 140

Olga, Grand Duchess (1867) 317
Olga, Grand Duchess (c. 1906) 342, 343
Oliver, Isaac 64
Oliver, Peter 106, 107
Olonne, Comtesse d' 138, 142–43
Orders: Garter 98, 102, 103, 288–89, 289, 321; Golden Fleece 11, 13, 21, 35, 86, 204; Royal Family 284–85; St Andrew 303, 304, 306; St George 309; St Michel 21, 23; St Esprit 28; Star of India 238, 241; Teutonic 39; Victoria and Albert 238, 241
Orléans, Henriette d' 138
Orléans, Louis-Philippe, Duc d' and later King of France 233, 269, 272, 274, 275
Orléans, Marie-Louise d' 138; and see Maria Luisa, Queen of Spain
Orléans, Philippe d' 138, 140

Paar, Ludwig 259
Pahlen, Yulia see Samoilova
Passot, Gabriel-Aristide 278
Paul I, Emperor of Russia 244, 246
Pereda, Antonio de 86, 90
Perkhin, Mikhail 306, 307, 310, 318, 341
Peter the Great, Emperor of Russia 152, 152, 153, 221, 332, 332
Petitot, Jean I 106, 108, 109, 134, 138, 139–43, 144, 148, 149, 150–51, 152
Philip II, King of Spain 12, 13, 13, 14, 16–17, 18, 30
Philip III, King of Spain 64
Philip IV, King of Spain 130, 133
Phillips, Thomas 286
Phoenix Jewel 40, 46–47
Pistrucci, Benedetto 234, 236, 238
Pius VII, Pope 243–44
Platov, Matvei Ivanovich 285, 286

Pompadour, Marquise de 6, 158, 159, 160, 161, 202
Prochet (Philippe Prochietto) 279
Pujos, André 190

Quentin de La Tour, Maurice 215

Rawlins, Thomas 83, 83, 99, 183
Regulski, Jan 173, 174
Reimer, Hans 45
Riley, John 102, 103
Rinehart, W. H. 249
Romano, Giancristoforo 6, 36, 37
Rondé, Claude-Dominique 191
Ross, William 285, 289, 292, 293
Rossi, Giovanni Antonio de' 19, 20, 21
Rouquet, Jean-André 214
Rousseau, Jean-Jacques 186, 189
Royal Institute of Painters in Water Colours 252, 253
Rozerot, Jeanne 280, 281, 283
Rubens, Peter Paul 48, 51
Ruiz, Magdalena 17
Rundell, Bridge and Rundell 215, 236, 237, 250, 251, 253, 285, 287, 327

Saint-Gaudens, Augustus 242, 243
Samoilova, Countess 300, 301
Sánchez Coello, Alonso 17
Saulini, Luigi 243, 244
Saulini, Tommaso 241, 244, 249
Schwabe, Nicolaus 48
Schwedler, Abraham 39, 39
Seaton, Lady 62, 63
Seymour-Conway, General Henry 216
Sicardi, Louis-Marie 195
Signac, Pierre 129, 130, 131, 132
Simon, Jean-Henri 165, 233
Simon, Thomas 83, 85, 99
Simpson, John 291
Sophia, Electress 39–40, 41, 59
Sophie Amalie, Queen of Denmark 123, 126–28
Spilman, Sir John 64
Spinelli, Gasparo 52, 54
Stanislaus Augustus, King of Poland 173, 174
Stephanie, Queen of Portugal 289, 291
Stieler, Joseph 282
Strachan, Alexander 251
Stuart, Prince Charles Edward 171, 172, 214
Sully, Thomas 238, 240
Sylvius, Balthasar 13, 15

Tabbert, Gottfried 101
Tatiana, Grand Duchess 342, 343
Taute, Christian 156
Taylor, Peter Alfred 248, 249
Theer, R. 336

Therese, Queen of Bavaria 282
Thyra, Princess of Denmark 319
Toledo, Eleonora da 20, 21
Toutin, Henri 106, 107, 109, 134, 136–37
Toutin, Jean 78
Tresca, Giuseppe 272
Trezzo, Jacopo da 6, 10, 12–13, 16, 18, 30, 344

Ulrika Eleonora the Elder, Queen of Sweden 128

Vachette, A.-J.-M. 162, 163
Van Dyck, Anthony 83, 99, 108–10, 183
Vasari, Giorgio 20, 21
Velásquez, Diego de Silva y 133
Vernier, Emile 258, 258
Vernon, Frédéric 258
Verschuur van der Voort 344, 344
Victoria, Queen of Great Britain and Ireland 238, 240–41, 250, 252, 253, 285, 289, 291, 292, 293, 309, 313, 314–15
Vladimir, Grand Duke 339, 340
Vogt, Daniel 91, 91
Voltaire 194, 200–201

Waechter, Johann Georg 183, 184
Wagner, Heinrich 34
Walsingham, Sir Francis 30, 33
Walsingham, Katherine 73, 76–77
Walters, Ellen 249, 249
Walters, William Thompson 249
Warin, Jean 92, 93
Watson Stuart, Anna 242, 243
Whitelocke, Sir Bulstrode 99, 101
Wigström, Henrik 5, 308
Wild, Elizabeth 31, 33
Wilhelm V, Duke of Bavaria 44, 45
Willem II, King of the Netherlands 283, 283
Willem III, King of the Netherlands 344, 344
William III, King of England 117, 118–19
William IV, King of Great Britain and Ireland 277, 285, 327, 327
Winberg, Ivan 334
Winterhalter, F. X. 278
Wolff, Tobias 39–40, 41
Wolffgang, G. A. 206
Wright, John Michael 83, 84
Wyon, Thomas I 251
Wyon, William 238, 241

Zanetti, Antonio Maria 180, 182
Zehngraf, Johannes 306, 307, 310
Zincke, Christian Friedrich 216
Zoffany, Johann 208, 209, 210
Zola, Emile 280, 281, 283
Zuiev, Vasili 308